D0363599

I pray that the God of our Lord Jesus Christ, the Father of glory, may give ou a spirit of wisdom and revelation as you come to know him... (Eph 1:17)

To Alistair,
Blessings in Christ!

$+3$

THE CHRIST-CENTERED LIFE

david.broderick@thechrist-centeredlife.com

Twitter: @DavidBroderick7

www.thechrist-centeredlife.com

THE CHRIST-CENTERED LIFE

by David Broderick

Twitter: @DavidBroderick7

www.thechrist-centeredlife.com

The Christ-Centered Life

Deep Calls to Deep

This is the revelation that Jesus the Christ really is the very center of everything, that it is around him that everything revolves and is focused, and that everything testifies about him and points to him, whether it realizes it or not.

David Broderick

WestBow
PRESS
A DIVISION OF THOMAS NELSON

WestBow Press books may be ordered through booksellers or by contacting:

WestBow Press
A Division of Thomas Nelson
1663 Liberty Drive
Bloomington, IN 47403
www.westbowpress.com
1-(866) 928-1240

ISBN: 978-1-4497-9627-3 (sc)
ISBN: 978-1-4497-9628-0 (hc)
ISBN: 978-1-4497-9626-6 (e)

Library of Congress Control Number: 2013909396

Printed in the United States of America.

WestBow Press rev. date: 5/28/2013

All Scripture references from the Pradis 5 CD-ROM Leader's Edition of the New Revised Standard Version © 1989 in the USA. Italicized words in Scripture quotations are the author's own emphasis

Lord God of heaven and earth:
Please break out of the box that I keep you in.
Please break the cast that I have fashioned for you.
Please break the rules that I have put on you.
Please destroy the narrow ideas that I have about you.
Please reveal yourself far beyond the image that I have of you.
Build foundations of true gold in my life.
May you take pleasure in living in me in all your fullness.
Enable me to have a truly open heart to receive you in fullness.
Enable me to have truly empty hands to receive from you.
May you strengthen my knees.
May you warm my heart.
May Jesus be present in me.
May Jesus be glorified in me.
Lord God of heaven and earth,
Please ...
Come ...

Contents

Introduction

This book is about my journey into Christ-centeredness, a personal journey that continues daily for me and will continue throughout my life. I present this book as a beginning and as a foundation for the journey into Christ-centeredness that each of us can undertake as we grow in Jesus for ourselves. Therefore, this book gives you some starters and pointers for your own journey into Christ-centeredness.

Since Jesus the Christ really is the center of everything, everyone should be aware of looking at things that realize—make real—the centrality of Christ in everyday life. Of course, this requires revelation from God, and that is another reason why it is my deepest desire that nothing should prevent my readers from seeing Jesus for themselves and having a real and lasting encounter with him that leads to a life of Christ-centeredness.

Perhaps this book will cause people to think and then realize that there is more to being a Christian than just one flavor of orthodoxy or another. I hope so. Perhaps this book will cause people to consider the person of Jesus in a new way. I hope so. Perhaps many people will find many uses for this book. I do not know. What I do know is that this book's primary function is to point to Jesus, to make him seen and known. It aims to make Jesus known as he really is—not how we would like him to be. I constantly aim to look beyond my own prejudices, for we all have them, and I ask the Spirit of God to simply open my eyes so I may see Jesus. I hope that is why you read this book. I hope that you too can look beyond your own prejudices. If Jesus is known and worshipped by you as a result of this book, I will be very happy.

The reality of life is that we must be constantly growing to maturity. Our experience and knowing of God must be ever deepening. Remaining the same, day after day and year after year, is simply not an option. Furthermore, a gained mature perspective does not render an immature perspective as wrong or fake. It simply says that it is time to grow into a new experience, new knowing, and so a new understanding.

Of course, we do not teach children in the same way that we teach adults. We teach children according to where they are. For example, a child may be told to hold Daddy's hand when crossing a busy road. The child will probably object or ask, "Why?" The wise father does not sit the child down and discuss the consequences of a car hitting the toddler's body at thirty miles per hour. There is no point. Such a discussion lies outside the child's ability to engage with it. So the child is told, "Because Daddy says so." That is a totally appropriate response to the child. However, if that person is twenty-one years old, and Daddy still has to say to hold his hand when crossing a busy road, there is something very wrong. In the physical world in which we live, when children stop growing or healing, all the alarm bells start ringing. Why, then, do we accept a church culture in which it is the norm for Christians to remain stagnant, neither growing nor healing—and yet no alarm bells are ringing?

It cannot and must not be so in knowing God. We must grow daily in our experience of him. To stand still is to die the wrong kind of death. To stand still is to become entrenched in what we believe and to defend it against "heresy." Why are we content to remain as we are in experiencing God, while we do not accept such stagnation in any other areas of our lives? Why are alarm bells not ringing for those people whose experience with God has not grown or matured over years or even decades? This book aims to get every reader seeking to know Jesus better—whatever the cost.

Part of growing toward a mature perspective is recognizing the way things actually are, rather than the way they merely appear. This is a very important part of growth. In this regard, we must recognize that we cannot and do not put Jesus on any throne—even the throne of our own lives. We need revelation from God to see that Jesus is already on the highest throne and that everything, without exception, is subject to him. Therefore, we cannot enthrone Jesus. We can only receive revelation that he is, in fact, truly enthroned already. We cannot even enthrone Christ in our own lives; we can only live a Christ-centered life in simple recognition of the fact that Jesus is enthroned. Jesus Christ truly is Lord, to the glory of God the Father. This is reality, not mere theology.

Therefore, our voyage of discovery into the Christ-centered life does not change Jesus one iota. It changes us. Our voyage of discovery is to be one of revelation in which we continually discover how things really are, not how we would like them to be.

A Christ-centered life is one in which I will always be growing until the day I see him face-to-face, jump into his outstretched arms, and marvel at the fullness of him who fills all in all. I cannot exhaust the knowing of God, although sometimes I may try his patience! I want to keep growing daily into him who is the Head. I want to keep growing in relationship with Jesus who is the Christ. I want to keep being transformed day-by-day into his likeness, from one degree of glory into another—the glory that belongs to Jesus and to Jesus alone. All praise belongs to Jesus alone; I belong to Jesus alone; everyone belongs to Jesus alone. Many people just don't know it yet, so it is not real for them. Everything and everyone belong to Jesus alone. They just don't know it yet. Jesus is the center. We need revelation to see that and to grow into that amazing truth.

Such revelation affects our whole lives and transforms how we read the Scriptures. We will explore that in the pages that follow. As one example, I have often heard it said that the early church in Acts met together for fellowship, but I do not think they did so at all. I believe they gathered together to meet the Jesus who was moving and working in their midst. True fellowship, then, is Christ-centered, not meeting-centered. So the Christ-centered life makes this statement: the aim of fellowship is to meet together with Christ, not simply to meet together. Therefore, as you read this book, be open to meeting with Jesus. Let him draw near to you, as you draw near to him.

As we explore the theme of the Christ-centered life, we will begin with my own journey into Christ-centeredness as well as looking at Scriptures from a Christ-centered perspective. We will then move on to look at the law of God—the first five books of the old covenant, not just the so-called Ten Commandments—and will see how the law itself is Christ-centered and finds its fulfilment in him. We will look at Christ-centered marriage and how critical that is for the day and age in which we live. Marriage on earth is a reflection of God himself—no sexuality implied—and we Christians need our marriages to show the world what it means to be Christ-centered. We will then look at prayer from a Christ-centered perspective and see how radically different that is from the common concept of prayer: that of asking for something and then receiving it or not. We will then consider the subject of leadership from a Christ-centered perspective and see how God ordained the kind of people we are meant to be in Christ. We will then see that the Gospels—far from being the work of four "evangelists"—are actually the work of four proclaimers, each of whom, from his own perspective, is declaring Jesus to be King over all.

As you read this book, I hope you will decide to deliberately journey into Christ-centeredness for yourself and will begin to discover the wonders that are found in Christ and no one else. I hope the beauty of Christ will so captivate you that you will never again be satisfied in standing still, that you will pursue the knowing of Christ with all your heart, all your soul, all your mind, and all your strength. I hope you will realize that Jesus is Lord of all—and that such revelation will cause you to encounter him afresh.

My prayer for all of those who read the pages of this book simply echoes that of the apostle Paul from long ago.

> I pray that the God of our Lord Jesus Christ, the Father of glory, may give you a spirit of wisdom and revelation as you come to know him, so that, with the eyes of your heart enlightened, you may know what is the hope to which he has called you, what are the riches of his glorious inheritance among the saints, and what is the immeasurable greatness of his power for us who believe, according to the working of his great power. God put this power to work in Christ when he raised him from the dead and seated him at his right hand in the heavenly places, far above all rule and authority and power and dominion, and above every name that is named, not only in this age but also in the age to come. And he has put all things under his feet and has made him the head over all things for the church, which is his body, the fullness of him who fills all in all. (Ephesians 1:17-22)

Part I

Christ-Centered Living

In the beginning was the Word, and the Word was with God, and the Word was God. He was in the beginning with God. All things came into being through him, and without him not one thing came into being. What has come into being in him was life, and the life was the light of all people. The light shines in the darkness, and the darkness did not overcome it. There was a man sent from God, whose name was John. He came as a witness to testify to the light, so that all might believe through him. He himself was not the light, but he came to testify to the light. The true light, which enlightens everyone, was coming into the world. He was in the world, and the world came into being through him; yet the world did not know him. He came to what was his own, and his own people did not accept him. But to all who received him, who believed in his name, he gave power to become children of God, who were born, not of blood or of the will of the flesh or of the will of man, but of God. And the Word became flesh and lived among us, and we have seen his glory, the glory as of a father's only son, full of grace and truth. (John testified to him and cried out, "This was he of whom I said, 'He who comes after me ranks ahead of me because he was before me.'") From his fullness we have all received, grace upon grace.

> The law indeed was given through Moses; grace and truth came through Jesus Christ. No one has ever seen God. It is God the only Son, who is close to the Father's heart, who has made him known. (John 1:1–18)

Whereas the old covenant literally began with "beginning God," John revised that and literally began his gospel with "beginning Word." In doing so, John declared that everything that has existed, does exist, and will exist came into being through the Word of God: Jesus, who is the Christ. Thus, for John, Jesus really and truly was the center of everything, the focus of everything, and it is only through Christ that anything finds its true meaning. John boldly proclaimed the supremacy of Christ, as he declared that everything was Christ-centered—whether it realized it or not.

This mirrors the concept that starts off the old covenant. Hebrew thought deals in pictures and stories, not in fact and precision. Hebrew thought is based on concepts, not mathematics. "Beginning God" is not a mere statement of fact. It is a concept that says that everything that has a beginning has that beginning in God. It is a concept that says that nothing can have a beginning except it has that beginning in God.

John refined that concept. "Beginning Word" is not a mere statement. It also is a concept. It is a concept that says that everything that has a beginning has that beginning in the Word. It is a concept that says that nothing could have a beginning except it had that beginning in the Word. For John, Christ was supreme. All of creation either acknowledges it now or will do so. Whether it realizes it or not, everything acknowledges the supremacy of Christ, who fills all in all.

This is especially true of the Scriptures: "You search the scriptures because you think that in them you have eternal life; and it is they that testify on my behalf" (John 5:39).

Jesus was not referring to our old covenant Scriptures (Old Testament) but to the Jewish Scriptures that he read and knew. Jesus boldly declared that all the Scriptures that the Jewish religious leaders were familiar with testified on his own behalf—whether the Jewish religious leaders realized it or not. Perception cannot alter reality. Jesus was declaring that all of the Scriptures should be read as Christ-centered Scriptures.

Therefore, both John and Jesus were saying that everything is to be understood and appreciated primarily in and through Christ. That is precisely why this book is called *The Christ-Centered Life*. The foundation on which I build is Christ himself. He is the center, focus, and meaning of everything, whether everything realizes it or not.

John's opening words in his gospel, "beginning Word," are not just mystical writing or a nice turn of phrase. They are in fact the foundational truth on which everything is based, appreciated, and understood. "Beginning Word" is not merely a fact to note or just a historical statement. It is foundational truth that must be allowed to radically affect our experience, our knowing, and our understanding of God. "Beginning Word," then, has massive implications for us and for the whole of creation.

The Word, then, is the expression of God himself and reveals his likeness, but the Word is also far more than that. The Word—who is Jesus the Christ—is himself the starting point of everything. He is the beginning and the end, the focus and the light, the life and the breath. The Word is God in fullness. Jesus said so himself, over and over again, to disciples who could hear but not listen, who could receive words but not the mighty truth that the words pointed to. What Jesus was saying was so radical that the disciples simply did not get it, though they did get it later. All too often, we do not get it, either. We acknowledge in our songs that everything is all about Jesus, we tag his name onto the ends of our prayers, and we speak of salvation as being in Jesus. But it is too easy not to live Christ-centered in daily reality. Jesus himself made clear that true life is in him alone. The danger for us is that, just like the Pharisees of Jesus' day, we refuse to come to him for life.

> Jesus said to Thomas, "I am the way, and the truth, and the life. No one comes to the Father except through me. If you know me, you will know my Father also. From now on you do know him and have seen him." Philip said to him, "Lord, show us the Father, and we will be satisfied." Jesus said to him, "Have I been with you all this time, Philip, and you still do not know me? Whoever has seen me has seen the Father. How can you

say, 'Show us the Father'? Do you not believe that I am
in the Father and the Father is in me? The words that I
say to you I do not speak on my own; but the Father who
dwells in me does his works. Believe me that I am in the
Father and the Father is in me." (John 14:6–11)

What is our reaction to all this? Is it to nod our heads in agreement
but then carry on exactly as before? Or is it to ask the Spirit of God
to radically transform our hearts and minds so that we are becoming
truly Christ-centered in everything we say and do? As I establish the
foundation of Christ-centered living on which my own life is based,
there is one certainty that I must face: Christ-centeredness excludes
self-centeredness. There is a cost to be paid if we are to be truly Christ-
centered. Nevertheless, the rewards of being Christ-centered are
enormous, and the cost of being Christ-centered is truly insignificant
when compared to the benefits of knowing Jesus.

On a personal level, my journey into Christ-centeredness involved
continually meeting with Jesus the Christ who is Lord, but those meetings
were not what I expected. I knew in theory that Jesus was Lord, but I
also knew that Jesus didn't seize power, dominance, might, or majesty.
These were given to him by his Father in heaven. That led me to an
amazing discovery. For as far back as I can remember, to the earliest days
of my life, I have been pushed around, bullied, and dominated by others.
Perhaps, then, you can imagine my astonishment when I looked back
over the decades and discovered that, in my own personal experience,
Jesus had never pushed me around, bullied me, or dominated me. I really
had to sit down and think about that for quite a while.

The one person who has every right to push me around never does.
The one person who has every right to bully me never does. The one
person who has every right to dominate me never does. Jesus' approach to
me has always been one of love, and that is precisely why I didn't recognize
him for so long. Simply put, I didn't know what love was. More correctly,
I didn't know who love was. This Jesus, who is love, brought me:

- *Joy.* This is the true joy of a love relationship with the one who
  truly loves me. I have learned that the life of the Christ-centered

person is not about happiness but joy. Happiness and other emotions come through circumstances, but joy comes through relationships—especially through a relationship with a special person. That special person is Jesus the Christ.

- *Peace.* This is true peace of his loving presence that invites me into his arms. I have learned that peace is not the absence of trouble. It is internal, not external. It is the presence of a person: Jesus the Christ.
- *Patience.* I have learned to be at least as patient with other people as Jesus is patient with me. His patience is inexhaustible, because he knows firsthand what it is to be human and weak. I have learned that one person can show amazing patience with me. That person is Jesus the Christ.
- *Kindness.* I have learned to practice acts of kindness to other people, even as Jesus practices acts of kindness to me. This is much less about what we do for people and more about who we are for people. I have learned that kindness is a person. That person is Jesus the Christ.
- *Generosity.* I am learning to truly receive that I might learn to truly have—in order that I might learn to truly give. I have learned that giving is far less about giving the things that I have and more about giving of myself. Such selfless giving is found in a person. That person is Jesus the Christ.
- *Faithfulness.* Jesus is passionately loyal and faithful to me, and I am wholeheartedly determined to be loyal and faithful to him. I have learned that faithfulness is related more to who I am than to the things I do. I learned that faithfulness is found in a very special person. That person is Jesus the Christ.
- *Gentleness.* The gentleness that can touch and transform me without my even realizing it can also touch and transform others through me without them even realizing it. I have learned that gentleness achieves far more than bullying and insisting. Gentleness wins me around and draws me close. That gentleness is a quality of a godly person, that person is Jesus the Christ.
- *Self-control.* This is not my own attempt to modify or control my behavior. True self-control is self under the loving direction of

5

The apostle Paul certainly believed it, and he himself knew that reality. Indeed, it is the apostle Paul who developed the reality of the presence of Christ: "To the (saints) God chose to make known how great among the Gentiles are the riches of the glory of this mystery, which is Christ in you, the hope of glory" (Colossians 1:27).

Christ in me! What a stunning reality Paul speaks of! But—and I must speak personally here—why on earth would Christ want to dwell in me? To be honest, I don't actually know why he would, but I do know that not only does Christ want to dwell in me but he actually does dwell in me. I can't explain it, but I can live it. And he's not just in me. He's in you too!

> I have heard of your faith in the Lord Jesus and your love toward all the saints, and for this reason I do not cease to give thanks for you as I remember you in my prayers. I pray that the God of our Lord Jesus Christ, the Father of glory, may give you a spirit of wisdom and revelation as you come to know him, so that, with the eyes of your heart enlightened, you may know what is the hope to which he has called you, what are the riches of his glorious inheritance among the saints, and what is the immeasurable greatness of his power for us who believe, according to the working of his great power. God put this power to work in Christ when he raised him from the dead and seated him at his right hand in the heavenly places, far above all rule and authority and power and dominion, and above every name that is named, not only in this age but also in the age to come. And he has put all things under his feet and has made him the head over all things for the church, which is his body, *the fullness of him who fills all in all*. (Ephesians 1:15–23)

How can Jesus fill all in all? I don't know, to be honest. It is a mystery to me and to my finite mind contained in my mortal body. However, it is the truth.

Now, here is a simple principle that I have learned through Christ-centeredness: where truth and I meet, I can be certain that it is I who need to change. Of course the Scriptures tell us that Jesus is the same yesterday, today, and forever, so I should know that. But my self-centeredness expected Jesus to change to suit me. My self-centeredness never succeeded. Thank God. Jesus' rightful place is becoming ever real to me, as I live in peace through Christ-centeredness.

True peace, then, is the presence of Jesus. Jesus himself is our peace. Don't take my word for it. The Scriptures say so. Jesus said so. True hope is the presence of Jesus. Jesus himself is our hope. Therefore, simply to "believe" in Jesus—whatever that means today—is not enough. Indeed, it is nowhere near enough! It is only the first step of a lifelong journey. We must be growing and realizing a daily love relationship with Jesus the Christ, who is transforming us day-by-day into his likeness.

> Blessed be the God and Father of our Lord Jesus Christ! By his great mercy he has given us a new birth into a living hope through the resurrection of Jesus Christ from the dead, and into an inheritance that is imperishable, undefiled, and unfading, kept in heaven for you, who are being protected by the power of God through faith for a salvation ready to be revealed in the last time. In this you rejoice, even if now for a little while you have had to suffer various trials, so that the genuineness of your faith—being more precious than gold that, though perishable, is tested by fire—may be found to result in praise and glory and honor when Jesus Christ is revealed. Although you have not seen him, you love him; and even though you do not see him now, you believe in him and rejoice with an indescribable and glorious joy, for you are receiving the outcome of your faith, the salvation of your souls. (1 Peter 1:3–9)

When the revelation of Christ-centeredness came into my life and started its transforming work in me, I read the Scriptures in a new way. Everywhere I looked in Scripture, I found the supremacy of Christ. The apostle Peter was centered firmly on Christ. For Peter, it really was all about Jesus. This set me to exploring another astonishing truth—that the whole of creation centers on relationship with its creator, in the first instance, but also on relationship with humankind. Indeed, the whole of creation centers on relationship with Jesus the Christ. Eternal and everlasting relationship is what the new creation is all about.

The Scriptures begin and end with relationship. "It is I, Jesus, who sent my angel to you with this testimony for the churches. I am the root and the descendant of David, the bright morning star. The Spirit and the bride say, "Come." And let everyone who hears say, "Come." And let everyone who is thirsty come. Let anyone who wishes take the water of life as a gift" (Revelation 22:16–17).

I was staggered to realize that, when everything has been wound up and handed over to the Father, it is the man Jesus who will appear at the end of the age. I expected it to be the Christ who would appear at the very end, or perhaps Jesus in the role of one of his many other titles. But no, it is the man Jesus himself.

My own new beginning began in Jesus, and it will surely find ultimate fulfillment in Jesus. Everything really is all about Jesus himself. My heart wanted to explore that as far as I possibly could. I want to be Jesus-the-Christ-centered in everything: in prayer, in Scripture reading, in doing everyday chores, in the whole of life. Therefore, it was time to dig deep and explore the depths of God. He wants to be known. He calls us to explore him. My Father in heaven has made it clear that in Christ is where I belong. He also made clear that in Christ I will not only find the Father, but myself as well.

> One of the scribes came near and heard them disputing with one another, and seeing that [Jesus] answered them well, he asked him, "Which commandment is the first of all?" Jesus answered, "The first is, 'Hear, O Israel: the Lord our God, the Lord is one; you shall love the Lord your God with all your heart, and with all your soul, and with all your mind, and with all your strength.' The second is this, 'You shall love your neighbor as yourself.' There is no other commandment greater than these." Then the scribe said to him, "You are right,

Teacher; you have truly said that 'he is one, and besides him there is no other'; and 'to love him with all the heart, and with all the understanding, and with all the strength,' and 'to love one's neighbor as oneself,'—this is much more important than all whole burnt offerings and sacrifices." When Jesus saw that he answered wisely, he said to him, "You are not far from the kingdom of God." After that no one dared to ask him any question. (Mark 12:28–34)

We Gentiles have been so influenced by Greek thought that we find it hard to think any other way. We like certainties. We like black-and-white. We like yes-and-no. We like zeros-and-ones. We like right-and-wrong. We like up-and-down. We are would-be mathematicians. We are precise. We like order. We don't like loose ends. We don't like imprecise expression.

The Hebrew people of old were so different. They thought in pictures, word descriptions, and stories. I am going to sum up their way of thinking by saying that they thought in concepts. When Greek thought is applied to what Jesus said here in Mark's gospel, it gives us a mathematical formula: loving God = heart + soul + mind + strength.

If that isn't enough to discourage anyone from trying to love God, I don't know what is. Who among us could ever claim to achieve that standard? But Jesus never meant it that way, and neither would his hearers have understood it that way. For what Jesus said is not a mathematical formula but a flowchart: "loving God flows first from the heart and then to soul to mind to strength.

Jesus was saying to all who would listen to him—and especially to the religious leaders—that their approach to God was warped and twisted. The religious leaders were ruled by their heads, not by their hearts, and that was precisely why they lacked compassion. Jesus made plain the way that people were designed to be. They were to be heart-driven.

Your heart is to lead, giving your soul direction with strategy from your mind, to be carried out with all your strength. The key to knowing God is your heart, not your head. But if this is so, surely that must be

11

reflected in the Scriptures? And so it is. Both the law of God and the wisdom of God speak primarily of the heart, not the head. There are around seven hundred references in the Scripture to "heart," but only just over a hundred that refer to "mind." (This depends upon the version used, of course, but the figures stay relative.) Let us consider just a few of the Scriptures.

First, let's look at the Law (Deuteronomy 4:29; 6:5; 8:2, 5; 10:12; 13:3; 26:16; 30:1–3, 6, 11–14; 32:45–47). Second, the preeminence of the heart is not only enshrined in the Law of God, it is also enshrined in the wisdom of God (Proverbs 3:1–3, 5; 4:23; 10:8; 14:30, 33; 15:13–14; 16:1, 23; 22:17–18; 24:32). God's design is that your heart should determine your direction and your goals, while your mind determines the best strategy for achieving those goals. We are to be heart-driven carers, not head-driven accountants.

Children are a prime example of the preeminence of the heart. A newborn baby deeply touches your heart the moment it is born, but it will be a long time before your mind can engage with it. You can and will talk to a newborn baby, but you don't hold your breath waiting for a reply.

We were made to be led by our hearts, not by our heads. The mind is to be the servant of the heart, never the other way around. Greek thought had the mind leading the heart. Hebrew thought had the heart leading the mind. Our culture has not only reversed the created order of things, it also makes us doubt that the heart has any value at all. Our culture frowns upon and even mocks ideas of love, compassion, caring, and self-sacrifice. Where the mind is in control, a hardened heart is the inevitable result. A hardened heart is a heart without hope. A soft and teachable heart is a heart that has hope. The apostle Paul emphasized the preeminence of the heart.

> Moses writes concerning the righteousness that comes from the law, that "the person who does these things will live by them." But the righteousness that comes from faith says, "Do not say in your *heart*, 'Who will ascend into heaven?'" (that is, to bring Christ down) "or 'Who will descend into the abyss?'" (that is, to bring

Christ up from the dead). But what does it say? "The word is near you, on your lips and in your *heart*" (that is, the word of faith that we proclaim); because if you confess with your lips that Jesus is Lord and believe in your *heart* that God raised him from the dead, you will be saved. For one believes with the *heart* and so is justified, and one confesses with the mouth and so is saved. (Romans 10:5–10)

What Jesus said and what Paul said in Romans highlight a law of human nature: the heart is relational, but the mind is individual. The heart focuses (outwardly) on others, but the mind focuses (inwardly) on self. Therefore, where the heart is in control, there will be community. But where the mind is in control, there will be individualism. Therefore, as God said to me personally long ago, the Scriptures need to be read with your heart, not with your head. God's truth is made manifest in relationships, not in individualism. The primary relationship for exploring God and his truth is our relationship with Jesus.

If we really want to love God with all of our hearts—and then to all of our souls, to all of our minds, to all of our strength—we will certainly need soft and teachable hearts. A soft and teachable heart will welcome God and his work into our lives. It will welcome the touch of those people that God will use to teach us. For I would declare this: you haven't had true fellowship with someone until you have opened your heart to them. This is supremely true of a relationship with Jesus. All too often, Christians may open their minds to God, but not their hearts.

The apostle Paul knew this very well: "We have spoken frankly to you Corinthians; our heart is wide open to you. There is no restriction in our affections, but only in yours. In return—I speak as to children—open wide your hearts also" (2 Corinthians 6:11–13).

Now, I am not saying that our minds should be abandoned or disregarded—far from it. I am saying that we need to be led by our hearts, not by our heads. An ever-deepening relationship with Jesus the Christ has taught me this about myself and humankind in general: the heart learns life, and the head learns the lessons of life.

We surely need both, but the heart must lead! In our relationships, we need to stop teaching each other the lessons of life and teach each other life. In our relationships, we need to stop speaking the language of the lessons of life, and speak the language of life. We must share life with one another, not merely the lessons of life!

Our hearts must lead us, because our hearts will take us where our minds would never want to go. Why? Because our hearts specialize in risk-taking, but our heads specialize in risk assessment. Our hearts find reasons to go, and our heads find reasons to stay. Our hearts recognize the potential blessing, and our heads recognize only the potential cost. Our hearts consider others before self, and our heads consider self before others. "So if you have been raised with Christ, seek the things that are above, where Christ is, seated at the right hand of God. Set your minds on things that are above, not on things that are on earth" (Colossians 3:1–2).

Jesus is God's heart revealed. Our hearts forgive, as God in Christ has utterly forgiven us. Our hearts forgive, but our heads keep score! That is precisely why we must be heart-driven people. I say again that Jesus is God's heart revealed. If God himself is not critical, judgmental, and condemnatory toward us, neither should we be toward each other.

As the apostle so clearly stated it: "As God's chosen ones, holy and beloved, clothe yourselves with compassion, kindness, humility, meekness, and patience. Bear with one another and, if anyone has a complaint against another, forgive each other; just as the Lord has forgiven you, so you also must forgive. Above all, clothe yourselves with love, which binds everything together in perfect harmony" (Colossians 3:12–14).

The expression "bear with" here does not mean to put up with or to tolerate. It means to underpin and support. Such underpinning and supporting requires the reality of forgiveness in our lives. I learned this from my own human nature as I grew in relationship with Christ. If you are controlled by your head, you will not forgive. If you are controlled by your heart, you will not keep score.

Let me put it another way to bring in the language of many Scripture translations. If you are controlled by your head, you will not forget. If you are controlled by your heart, you will remember no more.

I thank my God every time I remember you, constantly praying with joy in every one of my prayers for all of you, because of your sharing in the gospel from the first day until now. I am confident of this, that the one who began a good work among you will bring it to completion by the day of Jesus Christ. It is right for me to think this way about all of you, because you hold me in your heart, for all of you share in God's grace with me, both in my imprisonment and in the defense and confirmation of the gospel. For God is my witness, how I long for all of you with the compassion of Christ Jesus. And this is my prayer, that your love may overflow more and more with knowledge and full insight to help you to determine what is best, so that in the day of Christ you may be pure and blameless, having produced the harvest of righteousness that comes through Jesus Christ for the glory and praise of God. (Philippians 1:3–11)

Jesus was heart-driven when he walked among us. Paul longed for the Christians at Philippi with the compassion of Christ Jesus. The good work begun by God in their lives will be completed in the day of Jesus the Christ. Jesus was at the very center of Paul's theology, for Paul was Christ-centered. As he wrote to the Christians at Philippi, another facet of human nature was shown to me: the head excludes, but the heart includes.

The head looks for reasons to exclude, but the heart looks for reasons to include. Jesus is all-inclusive. My exploration of Jesus revealed my own heart—and it still does daily—and it brought me to an uncomfortable truth: being heart-driven is, especially for men, a radical departure from our normal way of life. Many things can stop us from being heart-driven, not least of which for many people is that fact that life has damaged us. That is why, when we begin to follow Jesus, God begins the healing of the heart.

What is truly remarkable is the fact that we are not the only ones with wounded hearts. "The LORD saw that the wickedness of humankind was great in the earth, and that every inclination of the thoughts of their hearts was only evil continually. And the LORD was sorry that he had made humankind on the earth, and it grieved him to his heart" (Genesis 6:5–6). God's heart was filled with pain.

God is the healer of our wounded hearts, yet he himself is the wounded healer. I could stop there and meditate on that for days and weeks and never find understanding. Jesus is the wounded healer. God knows my pain. Jesus has been there. Such revelation brought me still closer to Jesus, as I realized that the wounded healer does not treat the symptoms of the disease; he heals the person himself. Nor does God heal from a distance. He is healing me even as he dwells in me. That is the true wonder of the incarnation: Christ in us, the hope of glory. This also highlights a strange paradox of healing, and it is this: that which has damaged us (relationships) is also what heals us (relationships). Therefore, in our Christian communities and elsewhere, we need relationships that help us to look inside ourselves and face up to what is in there so that Jesus might heal us. For this, we need friends.

What is a friend? I do not mean acquaintances, colleagues, family, or anyone else who is a necessary part of our daily lives. I mean real friends, and I will explain this through a growing sentence. I will not comment on each step but will leave you to ponder each as you read it.

1. A friend is *someone* …
2. A friend is someone *you trust* …
3. A friend is someone you trust *yourself to* …
4. A friend is someone you trust yourself to be *vulnerable with* …
5. A friend is someone you trust yourself to be vulnerable with and in whom you will invest *yourself* …
6. A friend is someone you trust yourself to be vulnerable with and in whom you will invest yourself *without expecting anything in return* …

True friendship, then, is the outward expression of unconditional love. Even as I say this, I realize that we tend to look for those people who will perhaps love us like that. Do we rather seek those to whom we can be that kind of friend? Such friendship is costly, and Jesus knew the extent of that cost.

True friendship reveals my own heart, and I may not find that very comfortable. The biggest historical obstacle to my accepting and loving other people has been a sense of my own worthlessness, which has even stopped me from loving myself. That is a battle that goes on to this day and will surely go on beyond this day. But I have begun to learn that it is what Jesus says about me that matters, not what I think or what anyone else thinks or says. It was no surprise, then, that when I began to explore Jesus' friendship with me, I discovered that any meaningful friendship examined me.

Unconditional love was an easy concept to speak about, but it was much harder to make it a part of my everyday life. Indeed, I knew I could not do so by myself. Only a real work of God could make it so. I knew Jesus loved me unconditionally—at least, my head theology did—but living in the reality of that revelation on a daily basis was an altogether different thing.

I discovered that I had to be growing daily in the personal reality of Jesus' unconditional love. Otherwise I could never even begin to express unconditional love to others. After all, I felt that everybody else was worthy of God's love, but I surely was not. How my prejudices were challenged in this area! When I began to realize the reality of Jesus' unconditional love, it put a whole new light on his presence.

The testimony of Jesus' presence with me is like this:

- It's okay.
- I care about you.
- You are worth it.
- I put you first.

Jesus put me first. How could that possibly be? I was so insignificant. I was not worth anything. Life had clearly taught me this down through the years.

It was then that an encounter totally changed things for me. I took a journey into my total insignificance as I was walking on a beach. I saw the sand on the beach, and I saw my life as a single grain of that sand. Insignificant. Nothing.

My vision became larger, as if I moved skyward. I saw the beach in

17

the context of the surrounding area, and it was but a small part of that area. How small, then, was my life, my grain of sand.

I moved and looked, and there was the nation spread like a map before me. I could no longer see the beach, for even it was now too small. How small my grain of sand. How insignificant.

I moved and looked, and I saw the earth as from space—a globe of beauty. But where was the nation? Where was the beach? Where was my grain of sand?

I passed the sun, and the earth was now only a spot of light in the distance. Insignificant. Nothing. I passed the billions of stars that are in our galaxy. Our sun was now long lost to sight. Where now was the beach? Where now was my grain of sand? Insignificance of insignificance. It seemed there were billions of galaxies—I don't know about billions, but I passed so many that I couldn't count them. I could no longer see my galaxy. I could no longer see how it mattered anyway. Where was my sun? Where was my earth? Where was my nation? Where was my beach? Where was my utterly insignificant grain of sand? I stood and I looked, and I knew total insignificance.

Just then I felt a hand on my shoulder. I looked around and it was Jesus. He said, "I made all this for you."

I have a saying I used to pass on to others about being there for people. It goes like this: "People will always remember that you were there for them—long after they have forgotten what you did for them."

Oh, the power of what Jesus has done for me! Jesus has always been there for me. Often he has been silent, just sitting with me—never criticizing, never pointing a finger, never wearing a stern look on his face.

"You search the scriptures because you think that in them you have eternal life; and it is they that testify on my behalf. Yet you refuse to come to me to have life" (John 5:39–40). How often I made exactly the same mistake that the Jewish religious leaders made: I did not actually come to Jesus to have life. I learned over time that life itself is Christ-centered, that life was meant to be deep and ever-deepening, not everlastingly shallow. "For freedom Christ has set us free. Stand firm, therefore, and do not submit again to a yoke of slavery" (Galatians 5:1).

In the physical world in which we live, when children stop growing or healing, all the alarm bells start ringing and people take notice. Why, then, do we accept a church culture in which it is the norm for Christians to stay stagnant, neither growing nor healing for years or decades—and yet there are no alarm bells ringing? How can it be that Christians can still believe today in exactly the same way they did decades ago?

Speaking personally again, if I am not continually experiencing growth and healing in my life, then there is a serious heart blockage in me that urgently needs to be dealt with before I suffer a serious or even fatal heart attack. Staying the same is not an option for me. If this sounds scary, the alternative is far worse. Fortunately, the one in whom we find that healing salvation is himself love, and love is powerful to work in us. "Perfect love casts out fear" (1 John 4:18).

The deepest fears that we have inside us usually cause us to run away from healing by running away from the healer. If we run away from the healer, we pay the price of stunted growth. However, speaking personally again, what caused me to initially run away from God was not a deliberate choice on my part. I ran out of my sense of worthlessness, which was the result of certain things that had happened to me during my formative years. God's approach to me in Christ was not, therefore, one of dealing with sin in my life. Rather, it was one of wooing a badly wounded human being close enough to Jesus to begin to find the healing that is in him. Feeling worthless doesn't allow me to believe the truth about who I am in Christ, and therefore I cannot draw near to him. That does not, however, stop Christ from drawing near to me. But he has to do it in disguise, if am not to run off again.

The heart learns life, but the head learns the lessons of life. However, the damage that was done to me caused my heart to learn death, not life. Because the head learns the lessons of life, my head tried to protect my heart from further damage by isolating it, putting my heart into solitary confinement. By placing my heart in solitary confinement, my head believed that it was protecting my heart from further damage, when in fact it was condemning my heart to death. The isolated and lonely heart in solitary confinement will surely die.

But Jesus had other ideas. "Indeed, the word of God is living and active, sharper than any two-edged sword, piercing until it divides soul from spirit, joints from marrow; it is able to judge the thoughts and intentions of the heart" (Hebrews 4:12).

This is no theory. This is how the Spirit of God works in you and me. There could not be lasting and ongoing growth and healing in me unless the master surgeon was allowed to do his work in me. My deep healing and consistent growth required deep repentance on my part, but not repentance from sin, which is only basic repentance. I had to experience the deepest repentance: repentance from independence and individualism.

When that repentance brought Jesus closer to me and allowed his healing love to work in my life, a dramatic transformation began. I began to hear from the mouth of Jesus himself, who told me who I really was. The best person to tell us who we are is our Creator. Identity lies at the core of every human being on planet earth. It is both a strength and a weakness of human life that we get often get our identities from others. Therefore I say it again: the best person to tell us who we are is our Creator. This comes through revelation in relationship, not through explanation in isolation.

This, then, brought me to see a bigger picture for my life, summed up in this way: Healing is the journey. Wholeness is the destination. Worship is the way.

Worship is a personal, unique encounter with Jesus, one that must be ongoing and frequent. The healing is in Jesus. The wholeness is in Jesus. The worship is in Jesus. Everything is in Jesus, from beginning to end. I read again in the Gospels how patient Jesus was with his own disciples, and I so wanted to know that Jesus—especially through his acts of power. Surely if God was working in power in and through me, I would know Jesus better.

Then came a revelation from God that stopped me in my tracks: You will know Jesus far better through intimacy than you ever will through his acts of power.

God was teaching me not to seek signs and wonders of God for their own sake, but rather to seek the God of signs and wonders. I was learning that God never puts on a show. He does not show off, even though many of his people seem to do their best to get him to do exactly that. God was emphasizing what was of primary importance for me: who I am in Christ, my identity, and the growth of his character in me.

"For we know, brothers and sisters beloved by God, that he has chosen you, because our message of the gospel came to you not in word only, but also in power and in the Holy Spirit and with full conviction; just as you know what kind of persons we proved to be among you for your sake. You became imitators of us and of the Lord" (1 Thessalonians 1:4–6). Would I want people to imitate me because I knew that my life was Christlike? What motives would be seen in me? How would my heart show up? What kind of person would I be known as? What kind of person would others see in me? Such questions framed big challenges for me.

"For our appeal does not spring from deceit or impure motives or trickery, but just as we have been approved by God to be entrusted with the message of the gospel, even so we speak, not to please mortals, but to please God who tests our hearts. As you know and as God is our witness, we never came with words of flattery or with a pretext for greed; nor did we seek praise from mortals, whether from you or from others" (1 Thessalonians 2:3–6).

Paul was not directing the Thessalonians to focus on rules and regulations but on the character of God as seen in those apostles. The character of God in the apostles was accompanied by the power of the Holy Spirit, and this produced a response of whole-hearted welcome in the Thessalonians. In Paul's day, the apostles' committed and costly love for others was completely countercultural. Such a committed and costly love for others is no less countercultural today, especially in the church.

God was at work in me through Christ. I was growing in the knowing of God's heart for me. I was getting to know what moved him, what touched him, how he felt about something or someone; and I was receiving his mercy as his love washed through me. I was growing in the knowing of God's mind for me, the consequences of choices, and his leading on safe paths. I was growing in the knowing of God's will for me—what he would do, and when and why he would do it—and I saw his love in action. All of this was in Christ himself.

This Christ-centered life that I was growing in produced a dramatic and fascinating change in me over time. I became relevant to people. I was able to engage people where they were, just as Jesus did. I was able to be relevant in what was touching their hearts, just as Jesus was. I was able to be relevant in the issues of their lives, just as Jesus always is. I was at last able to listen to people—really listen to them with my heart. I was able to watch people and learn about them and so relate to them better, just as Jesus did.

1

Revelation

Then the disciples came and asked him, "Why do you speak to them in parables?" He answered, "To you it has been given to know the secrets of the kingdom of heaven, but to them it has not been given. For to those who have, more will be given, and they will have an abundance; but from those who have nothing, even what they have will be taken away. The reason I speak to them in parables is that 'seeing they do not perceive, and hearing they do not listen, nor do they understand.' With them indeed is fulfilled the prophecy of Isaiah that says: 'You will indeed listen, but never understand, and you will indeed look, but never perceive. For this people's heart has grown dull, and their ears are hard of hearing, and they have shut their eyes; so that they might not look with their eyes, and listen with their ears, and understand with their heart and turn—and I would heal them.' But blessed are your eyes, for they see, and your ears, for they hear. Truly I tell you, many prophets and righteous people longed to see what you see, but did not see it, and to hear what you hear, but did not hear it. (Matthew 13:10–17)

Jesus was sitting in a boat, speaking parables to the crowds that stood on the shore. Since it was somewhat out-of-the-ordinary for Jesus to address the crowd apart from the disciples, they approached him and asked why he had been speaking to the crowd in parables. Jesus used the parables to cause the listeners to express their creative curiosity about the kingdom of heaven so that they would follow Jesus to have their curiosity satisfied. Jesus' disciples had been given "the knowing of the secrets of the kingdom of heaven," but the crowds had not. The disciples had been given the path to the knowing of the secrets, but they had not been given the secrets themselves. The word secrets is the Greek *mysteria* ("mysteries"), which draws on a Semitic background that speaks of an end-of-times secret that is passed on in veiled speech to God's chosen. The term is found explicitly in Daniel 2:19: "Then the mystery was revealed to Daniel in a vision of the night." (Compare Job 15:8; Psalm 25:14; Proverbs 3:32; Amos 3:7.)

From the beginning, Jesus' message clearly declared that the kingdom of heaven had already arrived but that it hadn't always been apparent to observers. Jesus gave his disciples the revelation of that kingdom as it was then and as it would later be manifested in the world. The kingdom was present, but not in its fully manifested power. But there was a mystery. The mystery was that the kingdom had arrived in a form different from that which people had anticipated. And this secret was being revealed in veiled speech to God's chosen, Jesus' disciples, the mere nobodies that he had chosen. So, on the one hand, the parables revealed to the disciples how the kingdom of God would operate in this world before its final, powerful manifestation. On the other hand, the truth that was revealed to the disciples was concealed from the crowd because of their unresponsive hearts.

The disciples' initial understanding of the secrets of the kingdom of heaven, as given by God through Jesus, would be enlarged upon so they would have a fuller understanding. But whatever understanding the crowd had, even that would be taken away. In other words, not only did the parables not reveal truth to the crowd; they even took away what little understanding the crowd already had. Truth not pursued falls from sight. At first glance, then, this is a hard passage that speaks about the "haves" and the "have-nots." At second glance, the key to knowing the secrets of the kingdom of heaven is a person's heart.

The secrets of the kingdom of heaven are made available for

exploration to those who have personally accepted the new covenant in Jesus and are now personally bound by its terms. These people are now ready to explore the secrets of the kingdom of heaven in order that they might be being transformed into maturity by those secrets. This is not a prohibition, then, but a warning.

"Our Father in heaven, hallowed be your name. Your kingdom come. Your will be done, on earth as it is in heaven. Give us this day our daily bread. And forgive us our debts, as we also have forgiven our debtors. And do not bring us to the time of trial, but rescue us from the evil one" (Matthew 6:9–13).

More on this later. Just as in physical life, growth is essential for spiritual life.

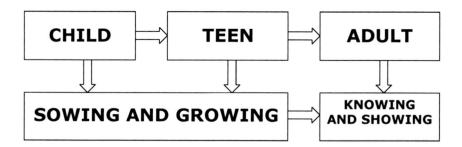

Childhood and teen years are very clear phases through which every individual needs to pass, both in the physical body and in the inner person. While learning never ceases in adulthood, it is clearly a different phase from the childhood and teen years that precede it. Both childhood and teen years are times of great sowing into the individual and great growing. Adulthood is a time of knowing (healthy relationships from a mature, wise, and discerning point of view) and a time of showing (living outwardly in maturity, wisdom, and discernment), and both have been enriched and enabled through the experiences of the childhood and teen years. Our earthly lives make a lot of sense when viewed in this way, but there is a much more important, significant, and urgent understanding to gain.

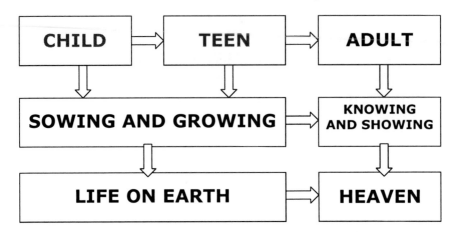

The whole of life on earth is actually about sowing and growing. It is a time of experience that feeds understanding, a time of relationship that feeds growth, a time of love that shapes a person. Whatever the heavenly life is going to be like, it will be a time of knowing and seeing (from a mature, wise, and discerning point of view) and a time of showing (living outwardly in maturity, wisdom, and discernment. Both of these will have been enriched and enabled through the years of life on earth.

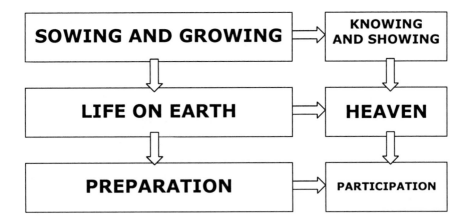

Life on earth is a time of preparation (sowing and growing), while our heavenly life will be a time of participation (knowing and showing). It is crucial that we realize the significance and importance of our preparation time here on earth, because the kingdom of heaven runs contrary to our earthly experience.

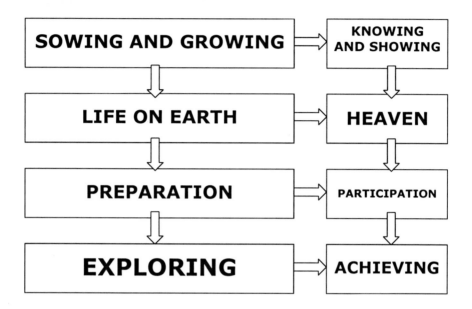

"When I was a child, I spoke like a child, I thought like a child, I reasoned like a child; when I became an adult, I put an end to childish ways. For now we see in a mirror, dimly, but then we will see face to face. Now I know only in part; then I will know fully, even as I have been fully known" (1 Corinthians 13:11–12).

If now, as adults, we see only dimly as in a mirror, then as children we didn't see at all, even though we thought we did. Before Christ was in us, we didn't see at all, even though we thought we did. Now, even though Christ is in us, we still see only dimly as in a mirror. That revelation, that realization, is crucial for us, because we must put away the idea that we can now see clearly and understand fully. If we believe that we can see and understand, we will never properly explore the secrets of the kingdom of heaven. In the unyielded or divided heart, the secrets of the kingdom of heaven will puff up, create arrogance, and destroy whatever remains of humility. That is why the exploration of the secrets of the kingdom of heaven is available only to those who have personally accepted the new covenant and are personally bound by its terms.

2

Glorification

Yet among the mature we do speak wisdom, though it is not a wisdom of this age or of the rulers of this age, who are doomed to perish. But we speak God's wisdom, secret and hidden, which God decreed before the ages for our glory. None of the rulers of this age understood this; for if they had, they would not have crucified the Lord of glory. But, as it is written, "What no eye has seen, nor ear heard, nor the human heart conceived, what God has prepared for those who love him—these things God has revealed to us through the Spirit; for the Spirit searches everything, even the depths of God. For what human being knows what is truly human except the human spirit that is within? So also no one comprehends what is truly God's except the Spirit of God. Now we have received not the spirit of the world, but the Spirit that is from God, so that we may understand the gifts bestowed on us by God. And we speak of these things in words not taught by human wisdom but taught by the Spirit, interpreting spiritual things to those who are spiritual. Those who are unspiritual do not receive the gifts of God's Spirit, for they are foolishness to them, and they are unable to understand them because they are spiritually discerned. Those who are spiritual discern all things, and they are themselves subject to no one else's scrutiny. "For who has known the mind of the Lord so as to instruct him?" But we have the mind of Christ. (1 Corinthians 2:6–16)

I must warn again that there is great danger here for the unyielded or divided heart. Before Christ was in us, we didn't see at all, even though we may have thought that we did. Now that Christ is in us, we see only dimly, as in a dark glass or smoked mirror. That revelation, that realization, is crucial for us, because we really must put away the idea that we can now see clearly and understand fully. We really must put away the idea that we have God sussed-out, that our theology of God somehow contains him. We must put away the idea that God is no greater than the sum of our combined theology. There are great depths of God to discover, but there are realities that we need to embrace if we are to explore them.

These are the critical realities that must become real to us personally if we are to explore the secrets of the kingdom of heaven.

- We have personal responsibility.
- Consequences are inevitable.
- Experience feeds understanding.
- Understanding rarely leads to experience.
- Argument springs from immaturity.
- The taking of offence is evidence of a divided heart.

In an era that is all about blame-shifting, personal responsibility is totally out-of-fashion. We behave in whatever way we like and then blame others for allowing or even causing our problems to happen. What nonsense! Before God, we cannot avoid personal responsibility. We cannot point to others and hope to deflect the gaze of God.

Part of personal responsibility is accepting that there are always consequences for what we do and say. They may be minor, or they may be major, but consequences are inevitable. Blame-shifting is an attempt to make others take the consequences for what we have done, and our society is full of that. Before God, we must never pass the buck. We cannot point to others and deflect the consequences of our words and deeds.

In an age that is dominated by Greek thinking, we imagine that knowledge will somehow lead us into new experiences. If it does, they are usually bad experiences. In the kingdom of God, it is experience that informs understanding, not the other way round. There is no substitute for personally meeting with Christ and knowing him. We cannot point to others and live off their experiences.

We sing, preach, and speak of a yielded heart to God, and then we argue with him. We tell him that the way he does things must fit in with our preferences and tastes. We tell him that if he wants our cooperation, he must do things our way. We give him permission to move! And then we wonder why God is distant and remote.

We take offence at his people who experience God in ways that we disapprove of. We are annoyed by someone else's exuberance in God. We look down on those people who behave in a "childish" way and criticize them. In other words, we quench the Spirit of God. And then we wonder why God is uncooperative and quiet. When will we learn?

The exploration of the secrets of the kingdom of heaven is available only to those who have personally accepted the new covenant in Jesus and are therefore personally bound by its terms. (We will explore this subject in depth later under the section on "Christ-Centered Law.") This is because the secrets of the kingdom of heaven will do untold damage in the heart of one who has not personally accepted the new covenant in Jesus and is therefore not personally bound by its terms. The apostle Paul was painfully aware of the damage that the secrets of the kingdom of heaven would do in an unyielded heart, because he was painfully aware of the background of his own heart.

Refer back to verse 6 in the passage above. Among the mature, we do speak wisdom. Maturity is evidenced in a person who is relationally-based—not theologically-based, academically-based, doctrinally-based, or biblically-based—and this relational basis is Christ-centered. Maturity is evidenced in a person who hears God's wisdom expressed from relationship, through relationship, and to relationship. This is "deep calling out to deep." This is God-to-God in human beings. Ah, but shallowness is so easy.

Look now at verse 7 in the passage above. We speak God's wisdom, secret and hidden, which God decreed before the ages for our glory.

God's wisdom shows how things link together (*shalom*), not how they are separated (*disintegration*). His wisdom shows how his plan is working out in human life and experience. God certainly is not distant and remote. His wisdom decreed that the incarnation was fulfilled by the ascension. How easily and conveniently we choose to forget that God's ways are far higher than our ways, that his understanding is far above our understanding.

Verse 9 in the passage above says, "But, as it is written, 'What no eye has seen, nor ear heard, nor the human heart conceived, what God has prepared for those who love him—these things God has revealed to us through the Spirit.'"

Paul knew the incarnation, and he described it in wondrous terms in Colossians 1:15–2:14:

> [Jesus] is the image of the invisible God, the firstborn of all creation; for in him all things in heaven and on earth were created, things visible and invisible, whether thrones or dominions or rulers or powers—all things have been created through him and for him. He himself is before all things, and in him all things hold together. He is the head of the body, the church; he is the beginning, the firstborn from the dead, so that he might come to have first place in everything. *For in him all the fullness of God was pleased to dwell*, and through him God was pleased to reconcile to himself all things, whether on earth or in heaven, by making peace through the blood of his cross.
>
> And you who were once estranged and hostile in mind, doing evil deeds, he has now reconciled in his fleshly body through death, so as to present you holy and blameless and irreproachable before him—provided that you continue securely established and steadfast in the faith, without shifting from the hope promised by the gospel that you heard, which has been proclaimed to every creature under heaven. I, Paul, became a servant of this gospel.

I am now rejoicing in my sufferings for your sake, and in my flesh I am completing what is lacking in Christ's afflictions for the sake of his body, that is, the church. I became its servant according to God's commission that was given to me for you, to make the word of God fully known, the mystery that has been hidden throughout the ages and generations but has now been revealed to his saints. To them God chose to make known how great among the Gentiles are the riches of the glory of this mystery, which is Christ in you, the hope of glory. It is he whom we proclaim, warning everyone and teaching everyone in all wisdom, so that we may present everyone mature in Christ. For this I toil and struggle with all the energy that he powerfully inspires within me.

For I want you to know how much I am struggling for you, and for those in Laodicea, and for all who have not seen me face to face. I want their hearts to be encouraged and united in love, so that they may have all the riches of assured understanding and have the knowledge of God's mystery, that is, *Christ himself,* in whom are hidden all the treasures of wisdom and knowledge. I am saying this so that no one may deceive you with plausible arguments. For though I am absent in body, yet I am with you in spirit, and I rejoice to see your morale and the firmness of your faith in Christ.

As you therefore have received Christ Jesus the Lord, continue to live your lives in him, rooted and built up in him and established in the faith, just as you were taught, abounding in thanksgiving.

See to it that no one takes you captive through philosophy and empty deceit, according to human tradition, according to the elemental spirits of the universe, and not according to Christ. *For in him the whole fullness of deity dwells bodily, and you have come to fullness in him,* who is the head of every ruler and authority. In him also you were circumcised with a spiritual circumcision, by putting off the body of the flesh in the circumcision of Christ; when you were buried with him in baptism, you were also raised with him through faith in the power of God, who raised him from the dead. And when you were dead in trespasses and the uncircumcision of your flesh, God made you alive together with him, when he forgave us all our trespasses, erasing the record that stood against us with its legal demands. He set this aside, nailing it to the cross. (Colossians 1:15–2:14)

The fullness of God dwelling bodily in those who have agreed to the new covenant in Christ and have come to union in him is an astonishing mystery that cannot begin to be explained. But it is an even more astonishing reality of experience that is intended to be the right of everyone who hears the deep call of God. Everything else pales into total insignificance compared to this reality of experience. Even the most godly, good, and right things of earth are as nothing compared to this reality of experience. The Spirit in us is the deposit that guarantees inheritance. Christ in us is the hope of glory. The Father in us is the certainty that we are now God's children.

Let's look back at 1 Corinthians 2:12 from the passage recorded at the beginning of this chapter. We have received not the spirit of the world, but the Spirit that is from God, so that we may understand the gifts bestowed on us by God. When we know in reality of experience the fullness of the incarnation, then we truly know and understand the gifts that God has bestowed on us—and how to use them.

Verse 13 of that same passage says that we speak of these things in words not taught by human wisdom but by the Spirit interpreting spiritual things to those who are spiritual. The deep things of God cannot be described or comprehended by logic. They can only be communicated by and to the heart that is in union and communion with God. (More on this later.) Deep calls out to deep. To receive the deep things of God requires a heart that is truly in control of the person and a head that is subservient to the heart. This is deep to deep—heart to heart—and much of it cannot be expressed by mere words. God expresses it by his eternal Word, his Son, and he finds his fullness of expression in Jesus. The deep things of God are in Christ and in Christ alone.

Verse 14 says that those who are unspiritual do not receive the gifts of God's Spirit. These gifts are foolishness to them, and they are unable to understand them because such gifts are spiritually discerned. This is not a prohibition. It is a warning that trying to use something you do not understand can be dangerous.

Verse 15 says that those who are spiritual discern all things, and they are themselves subject to no one else's scrutiny. How can any mortal human being judge Christ? Or how can any mortal human being judge what Christ is doing? Or how can any mortal human being judge those in whom Christ is? Or how can any mortal human being judge those in whom the fullness of God dwells bodily? Oh that we would put aside our competitive spirits and open our arms to each other!

Verse 16 says, "For who has known the mind of the Lord so as to instruct him?" But we have the mind of Christ. You cannot (and must not) judge, but you can know. You cannot (and must not) judge, but you can explore. You cannot (and must not) judge, but you can receive. You cannot (and must not) judge, but you can be one. There is great danger here for the unyielded or divided heart. There is treasure here for the heart that has personally accepted the new covenant in Jesus and is personally bound by its terms. This is deep. This is not for the fainthearted. This is personal.

3

Personification

I want their hearts to be encouraged and united in love, so that they may have all the riches of assured understanding and have the knowledge of God's mystery, that is, *Christ himself, in whom* are hidden all the treasures of wisdom and knowledge. I am saying this so that no one may deceive you with plausible arguments. For though I am absent in body, yet I am with you in spirit, and I rejoice to see your morale and the firmness of your faith *in Christ.*

As you therefore have received *Christ Jesus the Lord,* continue to live your lives *in him,* rooted and built up *in him* and established in the faith, just as you were taught, abounding in thanksgiving.

See to it that no one takes you captive through philosophy and empty deceit, according to human tradition, according to the elemental spirits of the universe, and not according to *Christ.* For *in him* the whole fullness of deity dwells bodily, and you have come to fullness *in him,* who is the head of every ruler and authority. *In him* also you were circumcised with a spiritual circumcision, by putting off the body of the flesh in the circumcision of *Christ*; when you were buried *with him* in baptism, you were also raised *with him* through faith in the power of God, who raised *him* from the dead. And when you were dead in trespasses and the uncircumcision of your flesh, God made you alive together *with him*, when he forgave us all our trespasses, erasing the record that stood against us with its legal demands. He set this aside, nailing it to the cross. (Colossians 2:2–14)

This passage is not just about the centrality of the Christ. It is about the personal centrality of the personal Christ and what Christ personally achieved for each of us. This passage speaks of the personal body of Christ, of which each of us is now a member, and the person of Christ as seen and known in his own people—his personal body. Think about these things.

- Christ himself is the one in whom are hidden all the treasures of wisdom and knowledge (vv. 2–3).
- Continue to live your lives in him, rooted and built up in him (vv. 6–7).
- In him also you were circumcised with a spiritual circumcision (v. 11).
- You were buried with him in baptism; you were also raised with him (v. 12).
- God made you alive together with him (v. 13).
- He forgave us all our trespasses (v. 13).
- He erased the record that stood against us with its legal demands (v. 14).
- He set this aside, nailing it to the cross (v. 14).

This inner reality needs to grow to become the normal Christian life inside. When there is absolutely nothing to stand in the way of my intimate relationship with God through Christ, there is nothing to stand in the way of the flow of living water that gushes from within and flows out to all who will receive. Explore the treasures that are in Christ. Live rooted and built up in Christ. Be raised up with Christ. Be alive in Christ. In Christ there is no record against you. In Christ there are no legal demands upon you. Be who you are in Christ.

4

Vindication

Vindication is about clearing oneself of blame, proving oneself right, proving oneself not wrong. Vindication is stronger than justification. But vindication prepares the way for failure. Vindication prepares the way for self to say, "I told you so." Vindication is a self-defense mechanism.

> Once while Jesus was standing beside the lake of Gennesaret, and the crowd was pressing in on him to hear the word of God, he saw two boats there at the shore of the lake; the fishermen had gone out of them and were washing their nets. He got into one of the boats, the one belonging to Simon, and asked him to put out a little way from the shore. Then he sat down and taught the crowds from the boat. When he had finished speaking, he said to Simon, "Put out into the deep water and let down your nets for a catch." Simon answered, "Master, we have worked all night long but have caught nothing. Yet if you say so, I will let down the nets." (Luke 5:1–5).

Peter was not here explaining why he was obeying Jesus. He was vindicating himself. Despite what Jesus said, Peter did not believe that they would catch anything. Peter believed in failure more than he believed in Jesus. Peter was paving the way for the coming failure. But he had reckoned without the grace of Jesus toward those who would follow him. Furthermore, Jesus believed in Peter more than Peter believed in Jesus.

"From that time on, Jesus began to show his disciples that he must go to Jerusalem and undergo great suffering at the hands of the elders and chief priests and scribes, and be killed, and on the third day be raised. And Peter took him aside and began to rebuke him, saying, "God forbid it, Lord! This must never happen to you." But he turned and said to Peter, "Get behind me, Satan! You are a stumbling block to me; for you are setting your mind not on divine things but on human things" (Matthew 16:21–23).

When things went wrong with Jesus' way of doing things, Peter wanted nothing more than to be vindicated, to be able to say, "I told you so" and "It's not my fault." Peter believed in himself more than he believed in Jesus. He was preparing the way for his own vindication, though he probably didn't recognize that he was doing so. His response was not about sin or deliberate choice; it was about what life had done to him. Peter didn't see this aspect of himself until later, but his need for vindication had to be dealt with, if Jesus was going to use Peter in a big way. By the time Pentecost came, Jesus had dealt with it. The events over which Peter sought to vindicate himself actually delivered him from his need for vindication.

> *You that are Israelites, listen to what I have to say:* Jesus of Nazareth, a man attested to *you* by God with deeds of power, wonders, and signs that God did through him *among you, as you yourselves know*—this man, handed over to *you* according to the definite plan and fore-knowledge of God, *you* crucified and killed by the hands of those outside the law. But God raised him up, having freed him from death, because it was impossible for him to be held in its power.
>
> For David says concerning him, "I saw the Lord always before me, for he is at my right hand so that I will not be shaken; therefore my heart was glad, and my tongue rejoiced; moreover my flesh will live in hope. For you will not abandon my soul to Hades, or let your Holy

One experience corruption. You have made known to me the ways of life; you will make me full of gladness with your presence."

Fellow Israelites, I may say to you confidently of our ancestor David that he both died and was buried, and his tomb is with us to this day. Since he was a prophet, he knew that God had sworn with an oath to him that he would put one of his descendants on his throne. Foreseeing this, David spoke of the resurrection of the Messiah, saying, "He was not abandoned to Hades, nor did his flesh experience corruption."

This Jesus God raised up, and of that *all of us* are witnesses. Being therefore exalted at the right hand of God, and having received from the Father the promise of the Holy Spirit, he has poured out this that you both see and hear. For David did not ascend into the heavens, but he himself says, "The Lord said to my Lord, 'Sit at my right hand, until I make your enemies your footstool.'" Therefore let the *entire house of Israel know with certainty that God has made him both Lord and Messiah*, this Jesus whom *you* crucified. (Acts 2:22–36)

Peter's address to the Israelites at Pentecost was personal and hard-hitting. Humanly speaking, Peter took a real risk in saying what he said. But he proclaimed God's word and did not vindicate himself over any part of it. Peter was free from the need for vindication. Peter was fit for purpose. He was perfect.

5

Realization

The need for vindication is only one of many symptoms that point to a damaged and hurting individual, whether the individual is aware of it or not. There are a great many other such symptoms, and so there is great danger ahead in terms of assumptions. Other symptoms of a damaged and hurting individual may include: an individual living in his own world, poor social skills, inability to see the obvious, and so on.

However, what has caused those symptoms or pathological signs is another question entirely. For many people, a group of such symptoms or pathological signs that consistently occur together is the direct result of what life has done to them in one way or another.

Especially critical in this regard are the ways that parents treat children—and even more so in how fathers treat sons. The family is at the center of how individuals grow and mature, and it shapes the individual. What kind of family determines what kind of shape. There is no standard way to define "normal" in relationship terms, for such a definition varies from culture to culture, place to place, age to age, experience to experience, religion to religion, and so on. There is no standard way to think about the world, for such thinking also varies from culture to culture, place to place, age to age, experience to experience, religion to religion, and so on.

For example, a person seemingly living in his own little world—for whatever reason—would probably display symptoms or pathological signs that could easily be labeled as Asperger's syndrome, and the person would then be duly written off. Since many such symptoms or pathological signs were evident in me personally—especially during my childhood and teen years, and sometimes even now—I work from the following basis: Such symptoms or signs are not always (or even nearly always) indicative of a permanent medical condition or irreversible fault that needs to be understood and coped with as best as one (and others) can. They only indicate stunted, damaged, or twisted growth during childhood and youth, probably caused in the first place by a person's upbringing and treatment by parents and other people.

Such a person needs to gradually leave his own self-centered world and come into a new world, but he is probably incapable of such a journey on his own. Even knowing where to go can be impossible if he undertakes the journey in isolation. Primary attention should therefore be given to helping such a person to grow in safe and secure relationships with others, which will enable him to gradually come out of his own little self-created, self-contained world and into the world of another person—or many people. Therefore, this person needs someone he trusts, someone he can invite into his world to lead him gently out of his own world and into another world. Nor is it enough for a person to leave his own world and come into the "real world," for the real world all around us is temporary, fluid, and deceptive.

The reality is that this person needs to be led and accompanied out of his own world into Christ's world. Only in Christ's world is there permanence, security, and safety. It is the best world to lead him into. And the best person to gradually lead the isolated person out of his self-world is someone who himself once lived in his own self-world and was led out of it and into Christ's world. The self-world is self-centered, but Christ's world is Christ-centered. Journeying with another person from one world to the other is a time- and energy-consuming journey that should never be undertaken lightly nor abandoned quickly. Such a journey is only possible in the security of a trusting love relationship and long-term commitment. Back in Jesus' day, no such name tag as "Asperger's syndrome" existed, but Jesus knew how to help people out of their own worlds and into his. So it is that we turn to Jesus for a deeper understanding of how he saw people and related to them.

> Jesus entered Jericho and was passing through it. A man was there named Zacchaeus; he was a chief tax collector and was rich. He was trying to see who Jesus was, but on account of the crowd he could not, because he was short in stature. So he ran ahead and climbed a sycamore tree to see him, because he was going to pass that way. When Jesus came to the place, he looked up and said to him, "Zacchaeus, hurry and come down; for I must stay at your house today." So he hurried down and was happy to welcome him. All who saw it began to grumble and said, "He has gone to be the guest of one who is a sinner." Zacchaeus stood there and said to the Lord, "Look, half of my possessions, Lord, I will give to the poor; and if I have defrauded anyone of anything, I will pay back four times as much." Then Jesus said to him, "Today salvation has come to this house, because he too is a son of Abraham." (Luke 19:1–9)

Zacchaeus was a "chief tax collector," which meant that he stood at the top of the collection pyramid in the area, taking a generous cut of commission from those who collected taxes for him. He was therefore a very wealthy but utterly despised man, and many would have considered his wealth ill-gotten. Zacchaeus was rejected by his own people, but he was not rejected by God. In Zacchaeus' heart, there was a deep longing, and God knew that. Zacchaeus was short in stature—both physically and internally—but he was determined to find out for himself who Jesus was.

In order to see Jesus, Zacchaeus climbed a sycamore tree, a tree with a short trunk and wide, lateral branches. Zacchaeus was not only climbing the tree to see Jesus but also to be seen. Furthermore, though he may not have known it, Zacchaeus' action was an invitation to Jesus to come into his own world. Jesus accepted that invitation by noticing Zacchaeus in the tree and accepting the invitation into Zacchaeus' world, since Zacchaeus had already issued the invitation by climbing the tree in the first place. Zacchaeus's seemingly incidental action revealed the desire of his heart, and Jesus responded to that desire. Jesus stopped and told him to come down out of the tree because Jesus "must" (*dei*) stay at his house that day. A despised and rejected man was given back his humanity—and his dignity—by Jesus.

Naturally, Jesus' choice of Zacchaeus as a host did not exactly meet with popular approval. The religious leaders judged that Jesus had chosen to be the guest of a "sinner," and they began to mutter. (The verb *diegongyzon* was used of the Israelites when they complained about being in the desert after the Exodus from Egypt (Exodus 16:7; 17:3; Numbers 11:1; 14:27–29; Luke 15:2)). Zacchaeus had long ago been written off by the crowd, the religious leaders, his own people, and even Zacchaeus himself. Yet somewhere deep inside the despised man, hope flickered.

Jesus did not write off those who remained open to God, even though they were isolated from the rest of humanity and even from themselves. He brought Zacchaeus out of his self-world and into Jesus' world. Zacchaeus expressed his appreciation of Jesus' acceptance of him by declaring his intent to show himself to be a different man. Now he was growing internally, shaking off the labels that had long stained his humanity. Because of his new relationship with God, Zacchaeus would do two things: give half of his possessions to the poor, and offer restitution to those he had wronged—at four times the amount taken.

Zacchaeus desired to right the wrongs he had done, and both actions stood out in light of what people expected. It was considered generous to give away twenty percent of one's possessions, and the restitution Zacchaeus gave was above the highest standard set by the law (Leviticus 5:16; Numbers 5:7). He actually penalized himself at the standard rate required of rustlers (Exodus 22:1; 2 Samuel 12:6), which was perhaps appropriate for a chief tax collector! This was indeed the thank offering of a changed heart.

But far more important and significant was the fact that it was the thank offering of a changed heart of a grown man who had found his humanity and dignity in Jesus' world. In Zacchaeus's changed heart, love for God expressed itself in love for others. Jesus endorsed Zacchaeus' response fully, noting that on that very day "salvation has come to [Zacchaeus'] house." This statement testifies to a heart changed by the presence of Jesus. The Lord had reclaimed a formerly lost and lonely child. Zacchaeus was now truly a son of Abraham: what Paul called a "child of faith" (Romans 4; Galatians 3). Zacchaeus's desire to make restitution met with Jesus' commendation, not as a requirement for the tax collector's salvation but as evidence that his new heart recognized a wrong that needed fixing.

Healing is in Jesus, for Jesus truly is the healer. But healing is not an incidental event detached from the person. Jesus always seeks to heal the whole person, not just the physical body. Any diagnosis, description, or recognition of symptoms (such as Asperger's) should not be seen as a blockage to healing but as an aid to healing. Jesus healed just as often through relationships as he did through acts of power. So should we. That is what makes the body of Christ so powerful and effective.

6

Personalization

"Of David. A Psalm. The earth is the LORD's and all that is in it, the world, and those who live in it; for he has founded it on the seas, and established it on the rivers. *Who shall ascend the hill of the LORD? And who shall stand in his holy place?* Those who have clean hands and pure hearts, who do not lift up their souls to what is false, and do not swear deceitfully. They will receive blessing from the LORD, and vindication from the God of their salvation. Such is the company of those who seek him, who seek the face of the God of Jacob. Selah" (Psalm 24:1–6).

In the past I lived in a horrible world that included an abusive father, and I was bullied almost everywhere I turned. Childhood was largely awful. Growing into teenage years, I was plagued by all sorts of problems, issues, addictions, weaknesses, and so on. So I lived in a make-believe world where I was loved, respected, and honored. This world existed in my own heart and mind, and no one else could get in and harm me there. In my world I was safe from harm; in the real world I was in perpetual crisis. But my depth of crisis was the peak of opportunity for God. God's answer to me was Jesus.

Jesus in me became, is becoming, and will become my hope of glory. My personal experience of that incarnation was my own, first, true Christmas. I gradually came out of my own little world into Jesus' world. Jesus' world is the only real world. I began a slow and painful climb of the hill of the Lord. When times were tough, I would run back into my own little world, and I did so often. Through the years, I have grown, as the incarnate Jesus has grown in me. Then, in early 2010, God spoke a word to me. The word was *vindication*. Jesus worked afresh in me. When I next came again into Jesus' world, my own world was demolished and destroyed even as I left it. I was in Jesus' world to stay.

"From there [Jesus] set out and went away to the region of Tyre. He entered a house and did not want anyone to know he was there. *Yet he could not escape notice*" (Mark 7:24). I cannot keep secret the presence of the incarnate Jesus in me. None of us can keep secret the presence of the incarnate Jesus in our midst. However, the glory for all of this goes to Jesus alone, never to anyone or anything else.

"How very good and pleasant it is when kindred live together in unity! … For there the LORD ordained his blessing, life forevermore" (Psalm 133:1, 3). Do you see what God's blessing is? Do you realize the implication of God's blessing? In this world, we each and all may ascend the hill of the Lord. In this world, we each and all may stand in his holy place. The place is holy because of who is there, not because of the place itself. In this world, we each and all may receive the blessing of life forevermore from the Lord. In this world, the world itself may be blessed by God.

"His divine power has given us everything needed for life and godliness, through the knowledge of him who called us by his own glory and goodness. Thus he has given us, through these things, his *precious and very great promises*, so that through them you may escape from the corruption that is in the world because of lust, and may become *participants of the divine nature*" (2 Peter 1:3–4).

I am speaking here and now of God's very great and precious promises to me personally. As the incarnation of Jesus was real in me, as the incarnate Christ continued to grow in me, as I had ascended the hill of the Lord, as I had stood in his holy place—so I have participated in the divine nature. This is the way that God said it would be. This is the normal Christian life for all who will receive it.

"For we did not follow cleverly devised myths when we made known to you the power and coming of our Lord Jesus Christ, but we had been *eyewitnesses of his majesty*. For he received honor and glory from God the Father when that voice was conveyed to him by the Majestic Glory, saying, 'This is my Son, my Beloved, with whom I am well pleased.' *We ourselves heard this voice* come from heaven, while *we were with him* on the holy mountain" (2 Peter 1:16–18).

I too am an eyewitness of his majesty. I myself heard that voice that came from heaven when I was with him on the sacred mountain, the hill of the Lord. This is no boasting or telling of fancy stories. What God said would be, is! Jesus is incarnate in me! What a gift! That gift to me was my first real Christmas.

Jesus is incarnate in us! Beloved, for us it is Christmas every day! Intimacy enables anointing. Intimacy is not a marketable product. Intimacy is not a destination at which we arrive. Intimacy is relationship without walls. Welcome to your world, Jesus. Welcome to your people. Come, Lord Jesus, come.

7

Dedication

"Of David. A Psalm. The earth is the LORD's and all that is in it, the world, and those who live in it; for he has founded it on the seas, and established it on the rivers. *Who shall ascend the hill of the LORD? And who shall stand in his holy place?* Those who have clean hands and pure hearts, who do not lift up their souls to what is false, and do not swear deceitfully. They will receive blessing from the LORD, and *vindication* from the God of their salvation. Such is the company of those who seek him, who seek the face of the God of Jacob. Selah" (Psalm 24:1–6).

Who shall ascend the hill of the LORD (YHWH) (v. 3)? The hill of the Lord is relational, not theoretical. The hill of the Lord is about meeting the Lord over and over again in greater and greater revelation. It is about knowing ourselves over and over again in greater and greater revelation. All of this is relationship-based, and every other interpretation can be put to one side for the moment. What is needed for growth in a relationship with God on the hill of the Lord?

- clean hands
- a pure heart
- not lifting up one's soul to what is false
- not swearing deceitfully

Clean hands are not the result of climbing the hill of the Lord; they are a prerequisite for doing so. This requires blamelessness and righteousness in relationships with other people—no hidden agendas, deceit, pretence, conjuring tricks, or oppressing of others. No broken human relationships are to prevent me from climbing the hill of the Lord. I know it is so, because the Lord himself told me. Before we can climb the hill of the Lord, our relationships must be clean. Climbing the hill of the Lord with dirty hands will result in judgment on the hill of the Lord.

A *pure heart* is required before we can climb the hill of the Lord. A pure heart is an undivided heart. An undivided heart will be renewed on the hill of the Lord. A naked and absolute determination to know God at all costs will be rewarded. The pure heart is pure because God himself has made it pure. Wanting or needing a pure heart is not the same as having a pure heart. Climbing the hill of the Lord with a divided heart will result in the divided heart being ripped apart on the hill of the Lord. Divided loyalties will quickly be revealed.

We are *not to lift up our souls to what is false.* Great wisdom is needed before anyone begins the ascent of the hill of the Lord. To lift the soul up to anything other than God is to risk severe soul damage. Only in God will the lifted soul find life and renewal. Before climbing the hill of the Lord, a person must be free of all idols that would damage the soul. You cannot serve God and another. All things have their places, but their places are not in place of God. Our hearts were made for God. They were made to know him. We were made to grow in that which is true, genuine, and pure: God himself. Do not let your heart be deceived into lifting up your soul to that which is not worthy of such a precious gift. Jesus alone is worthy of the gift of your whole self.

We are *not to swear deceitfully.* This has nothing to do with swear words. To swear deceitfully is to say that something is so when it is not, or to say that something is not so when it is. The danger of swearing deceitfully should always be uppermost in our heart understanding because of potential consequences; ask Ananias and Sapphira. Clean hands, a pure heart, and a soul free of idolatry are all needed if we are to avoid swearing deceitfully. To say that something is so when it is not so is a very dangerous thing. Likewise, to say that something is not so when it is so is also a very dangerous thing. Death and life are in the power of the tongue, and those who love it will eat its fruits. Unjust scales are an abomination to the Lord. The tongue dispenses death so easily and deceives so easily. The deceitful tongue on the hill of the Lord will result in death—what kind of death remains to be seen. The tongue that speaks out of integrity may ascend the hill of the Lord. The journey up the hill of the Lord is not an easy journey. Discovering God means discovering self. Not all discoveries of self are welcome discoveries.

These four requirements for growth in a relationship with the Lord are not the results of climbing the hill of the Lord; they are the prerequisites. This is a serious business that is open to all those who would be earnest in their pursuit of God to the point of utter dependence and total surrender. They will discover that it is actually God himself who is drawing them on, wooing them to come near.

The ascent of the hill of the Lord is a journey of wonder and awe for those who hunger and are drawn. Those who ascend the hill of the Lord will receive and participate in the blessing of the Lord: life forevermore.

Psalm 24:3 asks, "And who shall stand in his holy place?" Those who rightly ascend the hill of the Lord shall stand in his holy place, and that holy place is relational, not geographical. It is not the top of the mountain that is holy; it is the one who is there that is holy. Climbing a mountain does not change a life; meeting the God who is there changes a life. It is his holy place because it is where he meets a person, not because the place itself has been designated as holy in and of itself. The emphasis here is far less on the place itself and much more on the God who meets a person in that place.

> Then Moses and Aaron, Nadab, and Abihu, and seventy of the elders of Israel went up, and they saw the God of Israel. Under his feet there was something like a pavement of sapphire stone, like the very heaven for clearness. God did not lay his hand on the chief men of the people of Israel; also they beheld God, and they ate and drank. The LORD said to Moses, "Come up to me on the mountain, and wait there; and I will give you the tablets of stone, with the law and the commandment, which I have written for their instruction." So Moses set out with his assistant Joshua, and Moses

went up into the mountain of God. To the elders he had said, "Wait here for us, until we come to you again; for Aaron and Hur are with you; whoever has a dispute may go to them." Then Moses went up on the mountain, and the cloud covered the mountain. The glory of the LORD settled on Mount Sinai, and the cloud covered it for six days; on the seventh day he called to Moses out of the cloud. Now the appearance of the glory of the LORD was like a devouring fire on the top of the mountain in the sight of the people of Israel. Moses entered the cloud, and went up on the mountain. Moses was on the mountain for forty days and forty nights. (Exodus 24:9–18)

Meeting God on the hill of the Lord transcends time and imagination.

Now Moses used to take the tent and pitch it outside the camp, far off from the camp; he called it the tent of meeting. And everyone who sought the LORD would go out to the tent of meeting, which was outside the camp. Whenever Moses went out to the tent, all the people would rise and stand, each of them, at the entrance of their tents and watch Moses until he had gone into the tent. When Moses entered the tent, the pillar of cloud would descend and stand at the entrance of the tent, and the LORD would speak with Moses. When all the people saw the pillar of cloud standing at the entrance of the tent, all the people would rise and bow down, all of them, at the entrance of their tent. Thus the LORD used to speak to Moses face to face, as one speaks to a friend. (Exodus 33:7–11)

To encounter God face-to-face transcends prayer. For God to speak to a human being as a human being speaks to a friend transcends understanding. Such speaking is heart-to-heart, not mouth-to-mouth. Such union is being one with God. Such union in the holy place transforms everything about relationship with God. Known and expressed relationship becomes normality and everyday experience. When a leader meets with God in this way, there are serious implications for the people.

> While they were at Hazeroth, Miriam and Aaron spoke against Moses because of the Cushite woman whom he had married (for he had indeed married a Cushite woman); and they said, "Has the LORD spoken only through Moses? Has he not spoken through us also?" And the LORD heard it. Now the man Moses was very humble, more so than anyone else on the face of the earth. Suddenly the LORD said to Moses, Aaron, and Miriam, "Come out, you three, to the tent of meeting." So the three of them came out. Then the LORD came down in a pillar of cloud, and stood at the entrance of the tent, and called Aaron and Miriam; and they both came forward. And he said, "Hear my words: When there are prophets among you, I the LORD make myself known to them in visions; I speak to them in dreams. Not so with my servant Moses; he is entrusted with all my house. With him I speak face to face—clearly, not in riddles; and he beholds the form of the LORD. Why then were you not afraid to speak against my servant Moses?" And the anger of the LORD was kindled against them, and he departed. (Numbers 12:1–9)

To stand against the Lord's anointed is to take a terrible risk. The Lord's anointed carry a great responsibility.

> The LORD said to Moses, "Go down at once! Your people, whom you brought up out of the land of Egypt, have acted perversely; they have been quick to turn aside from the way that I commanded them; they have cast for themselves an image of a calf, and have worshipped

it and sacrificed to it, and said, 'These are your gods, O Israel, who brought you up out of the land of Egypt!'" The LORD said to Moses, "I have seen this people, how stiff-necked they are. Now let me alone, so that my wrath may burn hot against them and I may consume them; and of you I will make a great nation … When Joshua heard the noise of the people as they shouted, he said to Moses, "There is a noise of war in the camp." But he said, "It is not the sound made by victors, or the sound made by losers; it is the sound of revellers that I hear." As soon as he came near the camp and saw the calf and the dancing, Moses' anger burned hot, and he threw the tablets from his hands and broke them at the foot of the mountain. He took the calf that they had made, burned it with fire, ground it to powder, scattered it on the water, and made the Israelites drink it. (Exodus 32:7–10, 17–20)

There is always a very serious and very real price to be paid for willful idolatry. None are more aware of that very serious and very real price than those who have stood in the holy place. The hill of the Lord made me keenly aware that there was much in me that needed healing. The realization hit me that so much of what the Spirit of God has to deal with in me is not the result of deliberate sin or bad choices; it is the result of the damage that life has done to me. So much of what the Spirit of God has to deal with in me has to do with the very existence and presence of sin in me, the sin nature that I was born with.

This inherent sin nature in you and me will not be found by self-examination or counseling. It needs the master surgeon, the Holy Spirit, to expose it and remove it as and when he sees best. There is no personal guilt here, for this is not about deliberate sin on my part, neither is there any condemnation on God's part. This is about transforming a badly damaged human being into the likeness of Christ, growing in his love and character. It is about a heart transplant. This change of heart comes about as the Holy Spirit rewrites my DNA with the DNA of Christ and transforms me day-by-day with the love and character of Jesus.

This transformation goes far deeper than dealing with any willful sin. It is the transformation of my inner being, my real self, and such transformation will cause a real change in the external person that I am—that is, in the way I relate to and interact with others. Such transformation of the inner being is the transformation of union: Christ in me, the hope of glory. Such transformation, such union, had to take place before I was able to meet my Father. Yet if we resist the Spirit of God as he seeks to do his deepest work in us, we are cutting ourselves off from the union with God that allows us to meet our Father. Without that deep transformation brought about by the Spirit of God and the union he brought me into, I would not have survived the encounter with my Father. That is why the Spirit of God must be allowed to do his deepest work in us. Without that deepest work, we will not be able to meet God and survive the encounter.

8

Transformation

"Abide in me as I abide in you. Those who abide in me and I in them bear much fruit ... If you abide in me, and my words abide in you, ask for whatever you wish, and it will be done for you" (John 15:4–5, 7).

What does *abide* mean? The original primary meaning is "remain in expectation." Jesus said, "Remain in expectation in me as I remain in expectation in you. Those who remain in expectation in me and I remain in expectation in them will bear much fruit. If you remain in expectation in me and my words remain in expectation in you, ask for whatever you wish, and it will be done for you." Consistent remaining in expectation in Jesus produces transformation.

Transformation begins with the hidden, inner self, but it certainly does not stop there. Transformation is an ongoing resulting effect, not an independent event. Transformation is the incarnation breaking out of the private place and into the public sphere. Transformation is all heaven breaking loose. Transformation is the magnet that draws people to the Jesus who has been lifted high. Here are some examples of how that was true for Jesus himself, who remained in expectation in his Father in heaven.

"[Jesus and his disciples] went to Capernaum; and when the sabbath came, he entered the synagogue and taught. They were astounded at his teaching, for he taught them as one having authority, and not as the scribes" (Mark 1:21–22). Why were they astounded at his teaching? Because Jesus knew exactly what he was talking about from his own remaining in expectation in his Father.

"Whoever does not love me does not keep my words; and the word that you hear is not mine, but is from the Father who sent me" (John 14:24). But it wasn't just Jesus' words, powerful though they were through his remaining in expectation in his Father. "Very truly, I tell you, the Son can do nothing on his own, but only what he sees the Father doing; for whatever the Father does, the Son does likewise" (John 5:19).

What was the result of Jesus remaining in expectation in his Father and hearing his words and speaking them, and seeing his actions and doing them? "They were all amazed and glorified God, saying, 'We have never seen anything like this!'" (Mark 2:12). Why had they never seen anything like this before? Because Jesus wasn't asking God to do things. He was simply declaring them done.

"From there Jesus set out and went away to the region of Tyre. He entered a house and did not want anyone to know he was there. Yet he could not escape notice" (Mark 7:24). Why could Jesus not keep his presence secret? Because transformation was breaking out of the private place into the public sphere. And nothing like that transformation had ever been seen before.

"One day, while he was teaching, Pharisees and teachers of the law were sitting near by (they had come from every village of Galilee and Judea and from Jerusalem); and the power of the Lord was with him to heal" (Luke 5:17). Why was the power of the Lord with him to heal? Because transformation was never intended for the primary benefit of the person for whom transformation was breaking out. Transformation was primarily for the benefit of anyone who would receive it with an open heart. Even transformation was not an end in itself. Transformation was intended to introduce people to the transformer, Jesus.

Transformation is the ongoing effect of the presence of the person of Jesus. Here on planet earth, Jesus could not keep his presence secret as he moved around. He was gaining fame. But Jesus had won the battle with fame during the time that he was tempted by the Devil. Even as I say this about Jesus, I am aware that fame is a great danger for all of us— and a danger for me personally. There is danger in becoming the latest Christian superstar who will be microscopically examined, discussed, and then dissected and discarded. Fame is an insidious master.

Despite the danger of fame, transformation must break out into the open, but the one held high for all to see must be Jesus alone, not me or you. If fame is allowed to grow unchecked and uncontrolled, it will destroy us sooner or later—and probably sooner. Nevertheless, transformation must be allowed to break out of the private place and into the public sphere so that Jesus may be lifted high and draw people to himself. Jesus' purpose is to draw people to himself, not to you or me.

Receiving and honoring those people whom God is lifting up produces praise, honor, and glory for Jesus, not for the people he is lifting up. The resultant breakout of transformation will not be attributed to any human being or organization but to Jesus himself. And that is the way it should be. It is all too easy for people to see the human being who is being used by God—instead of seeing God who is at work through a human being. It is even easier to set aside the wonders that God has prepared for his people because we are overly cautious in focusing on the human being rather than on God. We need to ask if the people God is using are known to us because they are part of our community or if they are unknown strangers? Are these people that God is using known to have character and integrity?

> Blessed be the God and Father of our Lord Jesus Christ, who has blessed us in Christ with *every spiritual blessing* in the heavenly places, just as *he chose us in Christ before the foundation of the world* to be holy and blameless before him in love. *He destined us for adoption as his children* through Jesus Christ, according to the good pleasure of his will, to the praise of his glorious grace that he freely bestowed on us in the Beloved. In him we have redemption through his blood, the forgiveness of our trespasses, *according to the riches of his grace that he lavished on us.* With all wisdom and insight *he has made known to us the mystery of his will,* according to his good pleasure that he set forth in Christ, as a plan for the fullness of time, to gather up all things in him, things in heaven and things on earth. In Christ *we have also obtained an inheritance,* having been destined according

to the purpose of him who accomplishes all things according to his counsel and will, so that we, who were the first to set our hope on Christ, might live for the praise of his glory. In him you also, when you had heard the word of truth, the gospel of your salvation, and had believed in him, were marked with the seal of the promised Holy Spirit; this is *the pledge of our inheritance* toward redemption as God's own people, to the praise of his glory. (Ephesians 1:3–14)

What God has given needs to be received. What God has given needs to be realized. What God has given needs to be returned.

In Christ we have every spiritual blessing in the heavenly places (v. 3). In the place of highest authority, heaven, we have every spiritual blessing. Is this true in our daily lives?

We were chosen before the foundation of the world (v. 4). We were chosen to be holy. We were chosen to be blameless. Is this true in our daily lives?

He destined us for adoption as his children (v. 5). Children grow into their inheritance as they grow into adulthood. Children know that they are dearly and wonderfully loved. Is this true in our daily lives?

The riches of his grace have been lavished upon us (v. 7–8). Grace abounds far more than we can believe or understand. Grace never ends, fades, or spoils. Is this true in our daily lives?

God has made known to us the mystery of his will (v. 9). God's purpose has been made clear to us, and it includes us. Is this true in our daily lives?

In Christ we have also obtained an inheritance (v. 11). Along with Christ we have been given all things. We are to grow into all things through exploration and realization. Is this true in our daily lives?

Our inheritance has been pledged to us (v. 14). God will keep his promise and make our inheritance ours. We need to live as those who are growing into an imperishable inheritance. Is this true in our daily lives?

What God has given needs to be received, realized, and returned. God has not withheld anything. But we can neglect to receive it. We can neglect to realize it and return it.

I pray that, according to the riches of his glory, he may grant that you may be strengthened in your inner being with power through his Spirit, and that Christ may dwell in your hearts through faith, as you are being rooted and grounded in love. I pray that you may have the power to comprehend, with all the saints, what is the breadth and length and height and depth, and to know the love of Christ that surpasses knowledge, so that you may be filled with all the fullness of God. Now to him who by the power at work within us is able to accomplish abundantly far more than all we can ask or imagine, to him be glory in the church and in Christ Jesus to all generations, forever and ever. Amen. (Ephesians 3:16–21)

9

Identification

If someone should ask you, "Who are you?," how would you answer this question? Does telling a person your name answer the question? If you tell someone your parentage, what you do for a living, or where you live, does that satisfy the inquiry? Who are you? Is this a question of the head or the heart? Is the question requesting information, or is it looking for much more than that?

Let us consider the question that is on the lips of those people whose hearts are seeking reality: who is your God? How do we answer that question? Does telling a person God's name answer the question? If we describe his parentage, what he does for a living, or where he lives, does that suffice? The question, "Who is God?," is found all the way through Scripture. Here are just a few examples:

"Who is like you, O LORD, among the gods? Who is like you, majestic in holiness, awesome in splendor, doing wonders?" (Exodus 15:11).

"All my bones shall say, 'O LORD, who is like you?'" (Psalm 35:10).

"You who have done great things, O God, who is like you? (Psalm 71:19).

When someone with an open heart asks you, "Who is your God?," they are actually asking you, "Who is the God that you know by your own experience?" They don't want theory. They don't want a "proof" verse. They don't want cheap sayings, clichés, or intellectual persuasion. They want to know if the God you speak of is real in your life or just another concept. In other words, is your God a personal God or just a disinterested force?

The God who is love will always make himself known through acts of kindness, gentleness, and acceptance. Love expresses itself through grace, and grace ministers love. When someone asks you, "Who is your God?," that person is asking you to tell him what your God has done for you, how he has made himself real to you. Answer the question this person is actually asking. Yes, I know that we are mere human beings, but what about Christ who is in us, our hope of glory? Who is this Jesus? Who is this Christ?

"I saw one like a human being coming with the clouds of heaven. And he came to the Ancient One and was presented before him. To him was given dominion and glory and kingship, that all peoples, nations, and languages should serve him. His dominion is an everlasting dominion that shall not pass away, and his kingship is one that shall never be destroyed" (Daniel 7:13–14).

Jesus is the man in heaven so that God might be in us. When someone asks you, "Who is your God?," answer for yourself, and let God answer for himself. Those people with open hearts who ask the question will not reject you or walk away from you. They are seeking reality. They have had their fill of empty religion. They are tired of words that promise everything and deliver nothing. Christ in us is not just our hope of glory; he is the hope of glory for everyone we meet. Such identification lies at the heart of growing the character of God in us. It lies at the heart of the reality of Christ in us and his love made visible.

When you meet people who ask questions from an open heart, expect God to move, touch, speak, and make himself known. Love expresses itself through grace, and Jesus is the man of grace. "He is your praise; he is your God, who has done for you these great and awesome things that your own eyes have seen" (Deuteronomy 10:21). "Only fear the LORD, and serve him faithfully with all your heart; for consider what great things he has done for you" (1 Samuel 12:24).

Beloved people of the living God, expect God to move through you, to touch through you, to speak through you, and to make himself known through you.

And when Jesus had stepped out of the boat, immediately a man out of the tombs with an unclean spirit met him. He lived among the tombs; and no one could restrain him any more, even with a chain; for he had often been restrained with shackles and chains, but the chains he wrenched apart, and the shackles he broke in pieces; and no one had the strength to subdue him. Night and day among the tombs and on the mountains he was always howling and bruising himself with stones. When he saw Jesus from a distance, he ran and bowed down before him; and he shouted at the top of his voice, "What have you to do with me, Jesus, Son of the Most High God? I adjure you by God, do not torment me." For he had said to him, "Come out of the man, you unclean spirit!" Then Jesus asked him, "What is your name?" He replied, "My name is Legion; for we are many." He begged him earnestly not to send them out of the country. Now there on the hillside a great herd of swine was feeding; and the unclean spirits begged him, "Send us into the swine; let us enter them." So he gave them permission. And the unclean spirits came out and entered the swine; and the herd, numbering about two thousand, rushed down the steep bank into the sea, and were drowned in the sea.

The swineherds ran off and told it in the city and in the country. Then people came to see what it was that had happened. They came to Jesus and saw the demoniac sitting there, clothed and in his right mind, the very man who had had the legion; and they were afraid. Those who had seen what had happened to the demoniac and to the swine reported it. Then they began to beg Jesus to leave their neighborhood. As he was getting into the boat, the man who had been possessed by demons begged him that he might be with him. But Jesus refused, and said to him, "Go home to your friends, and tell them how much the Lord has done for you, and what mercy he has shown you." And he went away and began to proclaim in the Decapolis how much Jesus had done for him; and everyone was amazed. (Mark 5:2–20)

Beloved people of the living God, go home to your friends and tell them how much the Lord has done for you. When people ask you, "Who is your God?," tell them how much the Lord has done for you. When you meet the needy, the poor, the broken, or the abandoned, tell them how much the Lord has done for you. Then see what the Lord will do for them in front of your very eyes. Identification means much more than simply knowing who someone is. Identification joins one person to another. Being one with Christ and part of his body must bring a whole new order of things.

"Now before faith came, we were imprisoned and guarded under the law until faith would be revealed. Therefore the law was our disciplinarian until Christ came, so that we might be justified by faith. But now that faith has come, we are no longer subject to a disciplinarian, for in Christ Jesus you are all children of God through faith. As many of you as were baptized into Christ have clothed yourselves with Christ. There is no longer Jew or Greek, there is no longer slave or free, there is no longer male and female; for all of you are one in Christ Jesus" (Galatians 3:23–28).

Such a reality must be constantly transforming us inside, transforming the way we see and think about things and the way we do and receive things. This reality must be constantly transforming our identification of Christ, with Christ, and in Christ.

Do you not know that all of us who have been baptized into Christ Jesus were baptized into his death? Therefore we have been buried with him by baptism into death, so that, just as Christ was raised from the dead by the glory of the Father, so we too might walk in newness of life. For if we have been united with him in a death like his, we will certainly be united with him in a resurrection like his. We know that our old self was crucified with him so that the body of sin might be destroyed, and we might no longer be enslaved to sin. For whoever has died is freed from sin. But if we have died with Christ, we believe that we will also live with him. We know that Christ, being raised from the dead, will never die again; death no longer has dominion over him. The death he died, he died to sin, once for all; but the life he lives, he lives to God. So you also must consider yourselves dead to sin and alive to God in Christ Jesus. (Romans 6:3–11)

Is this a reality that is only for the future? If it is a reality that is to become real for us right here and now, then change is an ongoing requirement. There is a great deal of ongoing receiving and realizing to be done. Transformation must take place on a constant and ongoing basis. Otherwise the reality is of little or no value to us. It is time to focus less on speaking about the transformation that must happen, and focus more on giving time for the transformation to actually happen.

10

Purification

Jesus, full of the Holy Spirit, returned from the Jordan and was led by the Spirit in the wilderness, where for forty days he was tempted by the devil. He ate nothing at all during those days, and when they were over, he was famished. The devil said to him, "If you are the Son of God, command this stone to become a loaf of bread." Jesus answered him, "It is written, 'One does not live by bread alone.'"

Then the devil led him up and showed him in an instant all the kingdoms of the world. And the devil said to him, "To you I will give their glory and all this authority; for it has been given over to me, and I give it to anyone I please. If you, then, will worship me, it will all be yours." Jesus answered him, "It is written, 'Worship the Lord your God, and serve only him.'"

Then the devil took him to Jerusalem, and placed him on the pinnacle of the temple, saying to him, "If you are the Son of God, throw yourself down from here, for it is written, 'He will command his angels concerning you, to protect you,' and 'On their hands they will bear you up, so that you will not dash your foot against a stone.'"

Jesus answered him, "It is said, 'Do not put the Lord your God to the test.'" When the devil had finished every test, he departed from him until an opportune time.

> Then Jesus, filled with the power of the Spirit, returned
> to Galilee, and a report about him spread through all the
> surrounding country. He began to teach in their syna-
> gogues and was praised by everyone. (Luke 4:1–15)

The word translated "led" in verse one is a much more forceful word than merely led. The Holy was pushing, driving, urging Jesus into the wilderness. Jesus was full of the Holy Spirit, and yet the Spirit shoved him into the wilderness. It was a long, hard period of temptation at the hands of the Enemy, at the end of which Jesus was personally tempted by the personal enemy. But it was a vitally important time.

[Jesus] ate nothing at all during those days, and when they were over, he was famished (v. 2). The devil came personally to Jesus at the end of that hard period, when Jesus was at his weakest. But that personal temptation could not have been about sin. So, what was the personal temptation at the end of that period about? What was Jesus doing for the whole period that led up the devil's personal temptation? What was happening during that long and hard period?

"In the days of his flesh, Jesus offered up prayers and supplications, with loud cries and tears, to the one who was able to save him from death, and he was heard because of his reverent submission. Although he was a Son, he learned obedience through what he suffered; and having been made perfect, he became the source of eternal salvation for all who obey him, having been designated by God a high priest according to the order of Melchizedek" (Hebrews 5:7–10).

Since we know that Jesus was without sin, why did he have to learn obedience? If learning obedience had nothing to do with sin, what was its significance? How did Jesus learn obedience? We are not told any details here, nor are we told in the Luke passage. But when the Holy Spirit urged Jesus into the wilderness, it was so that Jesus could come face-to-face with his own human nature to discover in his own experience what it meant to be human. For Jesus had to be examined in what his own human nature was really like when it was naked and exposed. That period in the wilderness was critical for Jesus to fulfill his identity and do his Father's will. While Jesus did not have to battle inherent sin, he did have to battle the weakness of human nature. When that battle was close to being won, the Devil came personally to Jesus. After that temptation, the Devil was never again able to personally tempt Jesus away from his chosen path. And yet, even having gone through all of this struggle, it still wasn't over for Jesus in terms of facing up to his own weak human nature.

> They went to a place called Gethsemane; and he said to his disciples, "Sit here while I pray." He took with him Peter and James and John, and began to be distressed and agitated. And he said to them, "I am deeply grieved, even to death; remain here, and keep awake." And going a little farther, he threw himself on the ground and prayed that, if it were possible, the hour might pass from him. He said, "Abba, Father, for you all things are possible; remove this cup from me; yet, not what I want, but what you want." He came and found them sleeping; and he said to Peter, "Simon, are you asleep? Could you not keep awake one hour? Keep awake and pray that you may not come into the time of trial; the spirit indeed is willing, but the flesh is weak." And again he went away and prayed, saying the same words. And once more he came and found them sleeping, for their eyes were very heavy; and they did not know what to say to him. He came a third time and said to them, "Are you still sleeping and taking your rest? Enough! The hour has come; the Son of Man is betrayed into the hands of sinners. Get up, let us be going. See, my betrayer is at hand." (Mark 14:32–42).

During this final time of facing up to his own human nature, Jesus sweated profusely. This was a time of agonizing weakness for Jesus. He struggled to keep going along his chosen way. The immense weakness of his own human nature wanted to drag him aside. While he had faced up to his own human nature at the beginning of his ministry, Jesus had never faced it like this before. He was experiencing the stark reality of the cost of fulfilling his calling.

"Since, then, we have a great high priest who has passed through the heavens, Jesus, the Son of God, let us hold fast to our confession. For we do not have a high priest who is unable to sympathize with our weaknesses, but we have one who in every respect has been tested as we are, yet without sin. Let us therefore approach the throne of grace with boldness, so that we may receive mercy and find grace to help in time of need" (Hebrews 4:14–16).

Hebrews says that Jesus was tested in every respect as we are. That has an absolutely crucial flip side: if we really want to follow Jesus and be like him, then we can expect to be tested in every way that Jesus was tested. We can expect that we will face the temptation of the Enemy as he tries to derail us from fulfilling God's purpose for our lives. We can expect that our human nature will be revealed and tested as the Holy Spirit lays bare what it means for us as individuals to be human beings in Christ. We can expect to face the incredible weakness of our human frame as we come to face the reality of what it means to follow Jesus. We can expect that we will not enjoy any of this. We can expect that we will not enjoy being purified so that we as individuals might be fit for his purpose.

"Do you not know that all of us who have been baptized into Christ Jesus were baptized into his death? Therefore we have been buried with him by baptism into death … So you also must consider yourselves dead to sin and alive to God in Christ Jesus … While we were living in the flesh, our sinful passions, aroused by the law, were at work in our members to bear fruit for death. But now we are discharged from the law, dead to that which held us captive, so that we are slaves not under the old written code but in the new life of the Spirit" (Romans 6:3–4,11; 7:5–6).

The Spirit of God brings us face-to-face with the incredible weakness of our human frame so that we might be purified—and then terminated. Eternal life in Christ is for those who have died to self and who go on dying to self day-by-day, month-by-month, and year-by-year.

As we grow in and with Christ, we grow to face our own human nature—and we come again to the cross that we might die and go on dying. If we would truly live in Christ, then we must truly die. The kingdom of God of is populated by people who have died and been raised to life in Christ, people who go on dying and being raised to life in Christ day-by-day, month-by-month, and year-by-year.

11

Termination

The reason that the Spirit of God brings us face-to-face with the incredible weakness of our human frame is so that we might die. This does not mean dying in mere theological terms, in theory, in mental belief, or just in principle. It does not mean dying "in the heavenlies." It means actually dying to self. What does it mean to die? How does dying actually happen? Is dying what we really want? Are we really willing to die? Let me share seven truths that we need to realize if we are to truly die to ourselves.

1. *As citizens of God, we are at peace with God.* "Therefore, since we are justified by faith, we have peace with God through our Lord Jesus Christ, through whom we have obtained access to this grace in which we stand; and we boast in our hope of sharing the glory of God" (Romans 5:1–2). We are not the casualties of war. We are the sacrifice of peace. As we are walking in peace with Christ, we hear his call to come and die. "For if we have been united with him in a death like his, we will certainly be united with him in a resurrection like his" (Romans 6:5).

2. *Dying in Christ is not pointless.* Dying in Christ is not defeat. It is not a setback or God's second best for us. Dying in Christ is the only way to living in Christ. "You are in the Spirit, since the Spirit of God dwells in you. If the Spirit of him who raised Jesus from the dead dwells in you, he who raised Christ from

the dead will give life to your mortal bodies also through his Spirit that dwells in you" (Romans 8:9, 11).

3. *We do not die alone.* Not only has Christ died before us and for us, but the Spirit of God is in us, with us, and on us as we die daily. Indeed, we die daily in Christ, and it is the Spirit of God himself who daily gives our mortal bodies life. But the Spirit can only give life where there has been death. It is absolutely true that we do not face this death alone, but it is also true that the Spirit gives life the very moment that there is death. Death in Christ is not a lonely death. Death in Christ is not abandonment. "We know that all things work together for good for those who love God, who are called according to his purpose" (Romans 8:28).

4. *There are no circumstances in heaven or on earth that can stop God from fulfilling his purposes in us.* Everything that happens will be used by God to achieve what he wants to achieve. We have no need to worry about our next step. We do not need to panic about which way we should go. We should not get hung up on "right" and "wrong" decisions. In fact, we should not worry about the future at all. God will not be beaten. "What then are we to say about these things? If God is for us, who is against us? (Romans 8:31).

5. *Nobody can stand in the way of God fulfilling his purposes in our lives.* Many have tried, and many may yet try, but they will never succeed in thwarting the plans of God. There is no plan— no strategy, no cunning, no wisdom, no understanding, no anything—that can ever succeed against the Lord. The Devil himself stood in front of Jesus to oppose the Son of God, to derail him, and he was overcome by Jesus. Since the Devil himself could not defeat the Son who was the firstfruit, neither will the Devil be able to defeat those who follow the Son. "In all these things we are more than conquerors through him who loved us. For I am convinced that neither death, nor life, nor angels, nor rulers, nor things present, nor things to come, nor powers, nor height, nor depth, nor anything else in all creation, will be able to separate us from the love of God in Christ Jesus our Lord" (Romans 8:37–39).

6. *Love always triumphs in the end.* Remember that arriving at the destination is more important than the kind of journey we endure. Remember that the world order of things stands against us, so we should never expect an easy life. But we are already saved and in Christ—we are already in the image of God—though there is so much more to come. There are few certainties in life, but here is one: God's love in Christ is revealed to us. "I appeal to you therefore, brothers and sisters, by the mercies of God, to present your bodies as a living sacrifice, holy and acceptable to God, which is your spiritual worship" (Romans 12:1).

7. *Jesus is altogether worthy of our worship.* Jesus has done so much for us that anything we do for him is really insignificant. Yet the love of Jesus is such that he treasures our worship, our self-sacrifice, and our loyalty. He treasures us.

I appeal to you therefore, brothers and sisters, by the mercies of God, to present your bodies as a living sacrifice, holy and acceptable to God, which is your spiritual worship.

12

Incarnation

To the church of God that is in Corinth, to those who are sanctified in Christ Jesus, called to be saints, together with all those who in every place call on the name of our Lord Jesus Christ, both their Lord and ours: Grace to you and peace from God our Father and the Lord Jesus Christ. I give thanks to my God always for you because of the grace of God that has been given you in Christ Jesus, for in every way you have been enriched in him, in speech and knowledge of every kind—just as the testimony of Christ has been strengthened among you—so that you are not lacking in any spiritual gift as you wait for the revealing of our Lord Jesus Christ. He will also strengthen you to the end, so that you may be blameless on the day of our Lord Jesus Christ. God is faithful; by him you were called into the fellowship of his Son Jesus Christ our Lord. (1 Corinthians 1:2–9)

How does God want to make himself—the only living God—known in our culture? It is often said that we are living in a secular culture, but I do not believe that this is the best description of our society today. We are in a pluralist culture, which is a culture where anything goes, and there is an abundance of religions and spirituality to choose from. In our society today, there isn't just one way; there are many ways. If you don't like the god you worship, you can choose another. If you can't find another god you like, you can invent one. How, then, does God want to make himself known in such a culture? And how does he not want to be known?

I want to share with you my conclusion about how God wants to make himself known in our culture, about how he wants to be relevant to the people in our world, our culture, our cities, and our neighborhoods. I am not going to enlarge upon my thoughts or explore them in any depth. Rather, I will simply leave these ten points with you, so you can explore them further for yourself in your own time.

1. We may not believe in the world's religions or like them, but we must respect the people who do. People who already faithfully hold fast to their own religions are worthy of our respect and deserving of our good manners.

2. Christianity is not founded on high moral values but on the living person of Jesus himself. Without Christ, there is no Christianity. A "Christian" life that does not know Jesus personally is not a Christian life, no matter how morally high it may be.

3. Loudly and proudly shouting the gospel (as we see it) is of virtually no value in our world today. We will be dismissed as arrogant and loud-mouthed if we insist on trying to ram the gospel down people's throats, and rightly so.

4. The attitudes of those who have rammed the gospel (as they saw it) down people's throats through the decades have done immeasurable harm. We have taken the good news that is Jesus and mixed it with coercion and brute force, and we have somehow managed to think that we are doings God's work.

5. We do not possess the truth—Jesus will not be possessed— and we must never believe that we are the finished work. Such claims will be dismissed, and we will lose both credibility and the right to be listened to.

6. Separated from life experience and the action of the Holy Spirit, the Bible is simply another religious book. Appealing to the Scriptures as a final authority is something that Jesus did not do, and neither should we. Jesus himself is the final authority.

7. The Bible is an invaluable resource—if it is used properly. The Bible is not a collection of "proof" texts but a lens to help us see

better. The Bible is the lens through which we see God's world, and it is the provider of meaning in God's world.

8. Mission—whatever we perceive that to be—is actually not our mission but God's. It is God at work who creates the church, and the church's primary mandate is to make Jesus known.

9. The church should never claim to possess absolute truth, though that is all too often exactly what it does claim. Rather, the church knows who the absolute truth is: Jesus.

10. We, the church, were intended to influence, impact, and change people's lives exactly where we are in each of our daily lives. I believe God wants to make himself relevant to the people in our world, our culture, our cities, and our neighborhoods. How? Through thetransforming power of the Holy Spirit. There is no other way, and there never will be any other way.

"When I came to you, brothers and sisters, I did not come proclaiming the mystery of God to you in lofty words or wisdom. For I decided to know nothing among you except Jesus the Christ, and him crucified. And I came to you in weakness and in fear and in much trembling. My speech and my proclamation were not with plausible words of wisdom, but with a demonstration of the Spirit and of power, so that your faith might rest not on human wisdom but on the power of God" (1 Corinthians 2:1–5). Paul was not being arrogant here. Rather, he knew that only the power of the Holy Spirit could make a lasting difference.

Now let me remind you of some things that need careful thought and consideration. The power of the Holy Spirit is

- a realizing power
- a personal power
- a transforming power
- an examining power
- a purifying power

We must have the power of the Holy Spirit at work in us, if he is to work through us. The challenge of seeing the power of the Holy Spirit at work where we are at any given time of the day or night is to welcome the Holy Spirit in us to do his work day-by-day. Where the power of the Holy Spirit is at work, there is the kingdom of God. So, while I may ask, How much do you want the power of the Holy Spirit to be at work in your family, friends, colleagues, and enemies?, the real question is, How much do you want the power of the Holy Spirit to be at work in you yourself?

13

Separation

As we come to chapter six in the book of John, Jesus was nearing the end of his earthly life. Therefore, since his time was short, he was speaking to his disciples about his coming death in order to prepare them for what had to happen very soon. Jesus was speaking about the personal cost that he was about to pay as he moved unswervingly toward the cross.

> When many of his disciples heard it, they said, "This teaching is difficult; who can accept it?" But Jesus, being aware that his disciples were complaining about it, said to them, "Does this offend you? Then what if you were to see the Son of Man ascending to where he was before? It is the spirit that gives life; the flesh is useless. The words that I have spoken to you are spirit and life. But among you there are some who do not believe." For Jesus knew from the first who were the ones that did not believe, and who was the one that would betray him. And he said, "For this reason I have told you that no one can come to me unless it is granted by the Father." Because of this *many of his disciples turned back and no longer went about with him.* So Jesus asked the twelve, "Do you also wish to go away?" Simon Peter answered him, "Lord, to whom can we go? You have the words of eternal life." (John 6:60–69)

Jesus spoke very plainly of the cost he was about to pay. He did not mince his words or use flowery language here, and his disciples were complaining because they were offended by his words. In the opening events of John 6, Jesus then had well over a hundred disciples, but near the close of the chapter, he had lost all of them except his original twelve—and he was not even sure that the twelve would stay with him. To understand what happened here, we first need to look back at a few key points of Jesus' ministry.

"Jesus went throughout Galilee, teaching in their synagogues and proclaiming the good news of the kingdom and curing every disease and every sickness among the people. *So his fame spread throughout all Syria*, and they brought to him all the sick, those who were afflicted with various diseases and pains, demoniacs, epileptics, and paralytics, and he cured them. And *great crowds* followed him from Galilee, the Decapolis, Jerusalem, Judea, and from beyond the Jordan" (Matthew 4:23–25).

Jesus' fame spread rapidly, because crowds in the hundreds had never come across a rabbi like Jesus. They had not heard anyone speak like he spoke, and they were amazed at his deeds that surely meant that God was with him.

> Now when Jesus heard this, he withdrew from there in a boat to a deserted place by himself. But when the *crowds* heard it, they followed him on foot from the towns. When he went ashore, he saw a *great crowd*; and he had compassion for them and cured their sick. When it was evening, the disciples came to him and said, "This is a deserted place, and the hour is now late; send the *crowds* away so that they may go into the villages and buy food for themselves." Jesus said to them, "They need not go away; you give them something to eat." They replied, "We have nothing here but five loaves and two fish." And he said, "Bring them here to me." Then he ordered the *crowds* to sit down on the grass. Taking the five loaves and the two fish, he looked up to heaven, and blessed and broke the loaves, and gave them to the

disciples, and the disciples gave them to the *crowds*. And all ate and were filled; and they took up what was left over of the broken pieces, twelve baskets full. And those who ate were about *five thousand men, besides women and children*. (Matthew 14:13–21)

Before very long, the crowds that were following Jesus were numbering in the thousands. "After Jesus had left that place, he passed along the Sea of Galilee, and he went up the mountain, where he sat down. *Great crowds* came to him, bringing with them the lame, the maimed, the blind, the mute, and many others. They put them at his feet, and he cured them, so that the *crowd* was amazed when they saw the mute speaking, the maimed whole, the lame walking, and the blind seeing. And they praised the God of Israel" (Matthew 15:29–31).

Crowds of such magnitude were well beyond the Jewish leaders' ability to control. It must have looked like Jesus was preparing to lead an insurrection. Little wonder, then, that the Jewish authorities feared that this apparent uprising could bring the Roman army down on their heads. Multitudes of people were fed, healed, and delivered, and the crowds flocked to Jesus—at times in the tens of thousands. Yet in John chapter six, they had all abandoned Jesus, and he was back down to his own twelve disciples. Why? Why did the massive crowds abandon Jesus?

The answer is that, for the most part, they abandoned Jesus because they wanted benefit without cost. Of all the people who have followed Jesus down through the centuries and across the continents, this characteristic has marked out many of them. They have wanted:

- benefit without cost
- resurrection without crucifixion
- power without relationship
- everything as a free gift
- something for nothing

This needs heart consideration, so let your hearts consider with me. Matthew said that they brought to him all the sick—those who were afflicted with various diseases and pains, demoniacs, epileptics, and paralytics—and he cured them. How long did these healings and cures last? The physical benefits they received from Jesus only lasted as long as life lasted; the benefits they received were only short-term.

Matthew said that those who ate were about five thousand men, besides women and children. How long did the food that they received last? The benefit they received from Jesus only lasted until they were hungry again. It was short-term and temporary.

But Jesus wanted them to have a lasting benefit from following him. That was exactly why Jesus said to anyone who would listen to him, "Follow me." This was personal. Those who followed Jesus consistently would discover the lasting benefit of knowing him, but the massive crowds only had a short-term view.

For the most part, the massive crowds wanted benefit without cost. Therefore, the benefit they received was only temporary, and they missed the real point of what Jesus had given to them. The benefit they received was not an end in itself. Rather, it pointed to the one who had given them the benefit. The goodness God poured out pointed to Jesus. God's kindness, revealed through Jesus, was intended to get people to follow Jesus. That was the whole point of such kindness. From this come two very important principles.

- Lasting benefit comes from lasting change.
- Lasting change always comes at a lasting cost.

People's willingness (or unwillingness) to pay a lasting cost for a lasting benefit is what separates those who consistently follow Jesus from the massive crowds that only draw near for a quick fix. And across our land today—and in the world at large—many churches are only offering a quick fix, saying that we need only

- Make a "decision for Jesus"
- Believe, because believing is enough
- Believe that everything centers on the individual's choice
- Believe that everything is about the individual and what he wants

But there is a much deeper revelation to be gained here. The revelation that brings lasting benefit was highlighted by Peter, even as most of Jesus' disciples at that time were deserting Jesus: "Lord, to whom can we go? You have the words of eternal life." The cost of lasting benefit is sticking with Jesus himself through:

- the ever-deepening and ongoing revelation of what it means to be fallen human beings
- the ongoing deep and painful work of the Holy Spirit in our own individual, inmost being
- the ongoing pain of self-discovery
- the ongoing self-realization of utter helplessness
- the ongoing death of self

This is no quick fix. This is the lasting cost of sticking with Jesus. It is this ongoing payment that marks out Jesus' own disciples from the crowds who just want a quick fix. It is the payment of this lasting cost that separates Jesus' own disciples from the massive crowds. Through Jesus' own disciples who who pay the lasting cost, God will make himself known.

14

Preparation

"When I was a child, I spoke like a child, I thought like a child, I reasoned like a child; when I became an adult, I put an end to childish ways. For now we see in a mirror, dimly, but then we will see face to face. Now I know only in part; then I will know fully, even as I have been fully known" (1 Corinthians 13:11–12).

When Paul spoke here of becoming an adult, he was speaking of a change that had already happened in the past. Paul had once thought, spoken, and acted like a child, but he had put childish ways behind him when he had become an adult. For Paul, the time of becoming an adult was clearly very significant and important to him. I am certain that Paul was not just thinking about his physical growth but also about his growth in character and spirit. For each of us, there are significant and important times in life, and time and timing are fascinating subjects.

Consider what Paul said about the coming of Jesus. "For while we were still weak, at the *right time* Christ died for the ungodly" (Romans 5:6). There was a right time for Christ to die for the ungodly. How could there have been a wrong time for Christ to die for the ungodly? Let's look at some things that Jesus had to say about time and timing.

When Jesus attended a wedding with his disciples and family, the host's wine ran out. Such an occurrence would have brought shame on the host for being unable to properly cater to all his guests. Jesus' mother tried to involve Jesus by telling him what had happened, and this was his response: "Jesus said to his mother, 'Woman, what concern is that to you and to me? *My hour has not yet come*'" (John 2:4).

On another occasion, Jesus was talking to a Samaritan woman at a well, something a Jew should never have done. The woman spoke of the traditional view that certain places were holy and set apart for worship. Jesus said this to her during their conversation: "Woman, believe me, the *hour is coming* when you will worship the Father neither on this mountain nor in Jerusalem. You worship what you do not know; we worship what we know, for salvation is from the Jews. But the *hour is coming*, and is *now here*, when the true worshippers will worship the Father in spirit and truth, for the Father seeks such as these to worship him" (John 4:21–23).

Again, when the Jewish authorities were persecuting Jesus and trying to kill him, Jesus said to them:

> Very truly, I tell you, the *hour is coming*, and is *now here*, when the dead will hear the voice of the Son of God, and those who hear will live. For just as the Father has life in himself, so he has granted the Son also to have life in himself; and he has given him authority to execute judgment, because he is the Son of Man. Do not be astonished at this; for the *hour is coming* when all who are in their graves will hear his voice and will come out—those who have done good, to the resurrection of life, and those who have done evil, to the resurrection of condemnation." (John 5:25–29)

If persecution from the Jewish authorities wasn't enough, Jesus' own family started in on him as well.

> After this Jesus went about in Galilee. He did not wish to go about in Judea because the Jews were looking for an opportunity to kill him. Now the Jewish festival of Booths was near. So his brothers said to him, "Leave here and go to Judea so that your disciples also may see the works you are doing; for no one who wants to be widely known acts in secret. If you do these things, show yourself to the world." (For not even his brothers

believed in him.) Jesus said to them, *"My time has not yet come, but your time is always here. The world cannot hate you, but it hates me because I testify against it that its works are evil. Go to the festival yourselves. I am not going to this festival, for my time has not yet fully come."* After saying this, he remained in Galilee. (John 7:1–9)

Jesus told his disciples that his time had not yet come—but that any time was right for them. In the examples we have looked at, Jesus had a real sense of time and timing. He knew when things were going to happen and when they could not yet happen. Other people might not have had that sense of time and timing, but that didn't prevent them from being subject to it. "Then they tried to arrest him, but no one laid hands on him, because *his hour had not yet come*" (John 7:30).

While Jesus was teaching in the temple one day, the Pharisees were getting increasingly angry with him and wanted to arrest him. "He spoke these words while he was teaching in the treasury of the temple, but no one arrested him, because *his hour had not yet come*" (John 8:20).

On another occasion, Jesus managed to infuriate everyone in the synagogue, and they determined to kill him right there and then."When they heard this, all in the synagogue were filled with rage. They got up, drove Jesus out of the town, and led him to the brow of the hill on which their town was built, so that they might hurl him off the cliff. But Jesus passed through the midst of them and went on his way" (Luke 4:28–30).

A sense of time and timing played a huge part in what happened—or didn't happen—to Jesus. But what of Jesus' disciples? Did they get the sense of God's time and timing? Yes ... and no. The disciples still had an important lesson to learn when they were with the risen Jesus:

In the first book, Theophilus, I wrote about all that Jesus did and taught from the beginning until the day when he was taken up to heaven, after giving instructions through the Holy Spirit to the apostles whom he had chosen. After his suffering he presented himself alive to them by many convincing proofs, appearing to them during forty days and speaking about the kingdom of God. While staying with them, he ordered them not to leave Jerusalem, but to *wait there* for the promise of the Father. "This," he said, "is what you have heard from me; for John baptized with water, but you will be baptized with the Holy Spirit *not many days from now.*" So when the disciples and Jesus had come together, they asked him, "Lord, is *this the time* when you will restore the kingdom to Israel?" Jesus replied, "It is not for you to know the times or periods that the Father has set by his own authority." (Acts 1:1–7)

It is very important to realize that no one may know the times or seasons that the Father has fixed by his own authority. Oh, that people would really believe this! So many people down through the centuries have claimed to know the Father's timing on a great many things—especially the end of the world. Even a fool who keeps quiet is considered wise.

But what of times and seasons that are set by the authority of Jesus himself? What of times and seasons that are set by the authority of the Holy Spirit? What of times and seasons that are fixed by the authority of the Father, Son, and Holy Spirit together? Jesus had a very real sense of time and timing. He knew when things could and could not happen.

The disciples knew that something was going to happen soon for them, for the risen Jesus had given them specific instructions that included timing. The disciples believed Jesus, so they stayed where he told them to be—until the time was right. The disciples had caught Jesus' sense of timing, so they waited until God fulfilled his promise. The disciples knew that something was going to happen, but they had no idea what. The timing of what happened at Pentecost didn't take the disciples by surprise, because they knew that something was going to happen soon. What of us? Do we have a sense of time and timing? Can we have a sense of time and timing?

What no eye has seen, nor ear heard, nor the human heart conceived, what God has prepared for those who love him—these things God has revealed to us through the Spirit; for the Spirit searches everything, even the depths of God. For what human being knows what is truly human except the human spirit that is within? So also no one comprehends what is truly God's except the Spirit of God. Now we have received not the spirit of the world, but the Spirit that is from God, so that we may understand the gifts bestowed on us by God. (1 Corinthians 2:9–12)

Can we as human beings really anticipate what God may do in our midst? Could it be that we have been experiencing a time of preparation for something special? Do we have that sense of time and timing? Just as there have been times and seasons when God has moved in quite remarkable ways in the past, could it be that God is about to do a new thing in our midst? In that sense, what time is it?

At Pentecost the disciples were as prepared as they knew how to be. They were in the place where Jesus told them to be, and they were waiting for the time that Jesus had told them to wait for. And the promise they waited for was fulfilled. Lord, may your will be done here as it is in heaven.

15

Motivation

What motivates us to share Jesus with other people? Grace? Pride? Duty? Guilt? Mission? Service? A full church? Reputation? What really motivates us? Are we sharing Jesus with others, or are we merely sharing our faith, values, morality, beliefs, prejudices, doctrines, or pride? Are we really sharing Jesus himself with others?

Is this all about mission? Are we all missionaries or a missionary people—or none of the above? There is a problem here. Mission isn't a scriptural word. Paul could not have undertaken "missionary" journeys because he wasn't a missionary. Paul never described himself as a missionary. He repeatedly said that he was an apostle, but much of the church today is frightened of that word. He repeatedly said that God, through Christ, had sent him out. Therefore, Paul's journeys were apostolic journeys. Since Paul continually described himself as an apostle, why do we insist that he was a missionary? And that brings me to a very important question: what is the correct, God-appointed reason for God's people to go in his name?

Rather than take you exhaustively through the Scriptures, I will give you some examples of people you can check out for yourself—and there are plenty of others in the Scriptures. Then I will give you what I believe is the only basis on which God's people should ever go out. Consider the following:

- Moses and the burning bush (Exodus 3:6, 10)
- Isaiah in the temple (Isaiah 6:1–9)

- Abraham and his journey to an unknown destination (Genesis 12:1)
- Jonah (1:1–3)
- Joshua and the Promised Land (Joshua 1:1–9)

Also check out the following Scriptures: Genesis 17:1, 3; 18:1; 22:1; 24:6; Deuteronomy 4:32, 39; Isaiah 29:13; Matthew 2:1–3; 4:9; 17:1–8; 28:16–17.

And here is the principle that is validated by these examples: the only valid reason for me to go out is that I have personally met God in worship and that he has personally sent me out. There is no other valid reason for going.

That raises the question: what is worship? Worship is a personal, unique submission before a holy God. Those whom God calls to go are always called to go through a personal and unique encounter with God that leaves them with absolutely no doubt about the call or about the God who has called them. There is no other valid reason for going. Those who go out for any other reason will crash and burn, sooner or later.

If we must use the word mission, then I will declare that any mission must always begin with worship. True worship—a personal, unique submission before a holy God—is central to mission. But mission is not about us doing work for God. It is much more about God doing work in us and through us. It is really about working with God, not for God. If you are not being the person that God wants you to be—here, now, and where you are—there is absolutely no virtue in going out on any mission anywhere. Unless you are going with the express desire for God to change you, and even then, you must ask yourself if you believe that God can change you where you are now. Before we can meaningfully reach out to others, we need the Spirit to reach out to us, as he is the master surgeon who is at work deep inside us. This is precisely where and why some people struggle. True mission needs be going on inside you before it can work through you.

Your mission—should you choose to accept it—does not begin with you. It begins in you. God can only work through you to the extent that you have welcomed him to work in you. And that is precisely why so many missions can be fruitless. We often think to ourselves, Change the world, Lord, but leave me alone! Here, then, is a three-part principle for our lives as the people of Christ.

- Wholeness is the destination.
- Healing is the journey.
- Worship is the way.

In a very real sense, all mission is God's mission, not ours. In this sense, who was the first missionary?

> So when the woman saw that the tree was good for food, and that it was a delight to the eyes, and that the tree was to be desired to make one wise, she took of its fruit and ate; and she also gave some to her husband, who was with her, and he ate. Then the eyes of both were opened, and they knew that they were naked; and they sewed fig leaves together and made loincloths for themselves. They heard the sound of the Lord God walking in the garden at the time of the evening breeze, and the man and his wife hid themselves from the presence of the Lord God among the trees of the garden. But the Lord God called to the man, and said to him, "Where are you?" (Genesis 3:6–9).

If we must speak of mission, then YHWH himself was the first missionary. YHWH himself came to seek that which was lost. Anything that we call "mission" today only reflects that which God did in the beginning. Now consider Jesus.

> My Father is still working, and I also am working. Very truly, I tell you, the Son can do nothing on his own, but only what he sees the Father doing; for whatever the Father does, the Son does likewise. The Father loves the Son and shows him all that he himself is doing; and he will show him greater works than these, so that you

will be astonished. When you have lifted up the Son of Man, then you will realize that I am he, and that I do nothing on my own, but I speak these things as the Father instructed me. And the one who sent me is with me; he has not left me alone, for I always do what is pleasing to him. I have not spoken on my own, but the Father who sent me has himself given me a commandment about what to say and what to speak. And I know that his commandment is eternal life. What I speak, therefore, I speak just as the Father has told me. (John 5:17, 19–20; 8:28–29; 12:49–50)

If we are to share in the work of God, then we need to be people who hear what the Father says and see what the Father does. Therefore, we need to know how to hear what God is saying and how to see what God is doing. If we are to share in the mission of God, then we need to be people who say what the Father is says and do what the Father does. That is true evangelism!

16

Manifestation

We come now to two important questions that we need to carefully contemplate.

- Does God pour out his Spirit on people as a result of evangelism, or is the outpouring of the Holy Spirit the opportunity for evangelism?
- Is evangelism the prerequisite for the work and power of the Holy Spirit, or is the power and work of the Holy Spirit the opportunity for evangelism?

Examining the Scriptures leads me to the conclusion that evangelism has always been a strategic response to the manifestation of the work and power of the Holy Spirit in the lives of unbelievers. Therefore, in the days of the early church, evangelism had to do with reaping the harvest, not with sowing the seed.

Let us consider the early church. "But you will receive power when the Holy Spirit has come upon you; and you will be my witnesses in Jerusalem, in all Judea and Samaria, and to the ends of the earth" (Acts 1:8). This verse speaks of power to be, not power to do, because doing always flows from being. What you do and how you do something is a direct reflection of your inner self. The anointing of the Holy Spirit has to do with who we are in Christ through God's calling on our lives. Jesus told his disciples that something was going to happen soon. Here is the crowd's reaction to Pentecost:

Now there were devout Jews from every nation under heaven living in Jerusalem. And at this sound the crowd gathered and was bewildered, because each one heard them speaking in the native language of each. Amazed and astonished, they asked, "Are not all these who are speaking Galileans? And how is it that we hear, each of us, in our own native language? Parthians, Medes, Elamites, and residents of Mesopotamia, Judea and Cappadocia, Pontus and Asia, Phrygia and Pamphylia, Egypt and the parts of Libya belonging to Cyrene, and visitors from Rome, both Jews and proselytes, Cretans and Arabs—in our own languages we hear them speaking about God's deeds of power." All were amazed and perplexed, saying to one another, "What does this mean?" (Acts 2:5–12).

What utterly amazed these people was not the acts of the apostles but the manifestation of the work and power of the Holy Spirit that made Jesus known. Peter seized the opportunity, and his strategic evangelism was in response to the work and power of the Holy Spirit. Peter explained to the crowds about what they had just seen and heard. And what was the result? "So those who welcomed his message were baptized, and that day about three thousand persons were added" (Acts 2:41). Peter reaped.

Then notice carefully what happened next.

They devoted themselves to the apostles' teaching and fellowship, to the breaking of bread and the prayers. Awe came upon everyone, because many wonders and signs were being done by the apostles. All who believed were together and had all things in common; they would sell their possessions and goods and distribute the proceeds to all, as any had need. Day-by-day, as they spent much time together in the temple, they broke bread at home and ate their food with glad and generous hearts, praising God and having the goodwill of all the people.

And day-by-day the Lord added to their number those who were being saved. (Acts 2:42–47)

This was not a free-for-all. Notice who did the many wonders and miraculous signs. And the people were being saved. Present continuous tense.

Now let's consider Paul and the crippled man at Lystra. "In Lystra there was a man sitting who could not use his feet and had never walked, for he had been crippled from birth. He listened to Paul as he was speaking. And Paul, looking at him intently and seeing that he had faith to be healed, said in a loud voice, "Stand upright on your feet." And the man sprang up and began to walk" (Acts 14:8–10). Paul saw that "he had faith to be healed." In other words, Paul knew that the Holy Spirit was at work in that man at that time, so Paul seized the opportunity. Paul reaped.

Consider Peter and John with the cripple at the temple gate.

One day Peter and John were going up to the temple at the hour of prayer, at three o'clock in the afternoon. And a man lame from birth was being carried in. People would lay him daily at the gate of the temple called the Beautiful Gate so that he could ask for alms from those entering the temple. When he saw Peter and John about to go into the temple, he asked them for alms. Peter looked intently at him, as did John, and said, "Look at us." And he fixed his attention on them, expecting to receive something from them. But Peter said, "I have no silver or gold, but what I have I give you; in the name of Jesus Christ of Nazareth, stand up and walk." And he took him by the right hand and raised him up; and immediately his feet and ankles were made strong. Jumping up, he stood and began to walk, and he entered the temple with them, walking and leaping and praising God. All the people saw him walking and praising God, and they recognized him as the one who used to sit and ask for alms at the Beautiful Gate of the temple;

and they were filled with wonder and amazement at what had happened to him. (Acts 3:1–10)

Peter and John seized the opportunity, because they saw that the Holy Spirit was at work in that man at that time. God used this one incident to work in the hearts of a great many people, who were filled with wonder and amazement at what had happened to one crippled man. Peter and John reaped.

Evangelism is the strategic response to the manifestation of the work and power of the Holy Spirit in the lives of unbelievers. But the work and power of the Holy Spirit in someone's life may not be obvious. Therefore, we need discernment and wisdom to see where and when and in whom the Holy Spirit is at work so that we can be strategic in directing our reaping there.

Consider the parable of the sower.

Listen! A sower went out to sow. And as he sowed, some seeds fell on the path, and the birds came and ate them up. Other seeds fell on rocky ground, where they did not have much soil, and they sprang up quickly, since they had no depth of soil. But when the sun rose, they were scorched; and since they had no root, they withered away. Other seeds fell among thorns, and the thorns grew up and choked them. Other seeds fell on good soil and brought forth grain, some a hundredfold, some sixty, some thirty. Let anyone with ears listen! ... When anyone hears the word of the kingdom and does not understand it, the evil one comes and snatches away what is sown in the heart; this is what was sown on the path. As for what was sown on rocky ground, this is the one who hears the word and immediately receives it with joy; yet such a person has no root, but endures only for a while, and when trouble or persecution arises on account of the word, that person immediately falls away. As for what was sown among thorns, this is the one who hears the word, but the cares of the world and the lure of wealth choke the word, and it yields nothing. But as for what was sown on good soil, this is the one who hears the word and understands it, who indeed bears fruit and yields, in one case a hundredfold, in another sixty, and in another thirty. (Matthew 13:3–9, 18–23)

The Holy Spirit sows the seed. We should tailor our evangelism strategically according to how the seed is received rather than how or where it is sown. Evangelism then becomes a part of discipleship of people in whom the Holy Spirit is already at work. This is very important, because when God sends you out to work with him, he does not send you out to sow. He sends you out to discern the evidence of the work and power of the Holy Spirit in the lives of people in order to reap the harvest.

God makes converts; we make disciples. That is the remarkable partnership that he invites us into. We are partakers in the mission of God—if we really must use the word mission.

"Then Jesus went about all the cities and villages, teaching in their synagogues, and proclaiming the good news of the kingdom, and curing every disease and every sickness. When he saw the crowds, he had compassion for them, because they were harassed and helpless, like sheep without a shepherd. Then he said to his disciples, 'The harvest is plentiful, but the laborers are few; therefore ask the Lord of the harvest to send out laborers into his harvest'" (Matthew 9:35–38).

You do not go into a harvest field to sow. You go into a harvest field to reap. If God sends you out, he will send you where the sowing of the Holy Spirit is ready for harvest—for you to reap. But the work of the Holy Spirit may not be obvious, so we need wisdom and discernment in order to join with the Holy Spirit and be strategic in our evangelism. Furthermore, the aim of evangelism must always be to bring people to follow Jesus, not to follow the human beings that God uses to make Jesus known.

So, now let's consider a very important question. Is the church the means by which God is working in the world, or is the church the evidence that God is working in the world? If we are partakers in God's mission, then the church is primarily the evidence, the manifestation, the result of God at work in our world.

"And day-by-day the Lord added to their number those who were being saved" (Acts 2:47). The people were added by the Lord, not by the apostles. And those who were added were in the process of being saved. This is all about making disciples, not seeking converts. We are to be a people who partake fully with God by watching and listening for the evidence of the work and power of the Holy Spirit and by seizing the opportunity for a strategic response of appropriate evangelism.

We need to abandon our fixation with making converts and getting instant results. Making converts is the work of the Holy Spirit alone, and we need an effective strategy to make disciples.

"Woe to you, scribes and Pharisees, hypocrites! For you cross sea and land to make a single convert, and you make the new convert twice as much a child of hell as yourselves" (Matthew 23:15). Jesus' stinging rebuke to the Pharisees and the teachers of the law is a fascinating insight into the heart of God. Jesus focused on what they are making the convert into, rather than on the fact that they had gained a convert at all. Jesus is concerned about how we disciple the converts given to us by the Holy Spirit. If we will not or cannot disciple them, then the Holy Spirit will not give them to us. The state of the church in our land has nothing whatever to do with a lack of evangelism. It has to do with a lack of discipleship.

Now listen to Jesus. "All authority in heaven and on earth has been given to me. Go therefore and make disciples of all nations, baptizing them in the name of the Father and of the Son and of the Holy Spirit" (Matthew 28:18–19).

We have no mandate whatsoever to make converts, yet so much of church and mission is focused on making converts. We are obsessed with instant results. We live in a time when young people's lives are being eaten by the enemy of our souls. We live in a time and a land when families are being destroyed to such an extent that the whole concept of family is threatened. Our society is taking words like 'family' and 'marriage' and making them mean whatever they want. The enemy of our souls is hard at work. If we would only ask God to open our eyes and hearts, we would realize that God himself is at work in our land. The danger is that we ignore the work and power of the Holy Spirit and just "do" church.

17

Exploitation

Then Jesus entered the temple and drove out all who were selling and buying in the temple, and he overturned the tables of the money changers and the seats of those who sold doves. He said to them, "It is written, 'My house shall be called a house of prayer'; but you are making it a den of robbers." The blind and the lame came to him in the temple, and he cured them. But when the chief priests and the scribes saw the amazing things that he did, and heard the children crying out in the temple, "Hosanna to the Son of David," they became angry and said to him, "Do you hear what these are saying?" Jesus said to them, "Yes; have you never read, 'Out of the mouths of infants and nursing babies you have prepared praise for yourself'?" He left them, went out of the city to Bethany, and spent the night there. (Matthew 21:12–17)

To our eyes and ears, this incident at the temple may seem strangely out-of-character. Yet this incident and what took place around it are rooted and grounded in the old covenant.

The word that came to Jeremiah from the LORD: Stand in the gate of the LORD's house, and proclaim there this word, and say, "Hear the word of the LORD, all you people of Judah, you that enter these gates to worship the LORD. Thus says the LORD of hosts, the God of Israel: 'Amend your ways and your doings, and let me dwell with you in this place. Do not trust in these deceptive words: "This is the temple of the LORD, the temple of the LORD, the temple of the LORD." For if you truly amend your ways and your doings, if you truly act justly one with another, if you do not oppress the alien, the orphan, and the widow, or shed innocent blood in this place, and if you do not go after other gods to your own hurt, then I will dwell with you in this place, in the land that I gave of old to your ancestors forever and ever. Here you are, trusting in deceptive words to no avail. Will you steal, murder, commit adultery, swear falsely, make offerings to Baal, and go after other gods that you have not known, and then come and stand before me in this house, which is called by my name, and say, "We are safe!"—only to go on doing all these abominations? Has this house, which is called by my name, become a den of robbers in your sight? You know, I too am watching,' says the LORD." (Jeremiah 7:1–11).

Jesus was angry—but not about money or profit-making. The burning issue for Jesus was threefold:

- people willfully exploiting other people
- people allowing others to be exploited
- people allowing themselves to be exploited

Exploitation is deeply offensive to God, and it angers him. Exploitation is the inevitable manifestation of idolatry—especially, but by no means exclusively, the idolatry of money.

> If you lend money to my people, to the poor among you, you shall not deal with them as a creditor; you shall not

exact interest from them ... If any of your kin fall into difficulty and become dependent on you, you shall support them; they shall live with you as though resident aliens. Do not take interest in advance or otherwise make a profit from them, but fear your God; let them live with you. You shall not lend them your money at interest taken in advance, or provide them food at a profit ... You shall not charge interest on loans to another Israelite, interest on money, interest on provisions, interest on anything that is lent. On loans to a foreigner you may charge interest, but on loans to another Israelite you may not charge interest. (Exodus 22:25; Leviticus 25:35–37; Deuteronomy 23:19–20)

Of course, there is also exploitation to gain or keep power, position, status, and so on—though money is usually in there somewhere. Jesus' disciples knew how Jesus felt about exploitation, because he had already told them in no uncertain terms. "You know that the rulers of the Gentiles lord it over them, and their great ones are tyrants over them. It will not be so among you; but whoever wishes to be great among you must be your servant, and whoever wishes to be first among you must be your slave; just as the Son of Man came not to be served but to serve, and to give his life a ransom for many" (Matthew 20:25–28). "In everything do to others as you would have them do to you; for this is the law and the prophets" (Matthew 7:12).

Jesus clearly told the scribes and the Pharisees too. "Woe to you, scribes and Pharisees, hypocrites! For you tithe mint, dill, and cummin, and have neglected the weightier matters of the law: justice and mercy and faith. It is these you ought to have practiced without neglecting the others" (Matthew 23:23).

Justice, mercy, and faith are designed to develop and deepen covenant relationship—not to allow us to exploit others by demanding these characteristics from others without giving them ourselves. The money changers (and others) in the temple were exploiting people who were seeking to worship God. The chief priests and the Pharisees were turning a blind eye to that exploitation—and even joining in.

God's face is set against leaders who exploit other people or who willfully allow other people to be exploited. God's face is set against any organization that exploits people or that willfully allows other people to be exploited.

When Jesus overturned the tables in the temple, he sent out a very clear message that people were not to be exploited. He also sent out the message that the people arriving at the temple were not to allow themselves to be exploited. Exploitation is the hallmark of the enemy of our souls. Let those who are exploited find security in Jesus, for he will never exploit them. In Jesus is safety. In Jesus is healing. We must not let anyone settle for mere church or mere Christians. We must introduce others to Jesus himself. The people of God should never willfully exploit people. That is not the spirit within us. The Spirit within us liberates us.

18

Liberation

"Now the Lord is the Spirit, and where the Spirit of the Lord is, there is freedom" (2 Corinthians 3:17).

"Therefore, since we are surrounded by so great a cloud of witnesses, let us also lay aside every weight and the sin that clings so closely, and let us run with perseverance the race that is set before us" (Hebrews 12:1).

"This was in accordance with the eternal purpose that he has carried out in Christ Jesus our Lord, in whom we have access to God in boldness and confidence through faith in him" (Ephesians 3:11–12).

What is freedom? Freedom is the ongoing experience of healing and growing in Christ. Freedom has two hands: freedom from and freedom for. Freedom works in us by giving us two things: authority and power.

The ongoing experience of being set free from something is an essential step to realized freedom. We are set free from by authority. When we submit ourselves under the authority of God, we then live in the outworking of that authority. God wants us to experience ongoing healing and growing in a dynamic love relationship with him through Jesus. To that end, the Spirit of God labors in us to set us free from all that would hold us back. Authority is concerned with who and what we are. The ongoing experience of being set free for something is the greater part of freedom. When we experience the ongoing revelation of who and what we are in Christ, God will show us what he wants to do. In the authority of God, we will act in power. Authority is about being. Power is about doing.

Jesus gives his authority to those who trust him – but he only gives his power to those he can trust. The freedom of power is based on the freedom of authority. Generally speaking, God will not give us great things to do until he has settled with us the issue of who and what we are.

The subject of freedom cannot be considered without bringing another subject into the discussion. That subject is responsibility. Responsibility is concerned with realizing and accepting the consequences of who we are, what we say, what we do, and the whole way that we relate to and treat people. First and foremost, responsibility has to do with authority, the person that I am. Responsibility requires maturity. The greater the maturity, the greater the responsibility.

Children cannot accept responsibility, and responsibility should never be forced upon them. The immature cannot accept responsibility, and responsibility should never be forced upon them. Never treat children as adults. Never treat adults as children. In terms of our responsibility to live as people who are growing in Christ and have Christ growing in them, how do we treat adults as adults?

"So if anyone is in Christ, there is a new creation: everything old has passed away; see, everything has become new! All this is from God, who reconciled us to himself through Christ, and has given us the ministry of reconciliation; that is, in Christ God was reconciling the world to himself, not counting their trespasses against them, and entrusting the message of reconciliation to us" (2 Corinthians 5:17–19).

Because God has given us the ministry of reconciliation, he has also given us the message of reconciliation. A message of reconciliation that has been divorced from the ministry of reconciliation is a message that has been rendered bereft of its power. A message of reconciliation that has been divorced from the ministry of reconciliation will actually work against God instead of for him. Our primary responsibility is to realize—to make real—the ministry of reconciliation and to support that reality with the message of reconciliation. If God's reconciliation is not real and growing in you, he cannot make it real through you. Our responsibility as Christians is to live reconciled lives and to support that reality with the message of reconciliation. Such living is freedom.

The church, generally, has long proclaimed—and not always

gracefully—some kind of message of reconciliation. But the far greater part of freedom is to live in the reality of reconciliation, not just to talk about it. A form of religion that holds to some words of reconciliation but denies the reality of reconciliation is actually fighting against the very God it claims to work for. A house divided against itself cannot stand. A house divided against itself has no credibility. A house divided against itself has no anointing.

"For the kingdom of God depends not on talk but on power" (1 Corinthians 4:20). How is your power? When we do what we can do, God will do what he can do. When we show who we really are, God will show who he really is. Each and every one of us makes a daily choice about how we will live. A living and growing daily relationship with Christ is a choice, but it is not an easy choice. Who-you-are is what-you-do.

> Everyone then who hears these words of mine and acts on them will be like a wise man who built his house on rock. The rain fell, the floods came, and the winds blew and beat on that house, but it did not fall, because it had been founded on rock. And everyone who hears these words of mine and does not act on them will be like a foolish man who built his house on sand. The rain fell, and the floods came, and the winds blew and beat against that house, and it fell—and great was its fall! (Matthew 7:24–27)

Jesus was speaking very clearly here about the life choices people make, not the mere deeds they do. Jesus was speaking about the place where a person puts his trust, his security—where a person feels safe and secure. Jesus was saying that true safety and security—and true freedom—are found only in him! Our growth in Jesus will be reflected in the whole of our lives at home, at work, and with friends. Knowing and loving Jesus is the whole reason for our being and doing. In him we live and move and have our being.

Part II

Christ-Centered Law

I had been long bound-up in thinking that Christianity was all about behaving properly—and that somehow my right behavior would please God. Unfortunately, I had discovered in my own personal experience that I was actually helpless to change my behavior. Oh, I was able to tinker at the edges, of course, but lasting and meaningful internal change was far beyond any ability I had to make it happen. Because I wasn't changing, my worldview had to change. I needed to be ever Christ-centered, for sure, but there was so much rubbish in my life that it was obvious that new foundations needed to be built into me. And Christ was the one to do that.

Before foundations could be properly built, the ground had to be cleared. One massive foundational change for me concerned my understanding of Christ and the law. "He [Christ] has abolished the law with its commandments and ordinances, that he might create in himself one new humanity in place of the two, thus making peace, and might reconcile both groups to God in one body through the cross, thus putting to death that hostility through it" (Ephesians 2:15–16).

The word *abolished* does not mean "destroyed" or "annihilated." It means "ended" or "set aside." When you are building a house, the foundations go in first. Once the foundations are completed—or "ended"—the rest of the house can be built on top of those foundations. In building the rest of the house, you do not destroy or annihilate the foundations; you build on top of them. Christ did not destroy or annihilate the Law. He ended it, because he built on top of it. Inherent in the word abolished ("ended") is a new beginning. Simply ending something is not enough. Jesus abolished ("ended") the old Law of God, but something had to take its place. There could not just be a vacuum.

> The old covenant was set aside because the new covenant was there in person. Jesus himself made clear that the old covenant had not been annihilated. "Do not think that I have come to abolish the law or the prophets; I have come not to abolish but to fulfill. For truly I tell you, until heaven and earth pass away, not one letter, not one stroke of a letter, will pass from the law until all is accomplished" (Matthew 5:17–18).

For Jews, Jesus fulfilled the Law. For Gentiles, Jesus abolished ("ended") the Law. To understand what the Law was designed to achieve, we need to explore it—while constantly asking what God was trying to do through the Law and why he made it known. When we understand what the Law was designed to achieve and why God made it known, then we will far better understand and appreciate what Jesus has done for us. We will realize that what Jesus did for us actually built on top of the foundation of the Law rather than destroying the Law.

God made the Law known so that the Jews, his own people in the world, would fully know and understand all the consequences of life's choices. This was done so that the Jews would live lives full of good choices that would restore their intimate relationship with God and show the Gentile world the way back to a life of intimacy with their Creator. But the Law failed to achieve that. Why did it fail?

It failed because of an inherent weakness in the Law itself. The Law of God failed to achieve its intended objective because it could only address external behavior. It could not change the inner person, the thoughts and attitudes of the heart. However, the Law of God did prove beyond any shadow of doubt that not one person would ever be changed from the outside in. The Law of God proved that behavioral modification does not change a person's heart. The Law of God also failed to achieve its intended objective for another reason. It failed because fallen humanity took a law that was meant to be received on the basis of faith in God and turned it into a law that was instead based on works for God. This caused a dreadful misunderstanding that has remained predominant to the present day. When the religious leaders of Israel through the centuries changed the basis of God's law from faith to works, they turned it into a prohibitive law of rules and regulations. But the Law of God was never a prohibitive law. A prohibitive law outlaws specific actions and sets out the punishment for breaking those prohibitions. There are no benefits inherent in a prohibitive law; it is entirely based on behavioral conformity. A prohibitive law relies on the fear of punishment to keep behavior modified and conformed.

The Law of God is not a prohibitive law; it is a consequential law. Actions always have consequences, and specific actions have specific consequences. The law of consequences is a law that is made known for our own benefit. Remember that the Law of God is not just the Ten Commandments. (They are not actually commandments at all, but more on that follows later.) The Law is all of the first five books of the Bible together (Pentateuch). Consequential law makes all the consequences of choices known—both good and bad— before the choices are made. To know all the consequences of one's choices before one makes a choice is true freedom of choice.

There is no punishment from God for those who make bad choices. There are only the bad consequences that directly result from those bad choices. Furthermore, the consequences of all choices happen automatically and independently of the one who made the law known: God. The universe in which we live is governed by consequential laws, and God made those consequential laws known to us. Some are made known through revelation and some through discovery.

When we properly understand consequential law, we change our ways accordingly. And, very importantly, for the sake of those who do not know or understand consequential law, we turn it into prohibitive law for their own safety. Children are the best example of this. Hopefully, once children grow up, they will understand the consequential law for themselves, and then the prohibitive law can be removed. Now, having understood that, we need to return to the abolition ("ending") of the Law of God in order to see just how serious Paul was in contending that the Law of God was abolished (ended) in and through Christ.

"Now to one who works, wages are not reckoned as a gift but as something due. But to one who without works trusts him who justifies the ungodly, such faith is reckoned as righteousness. For the wages of sin is death, but the free gift of God is eternal life in Christ Jesus our Lord" (Romans 4:4–5; 6:23).

The inevitable consequence of sin is the willful damaging and potential death of relationships. That damage to or death of relationships is not a punishment from God. He is not directly involved in that consequence. It is simply the inevitable consequence of bad choices.

> Therefore, do not let sin exercise dominion in your mortal bodies, to make you obey their passions. No longer present your members to sin as instruments of wickedness, but present yourselves to God as those who have been brought from death to life, and present your members to God as instruments of righteousness. For sin will have no dominion over you, since you are *not under law* but under grace. In the same way, my friends, you have *died to the law* through the body of Christ, so that you may belong to another, to him who has been raised from the dead in order that we may bear fruit for God. While we were living in the flesh, our sinful passions, aroused by the law, were at work in our members to bear fruit for death. But now we are *discharged from the law*, dead to that which held us captive, so that we are slaves *not under the old written code* but in the new life of the Spirit. There is therefore now no condemnation for those who are in Christ Jesus. *For the law of the Spirit of life in Christ Jesus has set you free from the law of sin and of death.* For God has done what the law, weakened by the flesh, could not do: by sending his own Son in the likeness of sinful flesh, and to deal with sin, he condemned sin in the flesh, so that the just requirement of the law might be fulfilled in us, who walk not according to the flesh but according to the Spirit. For Christ is the *end of the law* so that there may be righteousness for everyone

who believes. (Romans 6:12–14; 7:4–6; 8:1–4; 10:4; emphasis mine)

When the Gentiles, who were never given the Law, subject themselves to the Law, there are dire consequences for them, because in subjecting themselves to the Law, they step outside of Christ. If Gentiles try to live by the Law, they will reap the consequences of their inability to do so. It is simply inevitable. Paul clearly says that knowing God is through Christ alone, not through obeying the Law—even if they could do so, which is manifestly impossible.

"When Gentiles, who do not possess the law, do instinctively what the law requires, these, though not having the law, are a law to themselves" (Romans 2:14). God is not directly involved in this, but there are always consequences to choices. If Gentiles are foolish enough to try and please God by attempting to live by the Law, they will inevitably fail and suffer the consequences. Step outside Christ at your peril.

"For freedom Christ has set us free. Stand firm, therefore, and do not submit again to a yoke of slavery. Listen! I, Paul, am telling you that if you let yourselves be circumcised, Christ will be of no benefit to you. Once again I testify to every man who lets himself be circumcised that he is obliged to obey the entire law. *You who want to be justified by the law have cut yourselves off from Christ; you have fallen away from grace*" (Galatians 5:1–4).

The Law cannot achieve what it was meant to achieve because of the condition of the human heart. The inevitable result of Gentiles trying to obey the Law is exactly the same as it was for the Jews. If Gentiles attempt to keep one part of the Law, they became subject to the whole Law. And since they are subject to the whole Law, they will reap the consequences of not keeping the whole Law.

"Gentiles, who did not strive for righteousness, have attained it, that is, righteousness *through faith*; but Israel, who did strive for the righteousness that is based on the law, *did not succeed in fulfilling that law*. Why not? Because they did not strive for it on the basis of faith, but as if it were based on works" (Romans 9:30–32).

When Gentiles strive to obey the Law, they do so on the basis of works like this:

Right thinking + right behavior = salvation

But all they actually achieve is becoming peddlers of rules and regulations. Salvation cannot be earned, and neither can relationship with God. Now, let us look in more detail at the Law of God in order to understand why it was given, what it was intended to achieve, and how it can help us today. I must say again that the Law of God is not a prohibitive law, but a consequential law.

> Then God spoke all these words: I am the LORD your God, who brought you out of the land of Egypt, out of the house of slavery; you shall have no other gods before me. You shall not make for yourself an idol, whether in the form of anything that is in heaven above, or that is on the earth beneath, or that is in the water under the earth. You shall not bow down to them or worship them; for I the LORD your God am a jealous God, punishing children for the iniquity of parents, to the third and the fourth generation of those who reject me, but showing steadfast love to the thousandth generation of those who love me and keep my commandments. You shall not make wrongful use of the name of the LORD your God, for the LORD will not acquit anyone who misuses his name. Remember the Sabbath day, and keep it holy. Six days you shall labor and do all your work. But the seventh day is a Sabbath to the LORD your God; you shall not do any work—you, your son or your daughter, your male or female slave, your livestock, or the alien resident in your towns. For in six days the LORD made heaven and earth, the sea, and all that is in them, but rested the seventh day; therefore the LORD blessed the Sabbath day and consecrated it. Honor your father and your mother, so that your days may be long in the land that the LORD your God is giving you. You shall not murder. You shall not commit adultery. You shall not steal. You shall not bear false witness against your neighbor. You shall not covet your neighbor's house; you

shall not covet your neighbor's wife, or male or female slave, or ox, or donkey, or anything that belongs to your neighbor. (Exodus 20:1–17)

Notice from this one passage all the elements that are found in a consequential law but are never present in a prohibitive law:

1. God reminds his people of who he is.
2. God reminds his people of what he has done for them.
3. God desires intimacy with his people.
4. God's love for his people endures.
5. God cares for his people.
6. God has a design for human families.
7. Idolatry kills life.

None of these things are found in a prohibitive law. In the garden of Eden, when man and woman hid themselves from their Creator, God went walking in the garden to be with his beloved, and they weren't there. God's heart cry was, "Where are you?" God was not looking for information! He knew perfectly well the physical whereabouts of Adam. It was a relational question.

All the way through the old covenant, the cry of God's heart is for his people to draw near to him and to know him in intimacy. Yet all the way through the old covenant is found the hurting heart of God, because his people keep refusing him. This is the heart cry of God: he wants to be with his people in an intimate way. The power of love far outweighs the consequences of bad choices.

When you read through the first five books (Pentateuch) of the old Covenant, you will come across a repeated theme that is summed up in the phrase "for your own well-being" or "for your own good." God did not make the Law known because he was bored, or because he wanted to burden his people, or because he wanted to cause them difficulty. He made the Law known "for their own well-being." It is because God is love that he made the Law known. Knowing all the consequences of the choices in life would help his children to consistently to make good choices in life, and any parent should want the same for their children.

Family was designed to be a community of love in which the children know each other and enjoy the intimacy that comes through love that is known and expressed in safety, because they are protected by parents who fully understand the power of consequences resulting from bad choices.

An intimate relationship with Jesus is incredibly good for us. We grow strong and heal because we know our God—which is why God does not want us in slavery to any idols. But just because we do not bow down to self-made idols of wood or stone, we must not think that we are free from idolatry. Here in the West, we are just as prone to idolatry as the children of Israel were—and probably more so. We so easily and so often worship idols of self, career, leisure, money, power, position, status, beauty, youth, houses, possessions, cars, and much more. It is very easy to give ourselves to other gods and to let our religious observance salve our consciences. But God knows that he is good for us—actually, he is the best for us—and he wants nothing less than the best for us.

A prohibitive law is not interested in who you are or how you are. It is only concerned with obeying the rules and punishing you when you break the rules. Actually, a prohibitive law isn't even interested in your obeying the rules. It simply waits for you to break the rules so that punishment can be invoked. A prohibitive law doesn't care about you; it cares only that the law is enforced. A prohibitive law keeps you at a distance, for it has nothing to do with relationships. A prohibitive law can itself become an idol, and many of the world's religions demonstrate that. The foundation of a prohibitive law is: behave—or else. The foundation of a consequential law is: love—at all costs. Look at Jesus and see the consequences of love. In Galatians 5:1–25, look at Jesus and see love.

> For freedom Christ has set us free. Stand firm, there-fore, and do not submit again to a yoke of slavery.
>
> Listen! I, Paul, am telling you that if you let your-selves be circumcised, Christ will be of no benefit to you. Once again I testify to every man who lets himself be circumcised that he is obliged to obey the entire law. You who want to be justified by the law have cut

yourselves off from Christ; you have fallen away from grace. For through the Spirit, by faith, we eagerly wait for the hope of righteousness. For in Christ Jesus neither circumcision nor uncircumcision counts for anything; the only thing that counts is faith working through love.

You were running well; who prevented you from obeying the truth? Such persuasion does not come from the one who calls you. A little yeast leavens the whole batch of dough. I am confident about you in the Lord that you will not think otherwise. But whoever it is that is confusing you will pay the penalty. But my friends, why am I still being persecuted if I am still preaching circumcision? In that case the offence of the cross has been removed. I wish those who unsettle you would castrate themselves!

For you were called to freedom, brothers and sisters; only do not use your freedom as an opportunity for self-indulgence, but through love become slaves to one another. For the whole law is summed up in a single commandment, "You shall love your neighbor as yourself." If, however, you bite and devour one another, take care that you are not consumed by one another.

Live by the Spirit, I say, and do not gratify the desires of the flesh. For what the flesh desires is opposed to the Spirit, and what the Spirit desires is opposed to the flesh; for these are opposed to each other, to prevent you from doing what you want. But if you are led by the Spirit, you are not subject to the law. Now the works of the flesh are obvious: fornication, impurity, licentiousness, idolatry, sorcery, enmities, strife, jealousy, anger, quarrels, dissensions, factions, envy, drunkenness, carousing, and things like these. I am warning you, as I warned you before: those who do such things will not inherit the kingdom of God.

> By contrast, the fruit of the Spirit is love, joy, peace, patience, kindness, generosity, faithfulness, gentleness, and self-control. There is no law against such things. And those who belong to Christ Jesus have crucified the flesh with its passions and desires. If we live by the Spirit, let us also be guided by the Spirit. (Galatians 5:1–25)

A prohibitive law does nothing to build relationships. It is exclusively concerned with law enforcement. That is why those who try to live their lives by obeying (if not worshipping) the Law of God are usually very strong on behavior but very weak on relationships. Since the Law of God is a consequential law and not a prohibitive law, that law itself is meant to provoke a response from those who hear it. The *you-shall*s were intended to provoke the response: "Why?" The *you-shall-not*s were intended to provoke the response: "Why not?"

The Law of God was designed to make God's people respond by saying, "Why?" or "Why not?" in exactly the same way that children do when they are told the same things. The *you-shall-not*s are not prohibitions; they are warnings of the inevitable consequences of making bad choices. Therefore, and in the same way, the Ten Commandments are not commandments at all. They are warnings to make us carefully consider consequences before we speak or act. A consequential law is for our own benefit. When we truly know and understand the consequences that follow our choices, then we truly have free will. The purpose of the Law of God was to give God's people true free will by making all the consequences of choices known to them before they made the choices. God makes the consequential law fully known to us so that we can make good choices that benefit us and maintain our well-being—and so that we can avoid the bad choices that cause us harm. That is what a consequential law is all about: good-and-bad, not right-and-wrong. Under the old covenant the law was an attempt to reestablish intimacy with God, but now our choices should flow from the intimacy with God that is ours through Christ. They should be our natural, loving response out of a desire to please our Creator.

The old covenant law of God has been set aside for us Gentiles, but we have not been set free from personal responsibility. In fact, we are much more responsible before God than the Jews ever were, because for them the Law could only address external behavior, but we (Gentile) Christians are personally responsible for the very thoughts and attitudes of our hearts.

Verse one presents every single one of us with a choice: freedom or slavery? Will we continue to grow in our experience of freedom in knowing Christ, or will we allow other gods to enslave us again? Will we continue to struggle in our experience of slavery, or will we choose to know Jesus in an ever-deepening relationship so that he might be continually setting us free? To choose to stand still in our Christian lives is to choose to be enslaved.

The law of love in Christ has its consequences too. If we persistently neglect or refuse to grow in Christ, then Christ will not grow in us, either. Discipleship, which is for everyone, does not happen all by itself. If we turn back to or remain in slavery, there is no shortage of false gods waiting to put a yoke of slavery on us. Blessed are those who, through faith, consistently, persistently, and relentlessly choose freedom in Christ. Faith is a fight, but it is mainly a fight with our own selves, with our own hearts. It's so much easier to go back, lie down, roll over, and give up. Personal responsibility may have gone out-of-fashion in our land today, but it is still at the very center of the kingdom of God in Christ.

But we are not responsible to the old Law of God, a written code of external behavior. This is not about behavior! What, then, are we to say about the way we behave? Does our behavior matter? And if behavior does matter, how are we to change our behavior if there isn't a set standard to adhere to? We are responsible in love to Christ himself. Our responsibility to Christ himself is a much greater responsibility than trying to keep the Law of God, because it involves every thought and motive of our hearts. It involves every part of us that is unseen to others but is an open book to Christ.

Remember that the first five books of the old covenant are the Law of God, not just the 'Ten Commandments'. As I have said, I find the "Ten Commandments" to be a most unhelpful title, and I disagree with it anyway. The Law of God was centered around relationships—and especially an intimate relationship with God. The account of creation and the fall in Genesis is an essential part of the Law of God, because it centers around an intimate relationship with God. The book of Genesis, like the rest of the Bible, was not given to teach us history. It was given to teach us about relationships and the break-up of relationships. The overall theme of the whole of Scripture, then, is: covenant relationship.

> In the same way, my friends, you have died to the law through the body of Christ, so that you may belong to another, to him who has been raised from the dead in order that we may bear fruit for God. While we were living in the flesh, our sinful passions, aroused by the law, were at work in our members to bear fruit for death. But now we are discharged from the law, dead to that which held us captive, so that we are slaves not under the old written code but in the new life of the Spirit. There is therefore now no condemnation for those who are in Christ Jesus. For the law of the Spirit of life in Christ Jesus has set you free from the law of sin and of death. (Romans 7:4–6; 8:1–2).

We ought not to imply (or openly teach) that the Law of God is prohibitive and that God's angry, vindictive punishment follows the breaking of that Law, because it simply is not true. Yet this is so often the focus of evangelism. "Accept Jesus or you are going to hell." Good news? I think not. Instead, we ought to be making clear that all the choices we make have consequences—and some have eternal consequences. That we can do without being judgmental, without criticizing how people live, and without rudely shouting "turn or burn" at them.

"Therefore we must pay greater attention to what we have heard, so that we do not drift away from it. For if the message declared through angels was valid, and every transgression or disobedience received a just penalty, how can we escape if we neglect so great a salvation?" (Hebrews 2:1–3).

And those Gentiles who are trying to please or appease God by keeping the Law need the revelation of who and what they are. They need to be set free from the Law that they were never actually subject to in the first place. Therefore, there are absolutely no laws surrounding our relationship with God and our knowing of him and each other. In Christ we have full and free access. Because God did not give the Law to the Gentiles, we must not live under the Law. But we can and should understand what the Law was designed to achieve (though it never fulfilled its purpose). To do that, we must continually ask what God was trying to do through the Law and why he gave it. We are called to freedom in Christ, not bondage!

"Jesus was praying in a certain place, and after he had finished, one of his disciples said to him, 'Lord, teach us to pray, as John taught his disciples'" (Luke 11:1). Jesus was being asked by one of his disciples, perhaps on behalf of the others, to "teach us to pray … as John taught his disciples." One Jew was asking another Jew to teach his Jewish disciples how to pray in the Jewish way of the Jew called John the Baptist—not in the way of the Jewish scribes and Pharisees. It is critical to realize that Jesus' disciples were not asking him to give them a model prayer to be used as a religious centrepiece. Here is where one of our fondest traditions gets shot down in flames.

Jesus, Jewish rabbi, was heard by his Jewish disciples as he prayed with his Father, and it was clear to those disciples that there was a close connection binding Jesus and his Father together, a close connection that those disciples had not known before. They realized that this close connection was far removed from what was common amongst other rabbis. The disciples did not say to Jesus, "Teach us to pray as Rabbi (Whoever) teaches his disciples to pray." Instead they looked to John the Baptist and his relationship with God and Jesus, and they asked Jesus to teach them to pray "as John taught his disciples."

Remember that Jesus had been baptized by John the Baptist. So Jesus' disciples wanted to learn about the connection between John the Baptist, Jesus, and his Father. What was the basis of the relationship between them that allowed Jesus to pray with such freedom and authority? Their question was actually a Jewish legal question, not a casual inquiry. What was the covenant between Jesus and his Father that allowed Jesus to do the astonishing things that he did? What was the covenant between Jesus and his Father that allowed Jesus to speak with such authority? His disciples had never heard anyone pray or speak

115

the way Jesus did. Where did his freedom come from? So they asked Jesus what the covenant was that allowed him to pray with God in that way. They asked Jesus a legal question. Their question was about the Law.

"Pray then in this way: Our Father in heaven, hallowed be your name. Your kingdom come. Your will be done, on earth as it is in heaven. Give us this day our daily bread. And forgive us our debts, as we also have forgiven our debtors. And do not bring us to the time of trial, but rescue us from the evil one. For if you forgive others their trespasses, your heavenly Father will also forgive you; but if you do not forgive others, neither will your Father forgive your trespasses" (Matthew 6:9–15).

Our discussion on the Law of God now reaches a critical fact. We are at the point where many Christians and churchgoers may immediately take offense at me and my words. Why? Because I am saying that this is not the "Lord's Prayer." This is not the "disciples' prayer." This is actually not a prayer at all. When we look at what Jesus said about prayer, as recorded in the Gospels, we need to remember that he said it to disciples who were trying to come to terms with the new covenant in Christ and what that meant for them.

It is critical to understand the Jewish-ness of what was happening here. The disciple's request was not to teach them a prayer. The disciple's request was to teach them to pray. What we have here is not a prayer. It is actually a covenant agreement.

What we have here is the new covenant agreement. It is the new covenant agreement through Jesus between the Jews and the covenant-keeping God. What is normally called the "Lord's Prayer" is in fact itself the new covenant through Jesus to the Jews. Therefore, what is normally called the Sermon on the Mount isn't a sermon at all. It is the terms of that new covenant through Jesus to the Jews. The rest of Matthew's gospel is the outworking of the new covenant through Jesus to the Jews.

I am not a Jew. Gentiles are not Jews. It is a serious error to take what Jesus said to Jews and apply it unthinkingly to Gentiles who are in a completely different context and culture. Now, consider the fact that Paul was the apostle to the Gentiles. If the "Lord's Prayer," which has gained such a massive hold on modern Christianity, was so central to Christianity, what use did Paul make of it? The answer is: none. Paul never quoted it. Paul never even quoted a line or phrase from it. How could such a central plank of Christian tradition be ignored by Paul, who was the God-sent apostle to the Gentiles?

Paul was a Jew who was steeped in the Jewish Scriptures, Jewish tradition, and an understanding of the covenant-keeping God. Paul did not ignore the covenant-keeping God, but neither did he take the "Lord's Prayer" (new Jewish covenant) and simply pass it on to the Gentiles. This was because Paul knew that it wasn't a prayer at all but a new covenant. It was the way that something had been communicated to God's own people, the Jews. It was an entirely inappropriate way to communicate to Gentiles, because they had never been subject to the first covenant.

So, another way was needed for the new covenant to be communicated to the Gentiles, and Paul was the perfect person to do so. Why? Well, he must have been the perfect person, because God chose him. What did Paul do to bring the new covenant in Christ to the Gentiles?

Paul took the *elements* of the new covenant (the Lord's Prayer) to the Gentiles and made them known to the Gentiles. Where Matthew made the terms of the new covenant through Jesus known to Jews through his gospel, Paul made the terms of the new covenant through Jesus known to Gentiles through his own letters. In this way, the new covenant through Jesus was extended to Jews and Gentiles alike. So, what are the elements of the new covenant in Christ? They are:

- Fatherhood
- name
- kingdom
- provision
- forgiveness
- trials
- the Evil One

Paul's letters are shot all the way through with these elements, because he brought the terms of the new covenant in Jesus to the

Gentiles in a way that the Gentiles could relate to and receive. There was absolutely no point in quoting the Law to the Gentiles, as they had never been subject to the Law. The Gentiles needed to comprehend the terms of the new covenant in Christ in a way they could receive and accept.

The elements of the new covenant through Jesus will not only help us to know God himself, but they will also help us to know his ways. In following Jesus, we are to know, understand, and ultimately accept the terms of the new covenant through Jesus for ourselves, and so fully and freely give ourselves utterly to God for him to do his work in us and through us. God wants us to joyfully join him in the new covenant agreement through Christ, thus binding ourselves to God in Christ for all time and eternity. As we grow in Christ, the Spirit of God will bring us to the place where we know (and hopefully accept) the terms of the new covenant in Christ. We will then enter into that covenant with God through Christ and come into the fullness of what God has for us as his children.

"Accepting Jesus as Savior" (whatever that means) will not bring you into new covenant relationship with God. It will bring you into relationship with God—but not yet covenant relationship. Believing the gospel will not bring you into covenant relationship with God. It will bring you into relationship with God, but not yet covenant relationship. The moment we begin to follow Jesus, the Holy Spirit begins to lead us toward the realization of what it means to be in covenant relationship with God so that we may personally and individually enter into that covenant relationship for ourselves. That is why so many Christians do not receive from God; they believe but they have stagnated. They remain the same. They have stood still. No one has taken them deeper into God. They are in relationship with God, but they are not yet in covenant relationship. And there is a serious problem with that.

Many, many Christians want the benefits of the new covenant without the cost of the new covenant. Benefit without cost has no place in the kingdom of God. Self-sacrifice is the cost that must be paid to enter into a new covenant relationship with God. If we are to enter into that new covenant with God through Christ, we must examine, understand, and accept every single one of the individual terms of the new covenant so that we can agree the whole covenant with God. There is no halfway house here. We cannot pick and choose the bits of the covenant we like and ignore the rest. It is all or nothing.

The terms of the new covenant are the elements of the new covenant as revealed by the apostle Paul in his writings. The elements of the new covenant through Jesus will not only help us to know God himself, but they will also help us to grow into mature citizens of the kingdom of God. Sooner or later, God wants us all to come to the place where we accept the terms of the new covenant with Jesus and bind ourselves with God in that covenant. God desires that we covenant with him, not as children but as mature adults who have bound themselves to him in an everlasting covenant through Christ.

Let us now examine the covenant itself.

19

Fatherhood

The old covenant Scriptures rarely speak explicitly about God being the Father of his children Israel, yet every page is full of the experience and outworking of that relationship. And so it can be found in the beginning. "Then God said, 'Let us make humankind in our image, according to our likeness'" (Genesis 1:26).

Creating in one's own image is the very essence of fatherhood. However, when looking at human biological fatherhood, it is important to remember that it is not so much the act of becoming a father that is really important but rather how the children are fathered. So it is with spiritual fatherhood. It is not the act of spiritual adoption by the Father that is most important but rather how the spiritual children are fathered. The moment the Holy Spirit begins his work in us to make us into God's adopted children, our Father in heaven begins the process of fathering us according to the Father that he is.

As a heavenly Father, God is not detached, distant, or disinterested in his children. As a heavenly Father, God is emotionally involved with his children, because he cares for them with an unconditional, unending, and undeserved (for us) covenant love. This love is God-centered to us, not us-centered from God. This love comes from the God who is love, but it does not come because we deserve it. Yet God's love does place a high value on us that we should not only be loved but should actually receive and know that love. God's heart breaks when he sees his precious children in captivity and bondage that prevents them from receiving his love.

"Hear and give ear; do not be haughty, for the LORD has spoken. Give glory to the Lord your God before he brings darkness, and before your feet stumble on the mountains at twilight; while you look for light, he turns it into gloom and makes it deep darkness. But if you will not listen, my soul will weep in secret for your pride; my eyes will weep bitterly and run down with tears, because the LORD's flock has been taken captive" (Jeremiah 13:15–17).

Love weeps not primarily for its own loss but for the sake of its children who are caught up in bondage and captivity. At the human biological level, the act of becoming a father is easy, enjoyable, and quick, but many men become biological fathers without really knowing what fatherhood is. Fatherhood, both biological and spiritual, is not an event. It is a lifetime commitment to love and care for one's offspring. It is a lifetime commitment of unconditional, unending, and undeserved (for the child) love, irrespective of how that child reacts to his father. A father always seeks the very best for his children, even if those children don't want the very best for themselves.

Our Father in heaven has given himself to a lifetime commitment of unconditional, unending, undeserved love for his children, irrespective of how those children react to their Father in heaven. He always seeks the very best for his children, even when those children don't want the very best for themselves. Because we share the same father as Jesus, Jesus is not ashamed to call us his brothers and sisters. The wonder is this: that you and I as God's adopted children now share exactly the same benefits as God's natural children do.

> Sing aloud with gladness for Jacob, and raise shouts for the chief of the nations; proclaim, give praise, and say, "Save, O LORD, your people, the remnant of Israel." See, I am going to bring them from the land of the north, and gather them from the farthest parts of the earth, among them the blind and the lame, those with child and those in labor, together; a great company, they shall return here. With weeping they shall come, and with consolations I will lead them back, I will let them walk by brooks of water, in a straight path in which they

> shall not stumble; for I have become a father to Israel,
> and Ephraim is my firstborn. (Jeremiah 31:7–9)

Fatherhood loves at great cost to the Father himself, even at the cost of losing his own Son to gain other children. The Father will not speak a word against his own children when the accuser comes to call. Anything that the Father has to say will be said to his children themselves. The Father never abandons his own children, even though they may abandon their Father. He never curses his children with self-worthlessness, even though they may curse their Father. He never leaves his children to languish in helplessness, even though they may not take his hand. Despite appearances, God has not abandoned his natural children Israel; nor has he abandoned his fatherhood of Israel. But as long as our Father's original children are still rebelling against him or refusing to recognize his only Son, those original children are wandering and stumbling, blind and hungry, poor and naked. But it will not always be so.

> I ask, then, has God rejected his people? By no means!
> I myself am an Israelite, a descendant of Abraham, a
> member of the tribe of Benjamin. God has not rejected
> his people whom he foreknew. Do you not know what
> the scripture says of Elijah, how he pleads with God
> against Israel? "Lord, they have killed your prophets,
> they have demolished your altars; I alone am left, and
> they are seeking my life." But what is the divine reply to
> him? "I have kept for myself seven thousand who have
> not bowed the knee to Baal." So, too, at the present time
> there is a remnant, chosen by grace. But if it is by grace,
> it is no longer on the basis of works, otherwise grace
> would no longer be grace. What then? Israel failed to
> obtain what it was seeking. (Romans 11:1–7)

Israel could not achieve intimacy with YHWH through the Law. Since they couldn't rise to God, God came down to them. Israel may not have recognized that their Father had sent them his Son, but that does not negate the Son or what he came to do. What the Son came to do was wonderful.

> It was fitting that God, for whom and through whom all things exist, in bringing many children to glory, should make the pioneer of their salvation perfect through sufferings. For the one who sanctifies and those who are sanctified all have one Father. For this reason Jesus is not ashamed to call them brothers and sisters, saying, "I will proclaim your name to my brothers and sisters, in the midst of the congregation I will praise you." And again, "I will put my trust in him." And again, "Here am I and the children whom God has given me." Since, therefore, the children share flesh and blood, he himself likewise shared the same things, so that through death he might destroy the one who has the power of death, that is, the devil, and free those who all their lives were held in slavery by the fear of death. (Hebrews 2:10–15)

Jesus, the one who sanctifies, and we, the ones who are being sanctified, share the same father. Because we share the same father—no matter that appearances might tell us otherwise—Jesus is not ashamed to call us his brothers and sisters. God became man to share in flesh and blood, to share in the same struggles and the same death. The Father gave his only Son for his lost children. God sacrificially loves his children and, in doing so, shows that even the best earthly fatherhood is merely a poor reflection of heavenly fatherhood.

The wonder is this: that you and I as God's adopted children now share exactly the same benefits as God's natural children. The Word became flesh that God might share in flesh and blood with all its struggles and death, in order that we might become like God and share in his being with its glory and eternal life. But becoming like God doesn't happen automatically. It needs to be grown into.

> Endure trials for the sake of discipline. God is treating you as children; for what child is there whom a parent

> does not discipline? If you do not have that discipline in which all children share, then you are illegitimate and not his children. Moreover, we had human parents to discipline us, and we respected them. Should we not be even more willing to be subject to the Father of spirits and live? For they disciplined us for a short time as seemed best to them, but he disciplines us for our good, in order that we may share his holiness. (Hebrews 12:7–10)

Discipline is not about rules and regulations, which are prohibitive law enforcement and punishment for breaking that law. True discipline is discipleship: showing by lifestyle the best way to live life. But the point is this: if the Father in heaven never abandoned his original children but still has a plan to draw them back to himself, then neither will he abandon his children of the new covenant in Jesus. But God's fatherhood means that he must raise his children in the best way for them, and that means that they need to grow in intimacy with him.

For a great many Christians, intimacy with God is spelled F-E-A-R. An inability or outright refusal to trust God lies in the hearts of many Christians—often as a result of abuse. Abuse is all too common in families, and the church family is no different. But family is family, and family is precious, irrespective of what is happening in the family.

> I give thanks to my God always for you because of the grace of God that has been given you in Christ Jesus, for in every way you have been enriched in him, in speech and knowledge of every kind—just as the testimony of Christ has been strengthened among you—so that you are not lacking in any spiritual gift as you wait for the revealing of our Lord Jesus Christ. He will also strengthen you to the end, so that you may be blameless on the day of our Lord Jesus Christ. God is faithful; by him you were called into the fellowship of his Son, Jesus Christ our Lord. (1 Corinthians 1:1–4)

What a lovely way to begin a letter to one's family. It is a letter of love, but it centers around God's love for his people. It is a letter about God's love and his heart of amazing generosity. Paul personally knew of God's love and immense generosity, and so did so the church at Corinth. But Paul also knew of the appalling damage that had been done—and was still being done at that time—in the church at Corinth, even as he wrote to them. It had stopped the Christians' growth in Christ and the growth of Christ in them, the hope of glory. So how did Paul address the people who were so hurt and wounded?

"And so, brothers and sisters, I could not speak to you as spiritual people, but rather as people of the flesh, as infants in Christ. I fed you with milk, not solid food, for you were not ready for solid food. Even now you are still not ready, for you are still of the flesh. For as long as there is jealousy and quarrelling among you, are you not of the flesh, and behaving according to human inclinations?" (1 Corinthians 3:1–3).

Paul was pretty straight with them about their situation, but he knew that the Christians in Corinth did not need church discipline. They needed love. Specifically, the church at Corinth needed the love of a father—a father filled with compassion for his children and acting with great care and tenderness to draw near to his children that they might draw near to him. Only such a father could bring healing to the Christians in the church at Corinth.

"I am not writing this to make you ashamed, but to admonish you as my beloved children. For though you might have ten thousand guardians in Christ, you do not have many fathers. Indeed, in Christ Jesus I became your father through the gospel. I appeal to you, then, be imitators of me. For this reason I sent you Timothy, who is my beloved and faithful child in the Lord, to remind you of my ways in Christ Jesus, as I teach them everywhere in every church" (1 Corinthians 4:14–17).

Paul became a father to the Christians in the church at Corinth, who desperately needed the care and tenderness of a compassionate father. They were his beloved children. Paul was not a biological father to these people; he didn't physically create them. It was the Spirit of God who created them. But they became Paul's spiritual children by adoption. The adopted children shared exactly the same benefits as the natural children. The father who adopts spiritual children has an astonishing responsibility.

"But by the grace of God I am what I am, and his grace toward me has not been in vain" (1 Corinthians 15:10). Paul literally said, "By the grace of God YHWH." He was not claiming to be God, but he was saying that YHWH himself was formed in him. That was why he could father spiritual children: because the heavenly Father himself was formed in him. That was why he could call the Corinthian Christians to imitate him: because the heavenly Father himself was formed in him.

"Be imitators of me, as I am of Christ" (1 Corinthians 11:1). Paul's call to the Christians to become spiritual fathers was based on his own experience in which YHWH, formed in Paul, made such fatherhood possible. This is an astonishingly high calling! Timothy was also a spiritual father, and that was why Paul sent him. There were hard things to be faced up to, and only a father could say and do what was needed.

"It is actually reported that there is sexual immorality among you, and of a kind that is not found even among pagans; for a man is living with his father's wife. And you are arrogant! Should you not rather have mourned, so that he who has done this would have been removed from among you?" (1 Corinthians 5:1–2).

Paul's great compassion, care, and tenderness were seen in the way that he dealt with his children. There was, among many other things, incest—sexual abuse—in the church at Corinth, so we must learn from Paul's reaction to that knowledge.

"I am not writing this to make you ashamed" (1 Corinthians 4:14). Paul knew the power of shame, and he would not shame anybody for anything. Being ashamed of myself is quite different from someone else shaming me.

"I am not writing this to make you ashamed, *but to admonish you*" (1 Corinthians 4:14). Neither was Paul attaching blame. He was not raising sexual abuse as an issue to be dealt with. Rather, he was bringing the Christians themselves to face up to their own reactions to what had happened to them in the church family in Corinth.

"I am not writing this to make you ashamed, but to admonish you *as my beloved children*" (1 Corinthians 4:14). Paul was a loving and wise father to those badly wounded people in Corinth. His message was not about punishing those who had sinned and throwing them out of the church. It was about carefully and lovingly bringing healing and restoration to those who had been deeply hurt and wounded. Where is this kind of fatherhood in the church today? Where is this kind of love?

Fatherhood for Paul was a lifetime commitment of unconditional, unending, and undeserved love, irrespective of how his children reacted to him. Paul's fatherhood always sought the very best for his children, even when those children didn't want the very best for themselves. Paul would not speak a word against his children when the accuser came to call. Anything that this father had to say would be said to the children themselves. Paul never abandoned his children, even though they may have abandoned him. He never cursed his children with self-worthlessness, even though they may have cursed him. He never left his children to languish in helplessness, even though they might not take his hand. Paul loved them at great cost to himself.

"But even if I am being poured out as a libation over the sacrifice and the offering of your faith, I am glad and rejoice with all of you—and in the same way you also must be glad and rejoice with me" (Philippians 2:17–18). Paul poured himself out before God on behalf of his children. Just like at Corinth, the church at Philippi needed fatherhood. So what was Paul's plan?

"I hope in the Lord Jesus to send Timothy to you soon, so that I may be cheered by news of you. I have no one like him who will be genuinely concerned for your welfare. All of them are seeking their own interests, not those of Jesus Christ. But Timothy's worth you know, how like a son with a father he has served with me in the work of the gospel. I hope therefore to send him as soon as I see how things go with me; and I trust in the Lord that I will also come soon" (Philippians 2:19–24).

Every church needs fathers like Paul and Timothy. Every church needs fathers to grow within the church. Fatherhood is an essential part of the new covenant in Jesus. Fatherhood was an essential part of life for Jesus himself. But things don't always go smoothly, even in Jesus' family!

> Now every year (Jesus') parents went to Jerusalem for the festival of the Passover. And when he was twelve years old, they went up as usual for the festival. When

the festival was ended and they started to return, the boy Jesus stayed behind in Jerusalem, but his parents did not know it. Assuming that he was in the group of travellers, they went a day's journey. Then they started to look for him among their relatives and friends. When they did not find him, they returned to Jerusalem to search for him. After three days they found him in the temple, sitting among the teachers, listening to them and asking them questions. And all who heard him were amazed at his understanding and his answers. When his parents saw him they were astonished; and his mother said to him, "Child, why have you treated us like this? Look, your father and I have been searching for you in great anxiety." He said to them, "Why were you searching for me? Did you not know that I must be in my Father's house?" (Luke 2:41–50).

Parents often don't fully understand that their sons must go through the process of relationally leaving their dependence upon their parents. Even before boys relationally leave their parents—and certainly after—they need a male role model, a father figure who will spiritually father them through to maturity. For every boy, a male role model is critical, vital, and irreplaceable. However, as Jesus had no such human arrangement, where did he go for his role model?

"Didn't you know I had to be in my Father's house?" (See John 2:16; 5:19–23, 31, 36–37; 7:16; 8:16,18–19, 28, 54–55; 10:34–38.)

It is no coincidence that these sayings about Jesus' Father are in John's gospel. As a son, Jesus learned obedience from his Father in heaven, who was his role model. Jesus was a Son to his Father in heaven, but he was also a father to John. The intimacy of Jesus and John's special relationship was there for all to see. John was "the disciple whom Jesus loved." John's gospel reveals his intimacy with Jesus in a way that no other gospel does. In his gospel, John contrasts the humanity and divinity of Jesus that lived together in the one human being who knew who he was and where he was going.

At his crucifixion, Jesus saw his own biological mother and his own spiritual son John standing near, and on Jesus' instruction, John took Jesus' mother into his own home and cared for her as his own mother. After the resurrection when the disciples had gone back to fishing, it was John who recognized Jesus on the shore. John's gospel was written from a place of intimacy with Jesus, for John included details that no other gospel writer knew, or certainly did not know in the same depth. He included occasions when Jesus wept, went to a wedding, was thirsty, was tired out, washed his disciple's feet, and so on. In other words, John's focus was on Jesus himself.

John named people who were not named elsewhere. John used Greek words that are either rare in other gospels or are not found at all (*life*, *light*, *world*, *witness*, and so on). John often recorded Jesus' "I am" sayings, yet no other gospel has this focus. Jesus was John's role model of fatherhood, and that shaped the man and the father that John became. See the way that Jesus became a father to his own disciples. See the way that his disciples, and especially John, became fathers to others. Jesus shaped the kind of father that John himself became. Consider how John frequently and repeatedly addressed those to whom he wrote his first letter:

- my little children
- beloved
- little children
- young people
- children
- children of God

If any church is to grow strong in Christ, it needs fathers who lovingly journey with their children and raise them in the knowing, loving, and following of God. The fatherhood of God is an essential part of the new covenant in Christ. To know that God is our Father is to know that he calls each and every one of us to intimacy with him. This means that we must face up to what is inside us, allowing the master surgeon, who is the Holy Spirit, to operate on us so that we may experience healing and wholeness. That is part of the fulfillment of our covenant with our Father in heaven.

20

Name

A name can be just a simple tag that parents give to a baby for any number of reasons. A name can be that which other people give to a person (nickname). A name can be related to reputation or experience (black sheep, Judas, Old Faithful, etc.). Whole races can be given a particular name or nickname (Irish, Poles, etc.). Names can simply be tags given to identify an individual. They may also be commemorative for a time, experience, or culture. Some children are named after heroes, such as a football team. Some names have family, historical, or religious significance.

Some names reflect the parents' expectations or traits. For example, Jews tended to name their children in line with their aspirations or experiences—or the child's behavior. We need to explore the Hebrew concept of a "name," if we are to discover the significance of this element of the new covenant in Jesus.

Jesus said this: "Pray then in this way: Our Father in heaven, hallowed be your name" (Matthew 6:9). But his Father in heaven doesn't have a name. That was the point YHWH made all through the old covenant Scriptures. Other gods have names so that they can be identified, separated, recognized, and distinguished from each other, but YHWH is the only true God. He has no name, because he needs no name. He cannot be identified as just another god, because he isn't just another god. He is the one and only true and living God. Therefore, YHWH doesn't need a name.

"Beginning God ..." (Genesis 1:1). That is literally how the Bible begins. Not only was God already there before there was anything or anybody else, but there was no need to say which God. There was only one God, for no other gods had been invented or claimed to be God yet. Every god, every idol on planet earth since humankind walked the earth was either invented, fashioned, or imaged by human beings—or were God-created beings with ideas above their stations.

The one true and living God was and is community, but he was and is still the only one, true, and living God. Until the one true and living God created, there was nothing else and nobody else. What need, then, was there for God to have a name as we know names? But the Hebrew concept of names is far removed from our concept of names as identification tags that distinguish one individual from another. In Hebrew thought and culture, names equaled identity and therefore character, and they spoke of ownership and power.

> Then God said, "Let us make humankind in our image, according to our likeness; and *let them have dominion over* the fish of the sea, and over the birds of the air, and over the cattle, and over all the wild animals of the earth, and over every creeping thing that creeps upon the earth." So God created humankind in his image, in the image of God he created them; male and female he created them. God blessed them, and God said to them, "Be fruitful and multiply, and fill the earth *and subdue it*; and *have dominion over* the fish of the sea and over the birds of the air and over every living thing that moves upon the earth." (Genesis 1:26–28).

Dominion is domain or territory outside the main kingdom of a particular king but under the sovereignty of that particular king and his delegated authority of rule. Humankind was made in God's image and likeness to be in community. It was to have dominion over the rest of creation by subduing it. Man and woman had God-given, delegated authority to have dominion over creation. This was their high calling, given to them by God himself who would never revoke that calling.

"So out of the ground the LORD God formed every animal of the field and every bird of the air, and brought them to the man *to see what he would call them*; and *whatever the man called every living creature, that was its name*" (Genesis 2:19).

Adam didn't call the animals *Fred* or *John* or *Thomas*, because he wasn't giving them that kind of name. He wasn't naming individual creatures so they could be distinguished from each other of the same species. Rather, he was naming whole species, and the names reflected their being and doing. For example, Adam called one type of creature "lion" and another "elephant." That was how the different species of creatures were to be distinguished from one another: by species names that revealed something about the species. Name wasn't about an individual lion compared to other lions. It was about each species of creature as distinct from other species. And remember that Adam named *every* species.

"Now the serpent was more crafty than any other wild animal that the LORD God had made" (Genesis 3:1). It was God who made serpent, but it was Adam who named serpent. Adam had dominion over serpent, but he gave that dominion away by submitting to serpent instead of subduing serpent. Therefore, in that moment, serpent named Adam, and the name serpent gave Adam was *Abdicator*. From that moment on, serpent had dominion over Adam, and it is no coincidence that serpent is one of humankind's most feared creatures here on planet Earth. If the situation was not already bad enough, it got worse.

"[Adam and his wife] heard the sound of the LORD God walking in the garden at the time of the evening breeze, and the man and his wife hid themselves from the presence of the LORD God among the trees of the garden" (Genesis 3:8).

At the moment that man and his wife hid themselves behind the trees of the garden, they gave their dominion away. From that moment on, the earth itself had dominion over humankind and would subdue humankind—instead of humankind subduing the earth. The creative order of things had now been completely reversed. At the precise instant that the created order of things was reversed, humankind lost its name and no longer knew its identity. Everything that God had given to them was now lost beyond their ability to reclaim. Instead of humankind living out of and operating in their identity, they began the search for that lost identity. And that search still goes on today in every human heart. Name equals identity. Authority flows from known and recognized identity. But only the Creator can give creation its identity.

"And to the man he said, 'Because you have listened to the voice of your wife, and have eaten of the tree about which I commanded you, "You shall not eat of it," cursed is the ground because of you; in toil you shall eat of it all the days of your life; thorns and thistles it shall bring forth for you; and you shall eat the plants of the field. By the sweat of your face you shall eat bread until you return to the ground, for out of it you were taken; you are dust, and to dust you shall return'" (Genesis 3:17–19).

Humankind was no longer capable of subduing the land. It was the complete reversal of the created order of things, and humankind could do absolutely nothing to change it back to the way it was meant to be. The situation was desperate, but it was actually about to get even worse.

"Then the LORD God said, 'See, the man has become like one of us, knowing good and evil; and now, he might reach out his hand and take also from the tree of life, and eat, and live forever'—therefore the LORD God sent him forth from the garden of Eden, to till the ground from which he was taken. He drove out the man; and at the east of the garden of Eden he placed the cherubim, and a sword flaming and turning to guard the way to the tree of life" (Genesis 3:22–24).

If humankind losing its identity wasn't bad enough, it also forfeited its home. Its sense of belonging was now completely destroyed.

"When God created humankind, he made them in the likeness of God. Male and female he created them, and he blessed them and named them "Humankind" when they were created" (Genesis 5:1–2). While humankind knew that they were called "Humankind," they now had no real idea of what that meant in terms of relationship with their Creator. They knew of God but they no longer knew God. Furthermore, humankind's life was no longer God-centered; it had become self-centered. Even those who would receive God's specific call to them down through history often struggled over this.

> Then the LORD said, "I have observed the misery of my people who are in Egypt; I have heard their cry on account of their taskmasters. Indeed, I know their sufferings, and

I have come down to deliver them from the Egyptians, and to bring them up out of that land to a good and broad land, a land flowing with milk and honey, to the country of the Canaanites, the Hittites, the Amorites, the Perizzites, the Hivites, and the Jebusites. The cry of the Israelites has now come to me; I have also seen how the Egyptians oppress them. So come, I will send you to Pharaoh to bring my people, the Israelites, out of Egypt." But Moses said to God, "Who am I that I should go to Pharaoh, and bring the Israelites out of Egypt?" He said, "I will be with you; and this shall be the sign for you that it is I who sent you: when you have brought the people out of Egypt, you shall worship God on this mountain."

But Moses said to God, "If I come to the Israelites and say to them, 'The God of your ancestors has sent me to you,' and they ask me, 'What is his name?' what shall I say to them?" God said to Moses, "I AM WHO I AM." He said further, "Thus you shall say to the Israelites, 'I AM has sent me to you.'" God also said to Moses, "Thus you shall say to the Israelites, 'The LORD, the God of your ancestors, the God of Abraham, the God of Isaac, and the God of Jacob, has sent me to you': This is my name forever, and this my title for all generations." (Exodus 3:7–15)

God observed the misery of his people in Egypt and he knew their sufferings—caused because they were no longer living in the name of God. Even Moses himself was self-centered in the face of God's call: he didn't want to go. And even in the face of the evidence that God was acting on their behalf, hard hearts prevailed, as God declared:

The LORD your God, who goes before you, is the one who will fight for you, just as he did for you in Egypt before your very eyes, and in the wilderness, where you saw how the LORD your God carried you, just as one carries a child, all the way that you travelled until you reached this place. But in spite of this, *you have no trust in the LORD your God,* who goes before you on the way to seek out a place for you to camp, in fire by night, and in the cloud by day, to show you the route you should take. (Deuteronomy 1:30–33)

Whatever God did for his beloved children made no difference to them. Their hard hearts were unmoved and unreceptive. Hard and unreceptive hearts have no trust in the Lord. Hard and unreceptive hearts miss out on the best route that they should take. It wasn't long before the true origin of humankind began to be lost in human memory as well as in human lifestyle, prompting the heart of God to cry out in pain.

"Do you thus repay the LORD, O foolish and senseless people? Is not he your father, who created you, who made you and established you? Remember the days of old, consider the years long past; ask your father, and he will inform you; your elders, and they will tell you. When the Most High apportioned the nations, when he divided humankind, he fixed the boundaries of the peoples according to the number of the gods; the LORD's own portion was his people, Jacob his allotted share" (Deuteronomy 32:6–9).

The Lord's portion was his own people. But his own people were already far removed from intimacy with their creator. God's heart must have been deeply wounded. He was the one true and living God with a people of his own, and yet that people were relationally far from him. Although restoration was still a long time off, there was hope. No matter how bad things were with his own people, God would remain faithful to his own people by remaining faithful to his own name.

Then you spoke in a vision to your faithful one, and said: "I have set the crown on one who is mighty, I have exalted one chosen from the people. I have found my servant David; with my holy oil I have anointed him; my hand shall always remain with him; my arm also shall strengthen him. The enemy shall not outwit him, the wicked shall not humble him. I will crush his foes before him and strike down those who hate him. My

faithfulness and steadfast love shall be with him; and in
my name his horn shall be exalted. I will set his hand on
the sea and his right hand on the rivers. He shall cry to
me, 'You are my Father, my God, and the Rock of my
salvation!' I will make him the firstborn, the highest of
the kings of the earth. Forever I will keep my steadfast
love for him, and my covenant with him will stand firm.
I will establish his line forever, and his throne as long as
the heavens endure." (Psalm 89:19–29)

Throughout history, YHWH was reminding his people about who
they were, about who he was, and about what he had done for them.
YHWH was forever reminding his people that their lives were not
accidents and that their identity was found in him alone. Israel itself
sang songs that reminded them of all of these things and more, but did
this relationship just seem like a dream? Was the true identity of God's
people like a dream in the night for them? Did they have to wake up
afterwards and just get on with life? God's promise of something new
to come that would change things for Israel must have seemed like a
dream to Israel—one that was often offered but never fulfilled.

But Israel was never without hope. Read Psalm 103 in the context
of the "name" of God. Put aside all other shades of meaning for the
moment and concentrate on the context of the name of God.

Of David. Bless the LORD, O my soul, and all that is
within me, bless his holy name. Bless the LORD, O my
soul, and do not forget all his benefits who forgives all
your iniquity, who heals all your diseases, who redeems
your life from the Pit, who crowns you with steadfast
love and mercy, who satisfies you with good as long as
you live so that your youth is renewed like the eagle's.

The LORD works vindication and justice for all
who are oppressed. He made known his ways to Moses,
his acts to the people of Israel. The LORD is merciful
and gracious, slow to anger and abounding in steadfast
love. He will not always accuse, nor will he keep his

anger forever. He does not deal with us according to our sins, nor repay us according to our iniquities. For as the heavens are high above the earth, so great is his steadfast love toward those who fear him; as far as the east is from the west, so far he removes our transgressions from us. As a father has compassion for his children, so the LORD has compassion for those who fear him. For he knows how we were made; he remembers that we are dust.

As for mortals, their days are like grass; they flourish like a flower of the field; for the wind passes over it, and it is gone, and its place knows it no more. But the steadfast love of the LORD is from everlasting to everlasting on those who fear him, and his righteousness to children's children, to those who keep his covenant and remember to do his commandments.

The LORD has established his throne in the heavens, and his kingdom rules over all. Bless the LORD, O you his angels, you mighty ones who do his bidding, obedient to his spoken word. Bless the LORD, all his hosts, his ministers that do his will. Bless the LORD, all his works, in all places of his dominion. Bless the LORD, O my soul. (Psalm 103)

The significance of God's name is actually found all the way through the old covenant, and God's people of old would not have missed that. Furthermore, as we have seen, the reminders were not just in the Law but in the wisdom literature that pointed toward God as well. "Trust in the LORD with all your heart, and do not rely on your own insight. In all your ways acknowledge him, and he will make straight your paths. Do not be wise in your own eyes; fear the LORD, and turn away from evil. It will be a healing for your flesh and a refreshment for your body ... My child, do not despise the LORD's discipline or be weary of his reproof, for the LORD reproves the one he loves, as a father the son in whom he delights" (Proverbs 3:5–8, 11–12).

Though the word *name* does not appear here, this is all about God's name—his identity—and what that means for his people. The Lord knew there would be a day when the reversed order of things would begin to find its restoration, and he pointed toward that day.

"For a child has been born for us, a son given to us; authority rests upon his shoulders; and he is named Wonderful Counselor, Mighty God, Everlasting Father, Prince of Peace. His authority shall grow continually, and there shall be endless peace for the throne of David and his kingdom. He will establish and uphold it with justice and with righteousness from this time onward and forevermore. The zeal of the LORD of hosts will do this" (Isaiah 9:6–7).

The name or identity of God was hallmarked all the way through history. One day that hallmark would be clearly seen in one human being who would walk among humankind because God would become humankind. When that day arrived, the identity of that man would be a source of endless speculation for many people. Consider how people reacted to Jesus.

"[Jesus and his disciples] went to Capernaum; and when the sabbath came, he entered the synagogue and taught. They were astounded at his teaching, for he taught them as one having authority, and not as the scribes" (Mark 1:21–22). Authority flows from known identity. So who was this man?

"'But so that you may know that the Son of Man has authority on earth to forgive sins'—he said to the paralytic—'I say to you, stand up, take your mat and go to your home.' And he stood up, and immediately took the mat and went out before all of them; so that they were all amazed and glorified God, saying, 'We have never seen anything like this!'" (Mark 2:10–12).

The people sensed someone special here, and they glorified God. The people's delight in Jesus showed that their own religious leaders had a complete lack of authority (from known identity), but Jesus showed total authority (from known identity) that they had never seen before in one person.

"After Jesus had left that place, he passed along the Sea of Galilee, and he went up the mountain, where he sat down. Great crowds came to him, bringing with them the lame, the maimed, the blind, the mute, and many others. They put them at his feet, and he cured them, so that the crowd was amazed when they saw the mute speaking, the maimed whole, the lame walking, and the blind seeing. And they praised the God of Israel" (Matthew 15:29–31).

The crowds realized the significance of this man, because they knew where he came from. That was why they praised the God of Israel.

"Jesus went up the mountain and called to him those whom he wanted, and they came to him. And he appointed twelve, whom he also named apostles, to be with him, and to be sent out to proclaim the message, and to have authority to cast out demons" (Mark 3:13–15).

In such a few words, we find striking examples of the name of God in Jesus. In contrast to normal procedure where students would choose the rabbi they wanted to follow, Jesus chose the people he wanted, and called them to himself. Jesus appointed twelve and named them apostles. They were to be with him, and they were to proclaim the message by demonstration. They had an authority delegated to them by Jesus. But even his own disciples only saw and understood as through a glass darkly.

> On that day, when evening had come, Jesus said to them, "Let us go across to the other side." And leaving the crowd behind, they took him with them in the boat, just as he was. Other boats were with him. A great wind-storm arose, and the waves beat into the boat, so that the boat was already being swamped. But Jesus was in the stern, asleep on the cushion; and they woke him up and said to him, "Teacher, do you not care that we are perish-ing?" He woke up and rebuked the wind, and said to the sea, "Peace! Be still!" Then the wind ceased, and there was a dead calm. He said to them, "Why are you afraid? Have you still no faith?" And they were filled with great awe and said to one another, "Who then is this, that even the wind and the sea obey him?" (Mark 4:35–41).

Jesus' own disciples were asking exactly the same question that the crowds were asking: Who is this man? In whose name—in whose authority and on whose behalf—was Jesus doing these things? But in the midst of the questions, there was great danger. Jesus was not only showing God's ways, which the religious leaders manifestly did not do; he was also revealing and making known God himself. Jesus' own disciples struggled with the ways of God as made known by Jesus, and they simply—and understandably—couldn't grasp that Jesus was making God himself known.

> Immediately Jesus made his disciples get into the boat and go on ahead to the other side, to Bethsaida, while he dismissed the crowd. After saying farewell to them, he went up on the mountain to pray. When evening came, the boat was out on the sea, and he was alone on the land. When he saw that they were straining at the oars against an adverse wind, he came toward them early in the morning, walking on the sea. He intended to pass them by. But when they saw him walking on the sea, they thought it was a ghost and cried out; for they all saw him and were terrified. But immediately he spoke to them and said, "Take heart, it is I; do not be afraid." Then he got into the boat with them and the wind ceased. And they were utterly astounded, for they did not understand about the loaves, but *their hearts were hardened*. (Mark 6:45–52)

The great danger was that, in the midst of questions about Jesus' identity, Jesus' disciples allowed their hearts to be hardened. A hardened heart is the greatest danger that all of us face as disciples of Jesus. And it is the miraculous work of Jesus that is most likely to cause us to allow our hearts to harden. A hard heart:

- denies God his identity
- removes God's "otherness"
- reduces God to just another idol

Religious leaders are most at risk of hardened hearts. Jesus will not be put in a box, labeled, and sussed out. He is God Almighty, not the embodiment of our theology. And sooner or later this God will offend our theology. Sooner or later he will break out of our box—if he was ever in it in the first place. Jesus will not take our name upon himself. That is why our hope of glory is Christ in us, not us in Christ.

> Now when the Pharisees and some of the scribes who had come from Jerusalem gathered around Jesus, they noticed that some of his disciples were eating with defiled hands, that is, without washing them. (For the Pharisees, and all the Jews, do not eat unless they thoroughly wash their hands, thus observing the tradition of the elders; and they do not eat anything from the market unless they wash it; and there are also many other traditions that they observe, the washing of cups, pots, and bronze kettles.) So the Pharisees and the scribes asked him, "Why do your disciples not live according to the tradition of the elders, but eat with defiled hands?" He said to them, "Isaiah prophesied rightly about you hypocrites, as it is written, 'This people honors me with their lips, but their hearts are far from me; in vain do they worship me, *teaching human precepts as doctrines.' You abandon the commandment of God* and *hold to human tradition.*" (Mark 7:1–8)

A hardened heart teaches human precepts as doctrines. A precept is a command or an instruction or rule regarding moral conduct. A hardened heart teaches a moral code as if it were doctrine. A hardened heart turns Christianity—a love relationship with Christ—into a mere moral code. A hardened heart abandons the call of God. The call of God is this: "You shall love the Lord your God with all your heart, and with all your soul, and with all your mind, and with all your strength, and you shall love your neighbor as yourself." A hardened heart abandons love in favor of a moral code. A hardened heart holds to human tradition and makes God's Word void through it. A hardened heart proclaims human tradition as if it was God's Word. Jesus' own disciples had a big battle with their own hardened hearts.

"Then Jesus began to teach his disciples that the Son of Man must undergo great suffering, and be rejected by the elders, the chief priests, and the scribes, and be killed, and after three days rise again. He said all this quite openly. And Peter took him aside and began to rebuke him. But turning and looking at his disciples, he rebuked Peter and said, "Get behind me, Satan! For you are setting your mind not on divine things but on human things" (Mark 8:31–33).

Jesus was sharing his inmost being, his deeply disturbed heart, and the agony of doing his Father's will because of the great cost involved. Peter dismissed the groans of Jesus' heart and actually rebuked him. In the context of name or identity, Jesus' disciples from then until now have had a tendency to trivialize the precious because of hardened hearts. A hardened heart trivializes the precious and rationalizes love—because of fear.

> Six days later, Jesus took with him Peter and James and John, and led them up a high mountain apart, by themselves. And he was transfigured before them, and his clothes became dazzling white, such as no one on earth could bleach them. And there appeared to them Elijah with Moses, who were talking with Jesus. Then Peter said to Jesus, "Rabbi, it is good for us to be here; let us make three dwellings, one for you, one for Moses, and one for Elijah." *He did not know what to say, for they were terrified.* Then a cloud overshadowed them, and from the cloud there came a voice, "This is my Son, the Beloved; listen to him!" Suddenly when they looked around, they saw no one with them any more, but only Jesus. (Mark 9:2–8)

Only much later would the disciples realize the significance of this time. In the meantime, they were terrified by the manifest presence of God. It is a human tendency to speak nonsense when the manifest presence of God bids us be quiet. When the manifest presence of God terrifies you, and you do not know what to say, say nothing. Trivialization of the precious causes hardened hearts to harden even further. Trivialization of the precious causes hardened hearts to no longer even see the precious. So does a competitive spirit.

"John said to him, 'Teacher, we saw someone casting out demons in your name, and we tried to stop him, because he was not following us.' But Jesus said, 'Do not stop him; for no one who does a deed of power in my name will be able soon afterward to speak evil of me. Whoever is not against us is for us. For truly I tell you, whoever gives you a cup of water to drink because you bear the name of Christ will by no means lose the reward" (Mark 9:38–41).

The issue of name or identity goes to the very heart of every one of us as human beings. It puts God's spotlight upon what is deep inside every one of us—to see if it is of God or merely of humankind, to see if it is of God or the work of the Devil. Sometimes the ungodly see what the godly cannot see.

> When it was noon, darkness came over the whole land until three in the afternoon. At three o'clock Jesus cried out with a loud voice, "Eloi, Eloi, lema sabachthani?" which means, "My God, my God, why have you forsaken me?" When some of the bystanders heard it, they said, "Listen, he is calling for Elijah." And someone ran, filled a sponge with sour wine, put it on a stick, and gave it to him to drink, saying, "Wait, let us see whether Elijah will come to take him down." Then Jesus gave a loud cry and breathed his last. And the curtain of the temple was torn in two, from top to bottom. Now when the centurion, who stood facing him, saw that in this way he breathed his last, he said, "Truly this man was God's Son!" (Mark 15:33–39)

A Roman centurion saw who Jesus really was. John, who wrote the last gospel, was especially close to Jesus, and it was he who knew most of the reality of the name or identity of Jesus. It was John who looked back in awe and wonder and proclaimed the name of Jesus.

> In the beginning was the Word, and the Word was with God, and the Word was God. He was in the beginning with God. All things came into being through him,

and without him not one thing came into being. What has come into being in him was life, and the life was the light of all people. The light shines in the darkness, and the darkness did not overcome it. And the Word became flesh and lived among us, and we have seen his glory, the glory as of a father's only son, full of grace and truth. From his fullness we have all received, grace upon grace. The law indeed was given through Moses; grace and truth came through Jesus Christ. No one has ever seen God. It is God the only Son, who is close to the Father's heart, who has made him known. (John 1:1–5, 14–18)

John began his gospel in a fashion similar to but in a different from the way Genesis began: "Beginning Word." And John not only proclaimed Jesus; he wrapped his proclamation in the mystery of the incarnation. Love can know what John was proclaiming, because the heart apprehends. Logic cannot know what John was proclaiming, because the head is confounded. For John, Jesus was supreme, and that supremacy shaped everything John said.

"When it was evening on that day, the first day of the week, and the doors of the house where the disciples had met were locked for fear of the Jews, Jesus came and stood among them and said, "Peace be with you" (John 20:19). Doors locked because of fear? Jesus' name is stronger than locked doors. Jesus' name is stronger than fear. Jesus gave his authority to all his disciples down through the centuries, he gave them his name. Jesus' followers became known as Christians because they were like Christ.

"Now the eleven disciples went to Galilee, to the mountain to which Jesus had directed them. When they saw him, they worshipped him; *but some doubted.* And Jesus came and said to them, *"All authority in heaven and on earth has been given to me.* Go therefore and make disciples of all nations, baptizing them *in the name of the Father and of the Son and of the Holy Spirit,* and *teaching them to obey everything* that I have commanded you. And remember, *I am with you always,* to the end of the age" (Matthew 28:16–20).

"But some doubted." Hardened hearts cannot grasp even the most astonishing manifestation of God.

"All authority in heaven and on earth has been given to me." This is the very essence of what *name* is all about.

"In the name of the Father and of the Son and of the Holy Spirit." *Name* is about the whole of God, not part of him.

"Teaching them to obey everything." *Name* is not about knowledge, the possession or accumulation of facts. It is about working out in experience what we hear from Jesus.

"I am with you always." This is the supreme truth about *name*. It centers around the person and presence of Jesus. So let us constantly explore our identity as Christians.

> Paul, called to be an apostle of Christ Jesus by the will of God, and our brother Sosthenes, To the church of God that is in Corinth, to those who are sanctified in Christ Jesus, called to be saints, together with all those who in every place call on the name of our Lord Jesus Christ, both their Lord and ours: Grace to you and peace from God our Father and the Lord Jesus Christ. I give thanks to my God always for you because of the grace of God that has been given you in Christ Jesus, *for in every way you have been enriched in him*, in speech and knowledge of every kind—just as the testimony of Christ has been strengthened among you—so that *you are not lacking in any spiritual gift* as you wait for the revealing of our Lord Jesus Christ. He will also strengthen you to the end, so that you may be blameless on the day of our Lord Jesus Christ. God is faithful; by him you were called into the fellowship of his Son, Jesus Christ our Lord. (1 Corinthians 1:1–9).

If we are Christ's and he is in us, then everything that belongs to him belongs to us. If we are Christ's and he is in us, then everything that belongs to us belongs to him. There is no gift that we need that we do not have. But all of this is in the name or identity of Christ Jesus, and it is not just for our own benefit.

> From now on, therefore, we regard no one from a human point of view; even though we once knew Christ from a human point of view, we know him no longer in that way. So if anyone is in Christ, there is a new creation: everything old has passed away; see, everything has become new! All this is from God, who reconciled us to himself through Christ, and has given us the ministry of reconciliation; that is, in Christ God was reconciling the world to himself, not counting their trespasses against them, and entrusting the message of reconciliation to us. So we are ambassadors for Christ, since God is making his appeal through us; we entreat you on behalf of Christ, be reconciled to God. (2 Corinthians 5:16–20)

Paul was speaking here about *name*. We no longer know Christ from a merely human point of view. We have been given the ministry of reconciliation. (Why has the church so long practiced the ministry of alienation?) We have been given the message of reconciliation. We are ambassadors for Christ, acting in his name, on his behalf, with his authority, with his favor, in his anointing. For all intents and purposes, Christ's ambassadors fully represent Christ.

> Only, live your life in a manner worthy of the gospel of Christ, so that, whether I come and see you or am absent and hear about you, I will know that you are standing firm in one spirit, striving side by side with one mind for the faith of the gospel, and are in no way intimidated by your opponents. For them this is evidence of their destruction, but of your salvation. And this is God's doing. For he has graciously granted you the privilege not only of believing in Christ, but of suffering for him as well—since you are having the same struggle that you saw I had and now hear that I still have.
>
> If then there is any encouragement in Christ, any consolation from love, any sharing in the Spirit, any

compassion and sympathy, make my joy complete: be of the same mind, having the same love, being in full accord and of one mind. Do nothing from selfish ambition or conceit, but in humility regard others as better than yourselves. Let each of you look not to your own interests, but to the interests of others. Let the same mind be in you that was in Christ Jesus, who, though he was in the form of God, did not regard equality with God as something to be exploited, but emptied himself, taking the form of a slave, being born in human likeness. And being found in human form, he humbled himself and became obedient to the point of death—even death on a cross. Therefore God also highly exalted him and *gave him the name that is above every name*, so that at the name of Jesus every knee should bend, in heaven and on earth and under the earth, and every tongue should confess that Jesus Christ is Lord, to the glory of God the Father. (Philippians 1:27–2:11)

Jesus was given the name that is above every name. Everything is subject to him. If we are growing in Christlikeness and living out that Christlikeness, then we are living in the name of Christ. Calling ourselves Christians doesn't make us like Christ. The people around us day-by-day can clearly see through superficiality, and none are better skilled at that than our own children. If our name, our identity, really is from Christ and Christ is growing in us, then our lifestyle is from Christ too. We will be what he is, and we will do what he did. If we take the name of Jesus but are not growing in Christlikeness, then the name of Jesus is for us is a mere technicality.

Who and what we are proves who and what we are. Who and what we are will be seen and known. It cannot and will not be hidden. How we live and breathe and have our being proves who and what we are. We may try to hide who and what we are from the people around us, and they may be fooled. But God will never be fooled. And people aren't really fooled, either. Our external being will always be reflective of our internal being. Who and what we are will find expression.

To the saints and faithful brothers and sisters in Christ in Colossae: Grace to you and peace from God our Father. In our prayers for you we always thank God, the Father of our Lord Jesus Christ, for we have heard of your faith in Christ Jesus and of the love that you have for all the saints, because of the hope laid up for you in heaven. You have heard of this hope before in the word of the truth, the gospel that has come to you. Just as it is bearing fruit and growing in the whole world, so it has been bearing fruit among yourselves from the day you heard it and truly comprehended the grace of God. *This you learned from Epaphras, our beloved fellow servant.* He is a faithful minister of Christ on your behalf, and he has made known to us your love in the Spirit. For this reason, since the day we heard it, we have not ceased praying for you and asking that you may be filled with the knowing of God's will in all spiritual wisdom and understanding, *so that you may lead lives worthy of the Lord*, fully pleasing to *him*, as you bear fruit in every good work and as you grow in the knowing of God. May you be made strong with all the strength that comes from his glorious power, and may you be prepared to endure everything with patience, while joyfully giving thanks to the Father, who has enabled you to share in the inheritance of the saints in the light. He has rescued us from the power of darkness and transferred us into the kingdom of his beloved Son, in whom we have redemption, the forgiveness of sins.

He is the image of the invisible God, the firstborn of all creation; for in him all things in heaven and on earth were created, things visible and invisible, whether thrones or dominions or rulers or powers—all things have been created through him and for him. He himself is before all things, and in him all things hold together. He is the head of the body, the church; he is the beginning, the firstborn from the dead, so that he might come to have first place in everything. For in him all the fullness of God was pleased to dwell, and through him God was pleased to reconcile to himself all things, whether on earth or in heaven, by making peace through the blood of his cross. (Colossians 1:9–20)

We are ambassadors for Christ, acting in his name, on his behalf, with his authority, with his favor, and in his anointing. For all intents and purposes, Christ's ambassadors fully represent Christ. There is no difference between him and us. If our name, our identity, really is from Christ and Christ is growing in us, then our lifestyle is from Christ too. We will be what he is, and we will do what he did.

If we are growing in Christlikeness, then Christ's DNA is changing, renewing, and restoring us daily. Christ's DNA will determine how we live, what we say, and what we do. Christ's DNA will shape us and grow us into his likeness. Just as Christ was the image of the invisible God here on earth, so we are the image of the invisible Christ here on earth. That is what the incarnation is all about. That is what it means to have the name of God upon us.

As we mature in prayer, seeking after Jesus for himself and seeking to draw near to God, an amazing thing may happen: God will reveal to each of us our true name—the name that he gives each one of us. But this is not an identification tag in the sense that we tend to use names. Rather it is a name that speaks of our character and identity in Christ. It is a spiritual name, not an earthly name. And that new name will continue the transformation of our lives.

Knowing our identity in Christ, as revealed by our new name, will transform our relationship with God through Christ. We are no longer in the mainstream of human history. We have been lifted into the name of God. We are being changed into his likeness by one degree of glory into another. We cannot live that change and remain the same!

I am now rejoicing in my sufferings for your sake, and in my flesh I am completing what is lacking in Christ's afflictions for the sake of his body, that is, the church. I became its servant according to God's commission that was given to me for you, to make the word of God fully known, the mystery that has been hidden throughout the ages and generations but has now been revealed to his saints. To them God chose to make known how great among the Gentiles are the riches of the glory of this mystery, which is *Christ in you*, the hope of glory. It is he whom we proclaim, warning everyone and teaching everyone in all wisdom, so that we may present *everyone mature in Christ* ... As you therefore have received Christ Jesus the Lord, continue to live your lives in him, *rooted and built up in him* and established in the faith, just as you were taught, abounding in thanksgiving. See to it that no one takes you captive through philosophy and empty deceit, according to human tradition, according to the elemental spirits of the universe, and not according to Christ. For *in him the whole fullness of deity dwells bodily*, and *you have come to fullness in him*, who is the head of every ruler and authority. (Colossians 1:24–28; 2:6–10)

Christ is being formed in you day-by-day, and Christ in you is the hope of glory. It really is all about Jesus. I want everyone to be mature in Christ. To have his name is to be rooted and built up in him. In Christ, the fullness of the Godhead dwells bodily, and you have come to fullness in Christ. This doesn't make any sense logically, but it is relationally true.

As *God's chosen ones*, holy and beloved, *clothe yourselves* with compassion, kindness, humility, meekness, and patience. *Bear with one another* and, if anyone has a complaint against another, *forgive each other; just as the Lord has forgiven you, so you also must forgive*. Above all, *clothe yourselves with love*, which binds everything together in perfect harmony. And let the peace of Christ rule in your hearts, to which indeed you were called in the one body. And be thankful. Let the word of Christ dwell

150

in you richly; teach and admonish one another in all wisdom; and with gratitude in your hearts sing psalms, hymns, and spiritual songs to God. And whatever you do, in word or deed, *do everything in the name of the Lord Jesus*, giving thanks to God the Father through him. (Colossians 3:12–17)

This is all about *name*, and it is all about choices. Whose name do we want to be known by? God's chosen ones are those in whom the Father is reproducing himself in Christ through the power of the Holy Spirit. Clothe yourselves with love, compassion, kindness, humility, meekness, and patience, because no one else is going to clothe you. Bear with one another. This does not mean to merely tolerate with one another. Bearing with (and bearing up) means to support, underpin, strengthen, and fortify one another. This is love that is actively caring for others.

Forgive each other. Just as the Lord has forgiven you, so you must also forgive. Forgiveness is a choice, but it's not an optional extra. If we are going to take the new covenant seriously, then we must be people who freely forgive. It is the peace of the presence of the Christ in you that is to rule in our hearts. It is the very word that the Christ speaks that is to dwell in us richly. Doing everything in the name of the Lord Jesus is not a technical exercise. We breathe every breath in the name of Jesus. This is all about *name* and choices. Whose name do we want to be known by?

Now let us consider what Jesus said to three churches in his letters to them.

And to the angel of the church in Pergamum write: These are the words of him who has the sharp two-edged sword: "I know where you are living, where Satan's throne is. *Yet you are holding fast to my name*, and you did not deny your faith in me even in the days of Antipas my witness, my faithful one, who was killed among you, where Satan lives … To everyone who conquers I will give some of the hidden manna, and I will give a white stone, and on the white stone is written *a new name* that no one knows except the one who receives it." (Revelation 2:12, 17)

Are we so determined to hold fast to Jesus and his name that we would give our lives?

"And to the angel of the church in Sardis write: These are the words of him who has the seven spirits of God and the seven stars: "I know your works; you *have a name of being alive*, but you are dead … If you conquer, you will be clothed like them in white robes, and I will *not blot your name out* of the book of life; *I will confess your name* before my Father and before his angels" (Revelation 3:1, 5). If we hold fast, Jesus will confess our name to his Father.

"And to the angel of the church in Philadelphia write: I know that you have but little power, and yet you have kept my word and *have not denied my name* … I will write on you *the name of my God*, and the *name of the city of my God*, the new Jerusalem that comes down from my God out of heaven, and *my own new name*" (Revelation 3:7–8). There is a lot here that we do not understand, but this one thing I know: I want to be known by God's name. I don't want him to be known by my name.

> Then I saw a new heaven and a new earth; for the first heaven and the first earth had passed away, and the sea was no more. And I saw the holy city, the new Jerusalem, coming down out of heaven from God, prepared as a bride adorned for her husband. And I heard a loud voice from the throne saying, "See, the home of God is among mortals. He will dwell with them as their God; they will be his peoples, and God himself will be with them; he will wipe every tear from their eyes. Death will be no more; mourning and crying and pain will be no more, for the first things have passed away." And the one who was seated on the throne said, "See, I am making all things new." Also he said, "Write this, for these words are trustworthy and true." Then he said to me, "It is done! I am the Alpha and the Omega, the beginning and the end. To the thirsty I will give water as a gift

from the spring of the water of life. Those who conquer will inherit these things, and I will be their God and they will be my children." (Revelation 21:1–7)

Oh, the wonder of what God has done and will do for his children! This is not for the fainthearted. Those who overcome will inherit and will be shown to be God's children.

I saw no temple in the city, for its *temple is the Lord God* the Almighty and the Lamb. And the city has no need of sun or moon to shine on it, for the *glory of God is its light*, and *its lamp is the Lamb*. The nations will walk by its light, and the kings of the earth will bring their glory into it. Its gates will never be shut by day—and there will be no night there. People will bring into it the glory and the honor of the nations ... But the throne of God and of the Lamb will be in it, and his servants will worship him; *they will see his face*, and *his name will be on their foreheads*. And there will be no more night; they need no light of lamp or sun, for the *Lord God will be their light*, and they will reign forever and ever ... Blessed are those who wash their robes, so that they will have *the right to* the tree of life and *may enter* the city by the gates. (Revelation 21:22–26; 22:3–5, 14)

Unlike the buildings of our world today, the temple in the new city will be God himself. Unlike the light in our cities today, the light of the new city will be God himself. Then we will see his face, and we will truly know his name. When we see his face, his name will be our name. When his name is our name, we will inherit everything that is now held in waiting for us. How does this happen?

153

21

Communication, Communion, Union

Physical growth begins with union (a baby in a mother's womb), continues to communion (a baby receiving sustenance from its mother's breasts), and becomes communication (a self-aware person communicating independently).

1. *Union* is exemplified by a mother carrying a baby in her womb. The two are inseparable until the time comes when the baby can survive outside its mother.
2. *Communion* is demonstrated by the mother feeding her baby at her breast. Her baby literally draws its life from her.
3. *Communication* applies to the mother relating to her grown-up child through external means, such as speech, nonverbal communication, and so on. The adult is no longer dependent upon its mother for life, because it has learned how to take care of itself.

In spiritual life, our experience is the other way around. The direction of spiritual growth is the opposite of physical (biological) growth. The moment we begin a love relationship with Christ, the Holy Spirit begins the work of taking us on our spiritual journey.

Communication

Usually, our Christian life begins at the shallowest level. Communication between persons (including God) is over distance, because we are separate persons. Therefore, communication takes place between separate and distinct persons. I recognize that there are different depths and types of communication. These vary by culture, geography, upbringing, and so on. In the beginning, it is usually the head that leads communication. Thought and speech are natural ways of expressing ourselves and making ourselves known. Depending upon our context and culture, we may learn new ways of communicating and expressing ourselves. Therefore, this leads me to a foundational statement: communication is learned and taught.

Communication is a skill base that must be constantly growing. People's abilities in using their skill base vary enormously and for any number of reasons. Once again, culture and context play a big part here, as do many other things, such as upbringing, career, and so on. Where people are damaged in any way, communication is usually inhibited by the damage, making relationships much more difficult. This can lead us into errors of communication, which are sometimes caused by ignorance. One example would be talking at people rather than with them. We ought to be listening patiently to people, giving them time and space to express themselves, but sometimes we think it's far more important for the other person to hear our point of view! We need to be listening carefully to people, hearing what they are saying and what they are not saying.

There are too many aspects of this subject to explore here, and that is not my purpose, but I will mention a few other aspects:

- *proactive* communication
- *reactive* communication
- *timing* of communication
- *intonation*: how you say something
- *NVC*: nonverbal communication, including silence, which is very important
- *situation*: where you choose to meet or must meet, and who else is around
- *surroundings*: public places with some (or no) privacy, or private places for confidentiality
- *individual*: speaking one-to-one
- *groups*: the dynamics of group work, and watching out for the individuals within the group

- *confidentiality*: not betraying trust, not promising confidentiality you cannot keep
- *openness*: being open to others before you expect them to be open to you

Communion

I am speaking of *communion* as literally drawing life from another person, and that person is Jesus the Christ. Consider his own words:

> I am the bread of life. Your ancestors ate the manna in the wilderness, and they died. This is the bread that comes down from heaven, so that one may eat of it and not die. I am the living bread that came down from heaven. Whoever eats of this bread will live forever; and the bread that I will give for the life of the world is my flesh." The Jews then disputed among themselves, saying, "How can this man give us his flesh to eat?" So Jesus said to them, "Very truly, I tell you, unless you eat the flesh of the Son of Man and drink his blood, you have no life in you. Those who eat my flesh and drink my blood have eternal life, and I will raise them up on the last day; for my flesh is true food and my blood is true drink. Those who eat my flesh and drink my blood abide in me, and I in them. Just as the living Father sent me, and I live because of the Father, so whoever eats me will live because of me. This is the bread that came down from heaven, not like that which your ancestors ate, and they died. But the one who eats this bread will live forever. (John 6:48–58)

If Jesus really meant this, then we are to quite literally draw our life from him. As a baby at its mother's breast literally draws its life from her, so we are feeding from Jesus and drawing our life from him. This is not doctrine or theology. This is reality. The Holy Spirit works tirelessly and ceaselessly in us and with us to make real to us the food and drink that is in Jesus for us. The food and drink that sustain us and give us life are in Christ and nowhere else. The words that Jesus spoke are spirit, and they are life. Separated from Jesus, we will starve. It really is as simple as that. Jesus was abundantly clear about this, and so are the Scriptures that testify about him.

"But if Christ is in you, though the body is dead because of sin, the Spirit is life because of righteousness. If the Spirit of him who raised Jesus from the dead dwells in you, he who raised Christ from the dead will give life to your mortal bodies also through his Spirit that dwells in you" (Romans 8:10–11).

"When many of his disciples heard it, they said, 'This teaching is difficult; who can accept it?' But Jesus, being aware that his disciples were complaining about it, said to them, 'Does this offend you? Then what if you were to see the Son of Man ascending to where he was before? It is the spirit that gives life; the flesh is useless. The words that I have spoken to you are spirit and life'" (John 6:60–63).

"I planted, Apollos watered, but God gave the growth. So neither the one who plants nor the one who waters is anything, but only God who gives the growth" (1 Corinthians 3:6–7).

We may (and should) create in our lives the very best conditions in which healing and growth can take place, but it is only God who heals and gives growth. We may also create in our lives the very worst conditions in which healing and growth can take place, and God would be unable to heal and give us growth. Healing salvation and growth in Christ are essential elements of who and what we are, who and what we are becoming, and who and what we will one day be.

Union

This is not about unity. The "oneness" we are discussing here is union, not unity. Unity is the condition where human beings come together with a joint purpose or goal. That is not what is in God at all. Jesus spoke often about being "one" with his Father. Unity is of purely human origin, human effort, and human recognition. Union is where two or more distinct persons are inseparably joined together and—in the case of human beings—wholly dependent on each other.

A mother-to-be and her unborn baby are in union. Likewise, I in Christ and Christ in me are permanently one, so that we can no longer be separated or even be considered separately. To touch one is to touch the other, to be touched by one is to be touched by the other. This is an organic union of two persons with one life source. It is not a meeting of minds or a common purpose. The Father, Son, and Spirit are union. They are not three separate persons in unity, but three in one.

Unity is about striving, doing, achieving, and maintaining. Union is about being and knowing. Union cannot be invoked, replicated, or manufactured. The church of Acts 2 and Acts 5 was not a people in unity but a people in union. There is only one source of union: Jesus himself. And the Spirit of God takes us on an ever-deepening journey into the very depths of God himself, the journey into union.

> [Christ] is the image of the invisible God, the firstborn of all creation; for in him all things in heaven and on earth were created, things visible and invisible, whether thrones or dominions or rulers or powers—all things have been created through him and for him. He himself is before all things, and in him all things hold together. He is the head of the body, the church; he is the beginning, the firstborn from the dead, so that he might come to have first place in everything. For in him all the fullness of God was pleased to dwell … For in him the whole fullness of deity dwells bodily, and you have come to fullness in him, who is the head of every ruler and authority. (Colossians 1:15–19; 2:9–10)

This is no theological flight of fancy. This no mere theological viewpoint. This is the reality that God is drawing us into. "In him we live and move and have our being" (Acts 17:28).

People who live lives only of communication cannot speak the languages of communion and union. For them, the languages of communion and union will not make sense, sounding like nonsense or gibberish. When you realize that a person can only speak at the level of communication, you must use communication as your common ground for speaking with them.

People who live lives of communion cannot speak the language of union. For them, the language of union will not make sense, sounding like nonsense or gibberish. However, those people who live lives of communion can speak the language of communication and are therefore able to relate to those who speak communication, as well as to those who speak communion.

People who live lives of union can speak the languages of both communion and communication, and they can therefore relate to those people who speak communion and communication—as well as to those who speak union. The people who speak union can therefore speak the language that is appropriate for anyone they are relating to.

People who live lives of union have only begun the real journey into Christ. They have not arrived. Those people who know union with Christ are those people whose company you should regularly seek as a matter of urgency.

22

Kingdom

What is the kingdom of God? Can we see it? Can we touch it? Is it real? What is real?

"Pray then in this way: Our Father in heaven, hallowed be your name. Your kingdom come. Your will be done, on earth as it is in heaven. Give us this day our daily bread. And forgive us our debts, as we also have forgiven our debtors. And do not bring us to the time of trial, but rescue us from the evil one" (Matthew 6:9–13).

What we have here, then, is the new covenant agreement through Jesus the Christ between the covenant-keeping God and the Jewish people. Paul, apostle to the Gentiles, did not ignore the covenant-keeping God, but neither did he take the new covenant and simply pass it on *per se* to the Gentiles. And neither did Paul take the wording of the new covenant to the Gentiles. Instead, He took the essential elements of the new covenant to the Gentiles. Where Matthew made the terms of the new covenant through Jesus known to Jews in his gospel to the Jews, Paul made the terms of the new covenant through Jesus known to Gentiles in his letters. In this way, the new covenant through Jesus was extended to Jews and Gentiles alike. Paul also spoke a lot about the kingdom of God.

Every kingdom can only have one king. Earthly kingdoms appoint kings (or queens) because they are kingdoms, and kingdoms must have a king. It is the other way around in the kingdom of God. There is a kingdom only because there is a king. Earthly kingdoms are based on the kingdom, and no king rules forever. In the kingdom of God, it is the king who is everlasting, and that is why the kingdom is everlasting. Earthly kingdoms are based on a place, not a person. The kingdom of God is based on Jesus alone. "All things have been handed over to me by my Father" (Matthew 11:27).

Jesus is the king through whom the kingdom is brought into being. Jesus will have all things in him and with him until everything has been completed.

> Surely you have already heard of the commission of God's grace that was given me for you, and how the mystery was made known to me by revelation, as I wrote above in a few words, a reading of which will enable you to perceive my understanding of the mystery of Christ. In former generations this mystery was not made known to humankind, as it has now been revealed to his holy apostles and prophets by the Spirit: that is, the Gentiles have become fellow heirs, members of the same body, and sharers in the promise in Christ Jesus through the gospel. Of this gospel I have become a servant according to the gift of God's grace that was given me by the working of his power. Although I am the very least of all the saints, this grace was given to me to bring to the Gentiles the news of the boundless riches of Christ, and to make everyone see what is the plan of the mystery hidden for ages in God who created all things; so that through the church the wisdom of God in its rich variety might now be made known to the rulers and authorities in the heavenly places. (Ephesians 3:2–10)

The promise and the gospel are in Christ Jesus, not in anyone or anything else. Christ Jesus is not in the gospel. The gospel is in Christ. The gospel is the messenger, not the message. The message is Christ and Christ alone. The message is that God's kingdom is extended to the Gentiles in Christ.

"I became its servant according to God's commission that was given to me for you, to make the word of God fully known, the mystery that has been hidden throughout the ages and generations but has now been revealed to his saints. To them God chose to make known how great among the Gentiles are the riches of the glory of this mystery, which is Christ in you, the hope of glory" (Colossians 1:25–27).

Christ and Christ alone is the hope of glory in you. The gospel itself is not the hope of glory; it points unerringly to Christ. The Scriptures and Paul himself point without wavering to Christ as the hope of glory.

"I want their hearts to be encouraged and united in love, so that they may have all the riches of assured understanding and have the knowledge of God's mystery, that is, *Christ Himself,* in whom are hidden all the treasures of wisdom and knowledge" (Colossians 2:2–3). All the treasures of wisdom and knowing are in Christ alone. The gospel, the Scriptures, and the apostle Paul all point to Jesus. I am pointing to Jesus. If you miss Jesus, you miss everything.

Matthew and Paul took the new covenant in Christ to Jews and Gentiles respectively. Did they follow a clear strategy in taking the new covenant to their respective peoples? Did Jesus or Paul have clear strategies in the way they related to people? What can we learn, understand, and practice with regard to the kingdom of God through Jesus and Paul? Can we learn about the advancement of the kingdom of God, working alongside God as he works, and complementing him? What was Jesus' strategy for working out the new covenant? How is that strategy evident in the way he related to people, including his own disciples? I will summarize Jesus' strategy like this:

1. Make initial contact through an act of kindness:
   - an act of power
   - an act of healing
   - an act of friendship
   - an act of acceptance
   - causing the kingdom of God to come near
2. "Follow me."
   - Go where I go.
   - See what I see.
   - Watch what I do.

- See how I react.
- Know who leads me.
- Disciple, mentor, and teach by lifestyle relationship with a living person.
3. Walk with Jesus.
    - Progressively know the cost of discipleship.
    - Death must precede resurrection.
    - Resurrection without crucifixion is insurrection.
    - My reputation must die.
    - I am a servant, not a master. I do the will of my Father.
    - Be in partnership, side-by-side, staying together.
4. Develop communication, communion, union.
    - As you walk with me, you will become like me.
    - As you walk with me, the Spirit will transform you.
    - As you walk with me, your will becomes my will.
    - As we walk together, we will become one.
    - Walk in oneness, inseparable. To touch me is to touch him.

It was clearly evident in Jesus' own ministry that, in one sense, he did not have to say "follow me" very often, because the crowds actually followed him in droves. But the following crowds needed to become disciples who walked with him rather than merely following him. We do not know how Jesus first made contact with his own disciples, but something significant had happened for each of them before Jesus called them. We know this because, when Jesus called them, they immediately dropped everything and followed him. Once they began following Jesus, he began to make clear to them the true cost of discipleship, the true cost of the name of Jesus.

While Jesus was here on earth, the disciples followed Jesus. Once Jesus ascended to heaven, the disciples walked with Jesus.

While following Jesus, communication should progressively deepen to communion. When walking with Jesus, communion should progressively deepen to union. When the disciples were anointed with the Holy Spirit at Pentecost, it was clear that communion had become union. When we are one with Jesus, striving ceases, and abiding in Jesus provides rest. Then the kingdom of God has been unbreakably established in human life. Then Christ in you is the hope of glory. That was Jesus' strategy.

What was Paul's strategy? Actually, Paul's strategy matured to become exactly the same as Jesus' strategy. It was true that, in Athens, Paul had tried preaching to people, but he quickly discovered that it was not very effective.

> Those who conducted Paul brought him as far as Athens; and after receiving instructions to have Silas and Timothy join him as soon as possible, they left him. While Paul was waiting for them in Athens, he was deeply distressed to see that the city was full of idols. So he argued in the synagogue with the Jews and the devout persons, and also in the marketplace every day with those who happened to be there ... When they heard of the resurrection of the dead, some scoffed; but others said, "We will hear you again about this." At that point Paul left them. But *some* of them joined him and became believers, including Dionysius the Areopagite and a woman named Damaris, and others with them. (Acts 17:15–17, 32–34)

Paul argued with the Jews in the synagogue, and with everyone else in the marketplace. But his approach was not very fruitful. So Paul learned from that. Paul's next stop was Corinth, and there he did things quite differently from his experience in Athens. He recounted to the Corinthians how he had come to them.

"When I came to you, brothers and sisters, I did not come proclaiming the mystery of God to you in lofty words or wisdom. For I decided to know nothing among you except Jesus Christ, and him crucified. And I came to you in weakness and in fear and in much trembling. My speech and my proclamation were not with plausible words of wisdom, but with a demonstration of the Spirit and of power, so that your faith might rest not on human wisdom but on the power of God" (1 Corinthians 2:1–5).

As Luke observed and recorded, Paul's new approach to the Gentiles began with God's acts of kindness to the people and produced fruit in Corinth quite different from his earlier approach in Athens.

> When Silas and Timothy arrived from Macedonia, Paul was occupied with proclaiming the word, testifying to the Jews that the Messiah was Jesus. When they opposed and reviled him, in protest he shook the dust from his clothes and said to them, "Your blood be on your own heads! I am innocent. From now on I will go to the Gentiles." Then he left the synagogue and went to the house of a man named Titius Justus, a worshipper of God; his house was next door to the synagogue. Crispus, the official of the synagogue, became a believer in the Lord, together with all his household; and *many of the Corinthians who heard Paul became believers and were baptized.* (Acts 18:5–9)

Likewise, when Paul went on to Ephesus, it was the manifest power of God at work that caused people to follow Jesus.

> God did extraordinary miracles through Paul, so that when the handkerchiefs or aprons that had touched his skin were brought to the sick, their diseases left them, and the evil spirits came out of them. Then some itinerant Jewish exorcists tried to use the name of the Lord Jesus over those who had evil spirits, saying, "I adjure you by the Jesus whom Paul proclaims." Seven sons of a Jewish high priest named Sceva were doing this. But the evil spirit said to them in reply, "Jesus I know, and Paul I know; but who are you?" Then the man with the evil spirit leaped on them, mastered them all, and so overpowered them that they fled out of the house naked and wounded. When this became known to all residents of Ephesus, both Jews and Greeks, everyone was awestruck; and the name of the Lord Jesus was praised. Also many of those who became believers confessed and disclosed

their practices. A number of those who practiced magic collected their books and burned them publicly; when the value of these books was calculated, it was found to come to fifty thousand silver coins. So the word of the Lord grew mightily and prevailed. (Acts 19:11–20)

Notice that the acts of kindness produced praise for Jesus, not Paul. Interestingly, the new covenant Scriptures contain Paul's letters to churches in both Corinth and Ephesus, but there are no letters to Athens. Whether God's acts of kindness were at work or not, the church at Corinth was about as messed up as one could get. But Paul was very clear to them about how he would come to them.

I am not writing this to make you ashamed, but to admonish you as my beloved children. For though you might have ten thousand guardians in Christ, you do not have many fathers. Indeed, in Christ Jesus I became your father through the gospel. I appeal to you, then, be imitators of me. For this reason I sent you Timothy, who is my beloved and faithful child in the Lord, to remind you of my ways in Christ Jesus, as I teach them everywhere in every church. But some of you, thinking that I am not coming to you, have become arrogant. But I will come to you soon, if the Lord wills, and I will find out *not the talk* of these arrogant people *but their power.* For the kingdom of God depends not on talk but on power. (1 Corinthians 4:14–20)

It may well be that we do not really understand just how Paul related to those people in the power of God.

"For though absent in body, I am present in spirit; and as if present I have already pronounced judgment in the name of the Lord Jesus on the man who has done such a thing. When you are assembled, and *my spirit is present with the power of our Lord Jesus,* you are to hand this man over to Satan for the destruction of the flesh, so that his spirit may be saved in the day of the Lord" (1 Corinthians 5:3–5).

"My spirit is present with the power of our Lord Jesus." We tend not to be very comfortable with verses like that or with the power of God at work—and in some ways, rightly so.

> I myself, Paul, appeal to you by the meekness and gentleness of Christ—I who am humble when face to face with you, but bold toward you when I am away!—I ask that when I am present I *need not show boldness* by daring to oppose those who think we are acting according to human standards. Indeed, we live as human beings, but we do not wage war according to human standards; for the weapons of our warfare are not merely human, but they have divine power to destroy strongholds. We destroy arguments and every proud obstacle raised up against the knowledge of God, and we take every thought captive to obey Christ. We are ready to punish every disobedience when your obedience is complete. Look at what is before your eyes. If you are confident that you belong to Christ, remind yourself of this, that just as you belong to Christ, *so also do we.* Now, even if I boast a little too much of our authority, which the Lord gave *for building you up and not for tearing you down*, I will not be ashamed of it. I do not want to seem as though I am trying to frighten you with my letters. For they say, "His letters are weighty and strong, but his bodily presence is weak, and his speech contemptible." Let such people understand that what we say by letter when absent, *we will also do when present.* (2 Corinthians 10:1–11)

Paul was making it quite clear that when he came to them he would do so in the power of the Spirit, not with discussions, debates, and committees. Paul was really quite serious about the ability of the power of the Spirit of God to change and transform people's lives from the inside out.

We have now looked at Jesus and Paul. But what about YHWH

himself? Did YHWH have a clear strategy in the way that he related to his people? If so, what was it?

Actually, it was exactly the same as Jesus' and Paul's strategy, because they got their strategy from YHWH. Let us consider God the Father's strategy, which was his from the very beginning. In the beginning there was nothing but formless void and darkness. So God created, and it was good. Then God fathered humankind in his own image.

"God saw everything that he had made, and indeed, it was very good" (Genesis 1:31). YHWH's act of kindness was to fashion a wonderful creation for his humankind, even before he had actually fathered them. Then, having fathered humankind and given them the wonderful gift of the whole of creation, YHWH went to walk in the garden with them. But they weren't there. The opportunity for communication, communion, and union for humankind was lost. Dominion was lost, intimacy with Creator was lost, and the kingdom's advancement was on-hold—and it stayed that way for a very long time.

Then, when Jesus came to earth, a remarkable thing happened: God walked with his people again. Such a thing had not been known since the garden. And the proclamation concerning this was no less remarkable. "In those days John the Baptist appeared in the wilderness of Judea, proclaiming, 'Repent, for the kingdom of heaven has come near'" (Matthew 3:1–2).

The kingdom was no longer on-hold. It was on the move. John the Baptist paved the way for the advance of the kingdom of God. When John the Baptist faded from view, Jesus came on the scene, and the message on his lips was no less remarkable: "From that time Jesus began to proclaim, 'Repent, for the kingdom of heaven has come near'" (Matthew 4:17).

Jesus proclaimed exactly the same message as John the Baptist, but it was no longer the herald who was proclaiming the kingdom; it was the king himself. And Jesus' proclamation that the kingdom was near was validated by what he did. "Then Jesus went about all the cities and villages, teaching in their synagogues, and proclaiming the good news of the kingdom, and curing every disease and every sickness" (Matthew 9:35). These were acts of kindness from God, who was once again walking with his people. Do you see the wonder of this?

But for Israel, their religious leaders' rejection of their Messiah meant that there was a difficult consequence for them to bear. "Jesus said to the [religious leaders in the temple], 'Have you never read in the scriptures: "The stone that the builders rejected has become the cornerstone; this was the Lord's doing, and it is amazing in our eyes"? Therefore I tell you, the kingdom of God will be taken away from you and given to a people that produces the fruits of the kingdom'" (Matthew 21:42–43).

The kingdom of God is amongst us. It is in us, and we are in it. The kingdom of God is not about impersonal rules and regulations but about abiding in a person, the person of Jesus the Christ. Jesus knew that he could not physically remain on earth. He had to ascend to the Father. But when Jesus ascended to heaven, he did not leave us as orphans.

"For the kingdom of God is not food and drink but righteousness and peace and joy in the Holy Spirit" (Romans 14:17). The kingdom of God does not abide in things or places or laws. It is in the person of God himself. Since the kingdom of God is in the person of God himself, it is for us a kingdom of constant transformation into his likeness.

"Now the Lord is the Spirit, and where the Spirit of the Lord is, there is freedom. And all of us, with unveiled faces, seeing the glory of the Lord as though reflected in a mirror, are being transformed into the same image from one degree of glory to another; for this comes from the Lord, the Spirit" (2 Corinthians 3:17–18).

The freedom of the Spirit of the Lord leaves behind everything that is not of freedom. Since the freedom of God is in the person of God himself, the freedom of God leaves behind everything that is impersonal. As we abide in God himself, our faces are becoming more and more unveiled. We are being transformed from one degree of glory to another, leaving far behind everything that is impersonal. The kingdom of God is a kingdom of love made personally known.

> For this is the message you have heard from the beginning, that we should love one another ... Little children, let us love, not in word or speech, but in truth and action ... And this is his commandment, that we should believe in the name of his Son Jesus Christ and love one

another, just as he has commanded us ... Beloved, let us love one another, because love is from God; everyone who loves is born of God and knows God ... Beloved, since God loved us so much, we also ought to love one another. No one has ever seen God; if we love one another, God lives in us, and his love is perfected in us ... God is love, and those who abide in love abide in God, and God abides in them ... The commandment we have from him is this: those who love God must love their brothers and sisters also ... Everyone who believes that Jesus is the Christ has been born of God, and everyone who loves the parent loves the child. By this we know that we love the children of God, when we love God and obey his commandments. For the love of God is this, that we obey his commandments. (1 John 3:11, 18, 23; 4:7, 11–12, 16, 21; 5:1–3)

If Jesus' disciples are recognized by their love, then consider this. When we show an act of kindness to someone else, God is walking with us, and his kingdom has drawn near to that person. That simple reality shows us that, while God has brought us into his kingdom, he has not merely put his kingdom into us. Somehow, wonderfully, we have become his kingdom. "To him who loves us and freed us from our sins by his blood, and *made us to be a kingdom*, priests serving his God and Father, to him be glory and dominion forever and ever. Amen" (Revelation 1:5–6).

Do you see the wonder of this? It is hard for our minds to grasp the wonder of what God has done for us in Christ, but our hearts can know that reality. It is all personal, not impersonal.

Then I saw between the throne and the four living creatures and among the elders a Lamb standing as if it had been slaughtered, having seven horns and seven eyes, which are the seven spirits of God sent out into all the earth. He went and took the scroll from the right hand of the one who was seated on the throne. When he had taken the scroll, the four living creatures and the twenty-four elders fell before the Lamb, each holding a harp and golden bowls full of incense, which are the prayers of the saints. They sing a new song: "You are worthy to take the scroll and to open its seals, for you were slaughtered and by your blood you ransomed for God saints from every tribe and language and people and nation; you *have made them to be a kingdom* and priests serving our God, and they will reign on earth." (Revelation 5:6–10)

The kingdom of God is near. It is here. But it is also yet to come. Then, when history as we know it is finally wrapped up, Jesus will consummate the kingdom.

But in fact Christ has been raised from the dead, the first fruits of those who have died. For since death came through a human being, the resurrection of the dead has also come through a human being; for as all die in Adam, so all will be made alive in Christ. But each in his own order: Christ the first fruits, then at his coming those who belong to Christ. Then comes the end, *when he hands over the kingdom to God the Father*, after he has destroyed every ruler and every authority and power. (1 Corinthians 15:20–24)

Destroyed does not mean "annihilated." It means "cancelled, voided, held in check, annulled." Our lives are an important part of the realization of the cancellation of every ruler and every authority and every power. We need to be growing into maturity to play our part in what Christ is achieving at this time in the world. Until the end comes, everything has been given into Jesus' hands. The kingdom of God is based on King Jesus alone. That means that the kingdom of God is not geographical but personal. The kingdom of God is not based on a place but a person. Where the king is, there is the kingdom of God. That is why Christ in you is the hope of glory. Everything has been handed over to Jesus, so everything is from him, in him, and through him.

171

When everything has been fulfilled, Jesus will hand the full kingdom over to his Father. Then the new covenant will be fulfilled, and the kingdom will truly have come. Beloved, do you see the wonder of this? Do you see the wonder of what Jesus has done for us? Do you see the wonder of who we are? Do you see the wonder of Jesus?

What was Jesus' strategy for working out the new covenant and making the new kingdom known? How is that strategy evident in the way that Jesus related to people, including his own disciples? How can we engage in that same strategy? Let us remind ourselves and see our own way.

1. The kingdom of God comes near because the people of God come near. We can make initial contact through acts of kindness:
   * an act of power
   * an act of healing
   * an act of friendship
   * an act of acceptance
   * by asking, "What shall I do for this person, Lord?"
   * by asking, "What do you want to do for this person, Lord?" (This is a dangerous question.)
2. "Follow me."
   * Go where I go.
   * See what I see.
   * Watch what I do.
   * See how I react.
   * Know who leads me.

If Jesus was led by the Spirit of God showing him what the Father was doing, so we should be also. This is what discipleship is about. This is not about what I should do but about what the Father is doing. If you see what the Father is doing, you can safely join in.

3. Walk with Jesus.
   * Progressively pay the cost of discipleship.
   * Death must precede resurrection.
   * Resurrection without crucifixion is insurrection.

- My reputation must die.
- I am a servant, not a master. I do the will of my Father.

Consider this. "Then Jesus went about all the cities and villages, teaching in their synagogues, and proclaiming the good news of the kingdom, and curing every disease and every sickness" (Matthew 9:35).

Acts of kindness are from God, who is once again walking with his people. The kingdom of God is among us. It is in us, and we are in it. The kingdom of God is not about impersonal rules and regulations. It is about abiding in a person, the person of Jesus the Christ. Since the kingdom of God is in the person of God himself, it is for us a kingdom of constant transformation into his likeness. And transformation into his likeness means doing the things that he did.

23

Provision

"Pray then in this way: Our Father in heaven, hallowed be your name. Your kingdom come. Your will be done, on earth as it is in heaven. *Give us this day our daily bread.* And forgive us our debts, as we also have forgiven our debtors. And do not bring us to the time of trial, but rescue us from the evil one" (Matthew 6:9–13).

The reference to "bread" is an example of a figure of speech for food, but it especially refers to all of the believer's needs, both physical and spiritual. Disciples are to rely on God for all of their needs. The emphasis here is not on the needs themselves, nor upon the one who has needs. The emphasis is on the one who covenants to meet the needs, doing so as he sees fit. God is not a slot machine or a self-service supermarket checkout. God sees a big picture that we can barely imagine.

In the same way that manna was only given one day at a time, disciples are to rely on daily provision for life from God. This helps them to develop a continuous and conscious dependence on him for everything. The emphatic position of "today" at the end of the Greek sentence emphasizes that the present day is to be the center of attention. (Give us our bread daily.) This squares with Jesus' later admonition not to be anxious about the future. If God cares for us today, then surely he will provide for us every day of our lives. The best way to prevent anxiety is to consciously trust God for today's bread and then trust him for tomorrow's bread.

Jesus does not renounce responsible activity. His disciples are to take care of their needs and those of their loved ones, as he indicated in his sound rebuke of the Pharisees when they avoided providing for parental needs. We are to rely on God for all sustenance, for everything that is needed. But we are to be concerned with only one day at a time. Nowhere is this more true than in our reliance on God for life itself.

> If Christ is in you, though the body is dead because of sin, the Spirit is life because of righteousness. If the Spirit of him who raised Jesus from the dead dwells in you, he who raised Christ from the dead will give life to your mortal bodies also through his Spirit that dwells in you. So then, brothers and sisters, we are debtors, not to the flesh, to live according to the flesh—for if you live according to the flesh, you will die; but if by the Spirit you put to death the deeds of the body, you will live. For all who are led by the Spirit of God are children of God. (Romans 8:10–14)

So God's people are dependent upon God for their daily food—and in wealthy countries today, we barely acknowledge that. Beyond that, however, we are actually dependent upon God for life itself. This is not a new covenant revelation, nor has it come to us for the first time in the new covenant in Jesus. It has always been so from the beginning of time. But how quickly we human beings forget who is the true source of all things.

God's provision encourages relationships, because we are all dependent upon God, interdependent with each other, and looking to the same Father. Without God, we are nothing. Without God's provision, we have nothing. YHWH is our provider, and his provision is extraordinary, extravagant, and outrageous.

God's provision extends to everything, including life itself. God's provision to you and me is the call to die—to utterly and completely die to self and be found in Jesus. God will always be able to fully care for children who fully rely on him. That is why the Spirit of God in you and me works the way he does.

"What then are we to say about these things? If God is for us, who is against us? He who did not withhold his own Son, but gave him up for all of us, will he not with him also give us everything else?" (Romans 8:31–32). Such words from Paul take us right back to the garden, where everything was given to humankind—even before humankind existed.

> In the beginning when God created the heavens and the earth, the earth was a formless void and darkness covered the face of the deep, while a wind from God swept over the face of the waters. Then God said, "Let there be light"; and there was light. And God saw that the light was good; and God separated the light from the darkness. God called the light Day, and the darkness he called Night. And there was evening and there was morning, the first day.
>
> And God said, "Let there be a dome in the midst of the waters, and let it separate the waters from the waters." So God made the dome and separated the waters that were under the dome from the waters that were above the dome. And it was so. God called the dome Sky. And there was evening and there was morning, the second day.
>
> And God said, "Let the waters under the sky be gathered together into one place, and let the dry land appear." And it was so. God called the dry land Earth, and the waters that were gathered together he called Seas. And God saw that it was good. Then God said, "Let the earth put forth vegetation: plants yielding seed, and fruit trees of every kind on earth that bear fruit with the seed in it." And it was so. The earth brought forth vegetation: plants yielding seed of every kind, and trees of every kind bearing fruit with the seed in it. And God saw that it was good. And there was evening and there was morning, the third day.
>
> And God said, "Let there be lights in the dome of the sky to separate the day from the night; and let them be for signs and for seasons and for days and years, and let them be lights in the dome of the sky to give light upon the earth." And it was so. God made the two great

lights—the greater light to rule the day and the lesser light to rule the night—and the stars. God set them in the dome of the sky to give light upon the earth, to rule over the day and over the night, and to separate the light from the darkness. And God saw that it was good. And there was evening and there was morning, the fourth day.

And God said, "Let the waters bring forth swarms of living creatures, and let birds fly above the earth across the dome of the sky." So God created the great sea monsters and every living creature that moves, of every kind, with which the waters swarm, and every winged bird of every kind. And God saw that it was good. God blessed them, saying, "Be fruitful and multiply and fill the waters in the seas, and let birds multiply on the earth." And there was evening and there was morning, the fifth day.

And God said, "Let the earth bring forth living creatures of every kind: cattle and creeping things and wild animals of the earth of every kind." And it was so. God made the wild animals of the earth of every kind, and the cattle of every kind, and everything that creeps upon the ground of every kind. And God saw that it was good. (Genesis 1:1–25)

In the beginning, God gave humankind all things, even before humankind itself existed. In this new covenant through Jesus, God gives us all things along with his Son, and the fullness of that has yet to be realized. In the beginning, God's creation was finished at that time, and everything that had been created was for humankind. God could not have made a greater provision for his humankind. All things had been given to humankind before humankind even existed. And then God topped it all when he fathered humankind.

Then God said, "Let us make humankind in our image, according to our likeness; and let them have dominion over the fish of the sea, and over the birds of the air, and over the cattle, and over all the wild animals of the earth, and over every creeping thing that creeps upon the earth." So God created humankind in his image, in the image of God he created them; male and female he created them.

God blessed them, and God said to them, "Be fruitful and multiply, and fill the earth and subdue it; and have dominion over the fish of the sea and over the birds of the air and over every living thing that moves upon the earth." God said, "See, I have given you every plant yielding seed that is upon the face of all the earth, and every tree with seed in its fruit; you shall have them for food. And to every beast of the earth, and to every bird of the air, and to everything that creeps on the earth, everything that has the breath of life, I have given every green plant for food." And it was so. God saw everything that he had made, and indeed, it was very good. (Genesis 1:26–31)

Humankind was fathered into a world in which all things had been provided for them. But the garden was not a perfect environment. Of course it wasn't. No place could be a perfect environment when sin was present in the environment. The garden was the proving ground of free will. Would humankind, who had all things, walk with God wholeheartedly, or would they allow themselves to be fatally distracted? As a direct result of the fall, God's provision had to change.

The LORD God made garments of skins for the man and for his wife, and clothed them. Then the LORD God said, "See, the man has become like one of us, knowing good and evil; and now, he might reach out his hand and take also from the tree of life, and eat, and live forever"—therefore the LORD God sent him forth from the garden of Eden, to till the ground from which he was taken. He drove out the man; and at the east of

the garden of Eden he placed the cherubim, and a sword
flaming and turning to guard the way to the tree of life.
(Genesis 3:21–24)

All things were lost: home, intimacy with God, and dominion.
What was 'gained' was a result of the fall: the Lord God made garments
of skins for the man and his wife and clothed them. God's provision
of animal-skin clothing testified that death had already come to the
garden. Who killed the animals? God's provision of clothing testified
to the fatal loss of humankind's intimacy with God and with each other.
Clothes were barriers: necessary barriers, but barriers nonetheless. But
the barriers on the hearts of people were much more significant than
the barriers on the body.

"The LORD saw that the wickedness of humankind was great in
the earth, and that every inclination of the thoughts of their hearts
was only evil continually. And the LORD was sorry that he had made
humankind on the earth, and it grieved him to his heart. So the LORD
said, 'I will blot out from the earth the human beings I have created—
people together with animals and creeping things and birds of the air,
for I am sorry that I have made them" (Genesis 6:5–7).

God's provision had changed from that which flowed from intimacy
with his people to that which flowed from a distance—remote and
impersonal—because the heart of humankind no longer sought after
knowing their Creator. Whereas the whole of humankind should have
been seeking after the knowing of their Creator, there was now only
the occasional individual.

> But Noah found favor in the sight of the LORD. These
> are the descendants of Noah. Noah was a righteous
> man, blameless in his generation; Noah walked with
> God. And Noah had three sons, Shem, Ham, and
> Japheth. Now the earth was corrupt in God's sight,
> and the earth was filled with violence. And God saw
> that the earth was corrupt; for all flesh had corrupted
> its ways upon the earth. And God said to Noah, "I have
> determined to make an end of all flesh, for the earth is

filled with violence because of them; now I am going to destroy them along with the earth. Make yourself an ark." (Genesis 6:8–14)

God provided Noah with precise instructions for making the ark and filling it. The earth flooded from above and below, and outside the ark, life ceased. Finally, the waters receded, and God again provided Noah with his instructions.

In the six hundred first year, in the first month, the first day of the month, the waters were dried up from the earth; and Noah removed the covering of the ark, and looked, and saw that the face of the ground was drying. In the second month, on the twenty-seventh day of the month, the earth was dry. Then God said to Noah, "Go out of the ark, you and your wife, and your sons and your sons' wives with you. Bring out with you every living thing that is with you of all flesh—birds and animals and every creeping thing that creeps on the earth—so that they may abound on the earth, and be fruitful and multiply on the earth." (Genesis 8:13–17)

God established a covenant with Noah and his sons that such a flood would never happen again, and God provided a sign that would assure them of it. From the ark, the whole earth was repopulated. God's provision was not random or irrelevant. His provision was given to create opportunity for fruitfulness.

When Abram was ninety-nine years old, the LORD appeared to Abram, and said to him, "I am God Almighty; walk before me, and be blameless. And I will make my covenant between me and you, and will make you exceedingly numerous." Then Abram fell on his face; and God said to him, "As for me, this is my covenant with you: You shall be the ancestor of a multitude of nations. No longer shall your name be Abram, but your name

shall be Abraham; for I have made you the ancestor
of a multitude of nations. I will make you exceedingly
fruitful; and I will make nations of you, and kings shall
come from you. I will establish my covenant between
me and you, and your offspring after you throughout
their generations, for an everlasting covenant, to be God
to you and to your offspring after you. And I will give
to you, and to your offspring after you, the land where
you are now an alien, all the land of Canaan, for a perpetual holding; and I will be their God." God said to
Abraham, "As for you, you shall keep my covenant, you
and your offspring after you throughout their generations." (Genesis 17:1–9)

Provision enabled fruitfulness. In the garden, God's provision had
enabled fruitfulness, but that fruitfulness had been derailed before it
even got going. Abram, like Noah, was a fresh start, yet humankind
could not shake off the sin that corrupted the human heart. Abram had
trouble believing that God meant what he said.

God said to Abraham, "As for Sarai your wife, you shall not call her
Sarai, but Sarah shall be her name. I will bless her, and moreover I will
give you a son by her. I will bless her, and she shall give rise to nations;
kings of peoples shall come from her." Then Abraham fell on his face
and laughed, and said to himself, "Can a child be born to a man who is
a hundred years old? Can Sarah, who is ninety years old, bear a child?"
(Genesis 17:15–17).

Where humankind does not believe that God means what he says,
humankind turns God's provision into human rights. Human rights deny
God's provision and say instead that humankind has automatic rights
by the simple fact of being humankind. Human rights are impersonal
and distant, and they flow from pride. God provides because he loves,
not because he has to. Human rights are a human invention of human
pride, and they actually do not exist in the kingdom of God.

The Lord said: Because these people draw near with
their mouths and honor me with their lips, while their

hearts are far from me, and their worship of me is a human commandment learned by rote; so I will again do amazing things with this people, shocking and amazing. The wisdom of their wise shall perish, and the discernment of the discerning shall be hidden. Ha! You who hide a plan too deep for the LORD, whose deeds are in the dark, and who say, "Who sees us? Who knows us?" You turn things upside down! Shall the potter be regarded as the clay? Shall the thing made say of its maker, "He did not make me"; or the thing formed say of the one who formed it, "He has no understanding"? (Isaiah 29:13–16)

The illusion of human rights hides the reality of God's provision. As human beings we have a right to absolutely nothing. As human beings, we have only what has been given to us.

Woe to you who strive with your Maker, earthen vessels with the potter! Does the clay say to the one who fashions it, "What are you making"? or "Your work has no handles"? Woe to anyone who says to a father, "What are you begetting?" or to a woman, "With what are you in labor?" Thus says the LORD, the Holy One of Israel, and its Maker: Will you question me about my children, or command me concerning the work of my hands? I made the earth, and created humankind upon it; it was my hands that stretched out the heavens, and I commanded all their host." (Isaiah 45:9–12)

The illusion of human rights tricks people into believing that they are owners, when they are actually only stewards.

The word that came to Jeremiah from the LORD: "Come, go down to the potter's house, and there I will let you hear my words." So I went down to the potter's house, and there he was working at his wheel. The vessel he was making of clay was spoiled in the potter's hand, and he reworked it into another vessel, as seemed good to him. Then the word of the LORD came to me: Can I not do with you, O house of Israel, just as this potter has done? says the LORD. Just like the clay in the potter's hand, so are you in my hand, O house of Israel. At one moment I may declare concerning a nation or a kingdom, that I will pluck up and break down and destroy it, but if that nation, concerning which I have spoken, turns from its evil, I will change my mind about the disaster that I intended to bring on it. And at another moment I may declare concerning a nation or a kingdom that I will build and plant it, but if it does evil in my sight, not listening to my voice, then I will change my mind about the good that I had intended to do to it. (Jeremiah 18:1–10)

The illusion of human rights tricks people into believing that they are masters of their own destiny, when they are actually children of their father—and children are never masters of their own destiny. The more that humankind believes in human rights, the less they believe in God's provision. But God is under no obligation of any description to anyone. God provides because he loves, not because he has to do so.

"Gentiles, who did not strive for righteousness, have attained it, that is, righteousness through faith; but Israel, who did strive for the righteousness that is based on the law, did not succeed in fulfilling that law. Why not? Because they did not strive for it on the basis of faith, but as if it were based on works" (Romans 9:30–32).

The Jews turned the law of faith into a law of works and changed it from the basis of provision to that of human rights. We Gentiles have made exactly the same mistake. Gentiles turned the provision of God from the basis of love to that of human rights. Human rights cause us to be individualistic, detached, self-centered, and impersonal in many ways.

We say that a fetus isn't a person: it's a disposable thing, because women have the right to choose.

We say that wives aren't people: they're disposable conveniences because the husband is supreme.

We say that employees aren't people: they're disposable assets because the account book is god.

And so on. God's provision focuses on the God who provides, not on the provision itself—and certainly not on the one who receives. God's provision makes us community, joined together, others-centered, and personal. Human rights can destroy relationships, actually causing one individual to take priority over another. God's provision encourages relationships, because we are all equally dependent upon God, interdependent with each other, and looking to the same Father. Therefore, I say it again: Without God we are nothing. Without God's provision, we have nothing.

YHWH is our provider, and his provision is extraordinary, extravagant, outrageous.

On the third day there was a wedding in Cana of Galilee, and the mother of Jesus was there. Jesus and his disciples had also been invited to the wedding. When the wine gave out, the mother of Jesus said to him, "They have no wine." And Jesus said to her, "Woman, what concern is that to you and to me? My hour has not yet come." His mother said to the servants, "Do whatever he tells you." Now standing there were six stone water jars for the Jewish rites of purification, each holding twenty or thirty gallons. Jesus said to them, "Fill the jars with water." And they filled them up to the brim. He said to them, "Now draw some out, and take it to the chief steward." So they took it. When the steward tasted the water that had become wine, and did not know where it came from (though the servants who had drawn the water knew), the steward called the bridegroom and said to him, "Everyone serves the good wine first, and then the inferior wine after the guests have become drunk. But you have kept the good wine until now." Jesus did this, the first of his signs, in Cana of Galilee,

and revealed his glory; and his disciples believed in him.
(John 2:1–11)

The direct result of God's provision (through Jesus) was that "his disciples believed in him." It was the act of kindness that caused them to follow him. This provision was far beyond what anyone would have expected of Jesus. Except his mother! God's provision extends to everything, including life itself.

> Jesus said to them, "Very truly, I tell you, the Son can do nothing on his own, but only what he sees the Father doing; for whatever the Father does, the Son does likewise. The Father loves the Son and shows him all that he himself is doing; and he will show him greater works than these, so that you will be astonished. Indeed, just as the Father raises the dead and gives them life, so also the Son gives life to whomever he wishes. The Father judges no one but has given all judgment to the Son, so that all may honor the Son just as they honor the Father. Anyone who does not honor the Son does not honor the Father who sent him. Very truly, I tell you, anyone who hears my word and believes him who sent me has eternal life, and does not come under judgment, but has passed from death to life." (John 5:19–24)

Since we are utterly dependent upon God for everything, including life itself, we have no rights of our own. Human rights are a human illusion. Of ourselves, we are nothing, and we are entitled to nothing. Of ourselves, we are a people of no rights. But when we have no rights—when we are empty—an extraordinary thing happens.

> Let the same mind be in you that was in Christ Jesus, who, though he was in the form of God, did not regard equality with God as something to be exploited, but emptied himself, taking the form of a slave, being born in human likeness. And being found in human

form, he humbled himself and became obedient to the point of death—even death on a cross. Therefore, God also highly exalted him and gave him the name that is above every name, so that at the name of Jesus every knee should bend, in heaven and on earth and under the earth, and every tongue should confess that Jesus Christ is Lord, to the glory of God the Father. (Philippians 2:5–11)

When Jesus had no rights—when he was empty—God lifted Jesus to the highest place. When we have no rights—when we are empty—God lifts us to be with, in, and of Jesus. Then everything is beneath our feet.

"What are human beings that you are mindful of them, or mortals, that you care for them? You have made them for a little while lower than the angels; you have crowned them with glory and honor, subjecting all things under their feet." Now in subjecting all things to them, God left nothing outside their control. As it is, we do not yet see everything in subjection to them, but we do see Jesus, who for a little while was made lower than the angels, now crowned with glory and honor because of the suffering of death, so that by the grace of God he might taste death for everyone. (Hebrews 2:6–9)

All things are subjected under our feet. Nothing is outside our control. It is true that we do not see the fullness of that yet, but it is both here and coming in the life that is eternal and everlasting. If we insist on our human rights before God, if we do things our own way, if we refuse to empty ourselves, if we refuse to take on the form of a slave—well, I am sure you can work it out for yourself.

"Very truly, I tell you, whoever believes has eternal life. I am the bread of life. Your ancestors ate the manna in the wilderness, and they died. This is the bread that comes down from heaven, so that one may eat of it and not die. I am the living bread that came down from heaven.

Whoever eats of this bread will live forever; and the bread that I will give for the life of the world is my flesh" (John 6:47–51).

This world in which we live is the world of flesh, and Jesus' flesh is the life of the world. The world that is to come will not be a world of flesh that decays and dies, and it will be too late then to want to eat of Jesus' flesh. God's provision to you and me is the call to die, to utterly and completely die to self and be found in Jesus. That is why the Spirit of God in you and me works the way he does.

"When the Spirit of truth comes, he will guide you into all the truth; for he will not speak on his own, but will speak whatever he hears, and he will declare to you the things that are to come. He will glorify me, because he will take what is mine and declare it to you. All that the Father has is mine. For this reason I said that he will take what is mine and declare it to you" (John 16:13–15).

In order to lead us into all life, the Spirit will first lead us into all death. That is God's provision. In a very real sense, God's provision is for the dead—those who are dead to themselves in Christ. In a very real sense, God's provision is for those who are nothing—nothing of themselves in Christ. Only the "dead" in Christ and the "nothing" in Christ will inherit.

> He is the image of the invisible God, the firstborn of all creation; for in him all things in heaven and on earth were created, things visible and invisible, whether thrones or dominions or rulers or powers—all things have been created through him and for him. He himself is before all things, and in him all things hold together. He is the head of the body, the church; he is the beginning, the firstborn from the dead, so that he might come to have first place in everything. For in him all the fullness of God was pleased to dwell ... As you therefore have received Christ Jesus the Lord, continue to live your lives in him, rooted and built up in him and established in the faith, just as you were taught, abounding in thanksgiving. See to it that no one takes you captive through philosophy and empty deceit, according to

human tradition, according to the elemental spirits of the universe, and not according to Christ. For in him the whole fullness of deity dwells bodily, and you have come to fullness in him." (Colossians 1:15–19; 2:6–10)

Only the "dead" in Christ and the "nothing" in Christ will receive God's provision. Do you want God's provision?

24

Forgiveness

"Pray then in this way: Our Father in heaven, hallowed be your name. Your kingdom come. Your will be done, on earth as it is in heaven. Give us this day our daily bread. And forgive us our debts, as we also have forgiven our debtors. For if you forgive others their trespasses, your heavenly Father will also forgive you; but if you do not forgive others, neither will your Father forgive your trespasses" (Matthew 6:9–12, 15).

A traditional and very common way of understanding forgiveness from God is this:

- We sin against God.
- We ask God for forgiveness.
- God forgives us.

It is summed up in this way. If you ask God to forgive you, he will forgive you. But should this really be our understanding? When does God forgive us? When you read the old covenant Scriptures, forgiveness is in one of two forms.

1. Present tense: God says, "I *do* forgive." When asked to forgive (in the present tense), God forgives (in the present tense).

Moses wrote: "The LORD is slow to anger, and abounding in steadfast love, forgiving iniquity and transgression, but by no means clearing the guilty, visiting the iniquity of the parents upon the children to the third and the fourth generation. Forgive the iniquity of this people according to the greatness of your steadfast love, just as you have pardoned this people, from Egypt even until now. Then the LORD said, 'I do forgive, just as you have asked'" (Numbers 14:18–20).

2. Future tense: God says, "I *will* forgive."

"The priest shall make atonement for them, and they shall be forgiven … Thus the priest shall make atonement on his behalf for his sin, and he shall be forgiven … Thus the priest shall make atonement on your behalf, and you shall be forgiven" (Leviticus 4:20, 26, 31). "If my people who are called by my name humble themselves, pray, seek my face, and turn from their wicked ways, then I will hear from heaven, and will forgive their sin and heal their land" (2 Chronicles 7:14).

Here are more Scriptures that demonstrate the tense in which forgiveness is given.

> So the men turned from there, and went toward Sodom, while Abraham remained standing before the LORD. Then Abraham came near and said, "Will you indeed sweep away the righteous with the wicked? Suppose there are fifty righteous within the city; will you then sweep away the place and not forgive it for the fifty righteous who are in it? Far be it from you to do such a thing, to slay the righteous with the wicked, so that the righteous fare as the wicked! Far be that from you! Shall not the judge of all the earth do what is just?" And the LORD said, "If I find at Sodom fifty righteous in the city, I *will forgive* the whole place for their sake." (Genesis 18:22–26)

> The priest shall make atonement for all the congrega-tion of the Israelites, and they *shall be* forgiven; it was unintentional, and they have brought their offering, an offering by fire to the LORD, and their sin offering

before the LORD, for their error. All the congregation
of the Israelites *shall be* forgiven. (Numbers 15:25–26)

In the old covenant Scriptures, forgiveness is something that will
happen in the future, provided that atonement is made. There are lots
more old covenant Scriptures about forgiveness, and they are all in either
the present tense (a few) or in the future tense (the majority). When
does God forgive us?

"After this, when Jesus knew *that all was now finished*, he said (in
order to fulfill the scripture), 'I am thirsty.' A jar full of sour wine was
standing there. So they put a sponge full of the wine on a branch of
hyssop and held it to his mouth. When Jesus had received the wine, he
said, "*It is finished*." (John 19:28–30).

When did God forgive us?

> See to it that no one takes you captive through philoso-
> phy and empty deceit, according to human tradition,
> according to the elemental spirits of the universe, and
> not according to Christ. For in him the whole fullness
> of deity dwells bodily, and you have come to fullness
> in him, who is the head of every ruler and authority.
> In him also you were circumcised with a spiritual cir-
> cumcision, by putting off the body of the flesh in the
> circumcision of Christ; when you were buried with him
> in baptism, you were also raised with him through faith
> in the power of God, who raised him from the dead.
> And when you were dead in trespasses and the uncir-
> cumcision of your flesh, God *made* you alive together
> with him, when *he forgave us all our trespasses, erasing* the
> record that stood against us with its legal demands. He
> *set this aside*, nailing it to the cross. He *disarmed* the rul-
> ers and authorities and *made* a public example of them,
> *triumphing* over them in it. (Colossians 2:8–15)

Everything that God has done through Jesus with regard to
forgiveness is in the past perfect tense, not in the future. It is done.

Completely. It will never be done again. It cannot be done again. Let us look at some more Scriptures to see if this holds true.

"As God's chosen ones, holy and beloved, clothe yourselves with compassion, kindness, humility, meekness, and patience. Bear with one another and, if anyone has a complaint against another, forgive each other; just as the Lord *has forgiven* you, so you also must forgive" (Colossians 3:12–13).

"Do not grieve the Holy Spirit of God, with which you were marked with a seal for the day of redemption. Put away from you all bitterness and wrath and anger and wrangling and slander, together with all malice, and be kind to one another, tenderhearted, forgiving one another, as God in Christ *has forgiven* you" (Ephesians 4:30–32).

It is Paul's frequent theme that our selves and our behaviors should be seen in the light of what Christ has already done. And Paul is not alone in this.

> Beloved, I am writing you no new commandment, but an old commandment that you have had from the beginning; the old commandment is the word that you have heard. Yet I am writing you a new commandment that is true in him and in you, because the darkness is passing away and the true light is already shining. Whoever says, "I am in the light," while hating a brother or sister, is still in the darkness. Whoever loves a brother or sister lives in the light, and in such a person there is no cause for stumbling. But whoever hates another believer is in the darkness, walks in the darkness, and does not know the way to go, because the darkness has brought on blindness. I am writing to you, little children, because your sins *are forgiven* on account of his name. (1 John 2:7–12)

To suggest or to teach people that God does not forgive until they repent or seek forgiveness is to keep people in false darkness. We are a people of forgiveness because of what Christ has completely done for us. We are to show the world at large that God's forgiveness has been given to them too and that they need to receive that forgiveness from him. God's action of forgiveness is complete. He has done everything he needed to do. Forgiveness in the new covenant is in the past tense.

God's action of forgiveness is complete, but the outworking of forgiveness in the lives of humankind is not yet complete. The outworking of God's complete forgiveness continues in human experience. For us, therefore, forgiveness is more about outworking than it is about an event. Because God's act of forgiveness is fully complete, we are now an utterly forgiven people. There is nothing else that God needs to do. We do not need to ask God for forgiveness; we already have it. But we do need to receive it and let his forgiveness go on working in us day-by-day.

God forgave me fully through Christ. It is finished. But there is a vital relationship distinction to be made here: God did not forgive people's sin; he forgave people their sin. We tend to focus on bad or wrong behavior, calling it sin, but God's focus is on the person. We tend to be issue-focused, whereas God is person-focused. When our heads remember what has been done to us, we tend to focus on issues; but when our hearts lead the way, we will focus on the person—and what is best for that person (and therefore best for us).

"From now on, therefore, we regard no one from a human point of view; even though we once knew Christ from a human point of view, we know him no longer in that way. So if anyone is in Christ, there is a new creation: everything old has passed away; see, everything has become new!" (2 Corinthians 5:16–17).

Only Christians who live daily in the reality of being a forgiven people can bring that reality into the lives of other people. In the old covenant, forgiveness was in the future or present tense, and forgiveness was conditional to the act of atonement. Therefore, it was common under the old covenant for God's people to plead for forgiveness for others.

"Then the LORD appeared to Solomon in the night and said to him: 'I have heard your prayer, and have chosen this place for myself as a house of sacrifice. When I shut up the heavens so that there is no rain, or command the locust to devour the land, or send pestilence among my people, if my people who are called by my name humble themselves, pray, seek my face, and turn from their wicked ways, then

I will hear from heaven, and *will forgive* their sin and heal their land"
(2 Chronicles 7:12–14).

No wonder, then, that the God of the old covenant was known to
be a forgiving God. But Jesus, in the new covenant, makes known the
God of forgiveness.

> When [Jesus] returned to Capernaum after some days,
> it was reported that he was at home. So many gathered
> around that there was no longer room for them, not
> even in front of the door; and he was speaking the word
> to them. Then some people came, bringing to him a
> paralyzed man, carried by four of them. And when
> they could not bring him to Jesus because of the crowd,
> they removed the roof above him; and after having dug
> through it, they let down the mat on which the paralytic
> lay. When Jesus saw their faith, he said to the paralytic,
> "Son, your sins *are forgiven*." Now some of the scribes
> were sitting there, questioning in their hearts, "Why
> does this fellow speak in this way? It is blasphemy! Who
> can forgive sins but God alone?" At once Jesus perceived
> in his spirit that they were discussing these questions
> among themselves; and he said to them, "Why do you
> raise such questions in your hearts? Which is easier, to
> say to the paralytic, 'Your sins *are forgiven*,' or to say,
> 'Stand up and take your mat and walk'? But so that you
> may know that the Son of Man has authority on earth
> to forgive sins"—he said to the paralytic—"I say to you,
> stand up, take your mat and go to your home." And he
> stood up, and immediately took the mat and went out
> before all of them; so that they were all amazed and
> glorified God, saying, "We have never seen anything
> like this!" (Mark 2:1–12)

One of the most remarkable things about this account is that the
paralytic man, who is central to the story, never says a word. As we
begin this passage, Mark tells us that Jesus has "come home," back to

Capernaum where he and the disciples were based. The crowds were crushing in around Jesus, and there was no room to move. The building committee would have been horrified at what happened next.

In those days, houses were made of rough igneous rock (compacted lava) without mortar. They could support little more than a sloping, thatched roof consisting of wooden cross beams overlaid with matted reeds, branches, and dried mud. This roof had to be renewed every autumn before the winter rains set in, and it would neither be difficult to break through the roof nor difficult to repair it afterward.

When Jesus saw the faith of those who dug through the roof, he said to the paralytic, "Son, your sins are forgiven." This is in the past perfect tense. Jesus declared forgiveness that had already happened and was complete. While Mark had little interest in medical matters (Luke would pick those up later), he once again described Jesus doing what only YHWH could do: forgiving sin. But Jesus was not treating the symptom; he was treating the cause. Mark was giving us yet more evidence that Jesus is God incarnate. One of the most significant aspects of personal healing is that it is often made possible through the healing of relationships. The crowds had quite literally never seen or heard anything like this. Only God could pronounce sin forgiven in the past perfect tense. It was finished and never to be repeated. Now consider this.

- Did the paralytic *confess* sin to Jesus?
- Did the paralytic *ask* for forgiveness from Jesus?
- Did the paralytic even *want* forgiveness from Jesus?

Yet Jesus pronounced forgiveness in the past perfect tense. Why? Didn't forgiveness only come through the cross? But Jesus hadn't been crucified then. As you examine the Scriptures for yourself, learn from what they say. But also take note of what the Scriptures do not say. Notice what Jesus did and did not say.

- Jesus did say, "Your sins *are forgiven*."
- But why didn't Jesus say instead, "I *forgive* your sins"?
- Why didn't Jesus say instead, "*God forgives* your sins"?

You see, Jesus had not yet died on the cross. Yet Jesus was here declaring that sins had been forgiven (in the past perfect tense) and that this forgiveness never needed to be—nor would it be—repeated again. How could this be, when he had not yet died on the cross?

The reason that Jesus was able to pronounce sins as forgiven in the past perfect tense is because forgiveness did not come through the cross, although that is commonly believed. (I do acknowledge that the price of forgiveness was paid at the cross.) In the old covenant, the year of Jubilee—a year of forgiveness and restoration—was calendar based, but the incarnation brought forth a remarkable transformation. God's Jubilee was no longer based on the calendar but on a person. Jesus was God's Jubilee. That was why he was able to pronounce sins as forgiven, in the past perfect tense.

Jesus is still God's Jubilee. The era of Jubilee is still with us. Sins are totally and utterly forgiven in Christ, and only in Christ, for only he is God's Jubilee. Therefore, forgiveness came through the incarnation, and the price of forgiveness was paid at the cross. The rest of the new covenant Scriptures agree and speak of forgiveness in the past perfect tense.

"In Christ, God was reconciling the world to himself, not counting their sins against them" (2 Corinthians 5:19).

"And when you were dead in trespasses and the uncircumcision of your flesh, God made you alive together with him, when he forgave us all our trespasses, erasing the record that stood against us with its legal demands. He set this aside, nailing it to the cross" (Colossians 2:13–14).

"As God's chosen ones, holy and beloved, clothe yourselves with compassion, kindness, humility, meekness, and patience. Bear with one another and, if anyone has a complaint against another, forgive each other; just as the Lord has forgiven you, so you also must forgive" (Colossians 3:12–13).

"Do not grieve the Holy Spirit of God, with which you were marked with a seal for the day of redemption. Put away from you all bitterness and wrath and anger and wrangling and slander, together with all malice, and be kind to one another, tenderhearted, forgiving one another, as God in Christ has forgiven you" (Ephesians 4:30–32).

"I am writing to you, little children, because your sins are forgiven on account of his name" (1 John 2:12).

"From now on, therefore, we regard no one from a human point of view; even though we once knew Christ from a human point of view, we know him no longer in that way. So if anyone is in Christ, there is a new creation: everything old has passed away; see, everything *has become* new! All this is from God, who *reconciled* us to himself through Christ, and has given us the ministry of reconciliation; that is, in Christ God was reconciling the world to himself, *not counting their trespasses against them*, and entrusting the message of reconciliation to us. So we are ambassadors for Christ, since God is making his appeal through us; we entreat you on behalf of Christ, be reconciled to God" (2 Corinthians 5:16–20).

There are lots more new covenant Scriptures dealing with our forgiveness, which you can explore for yourself—and they are all in the past tense. God's act of forgiveness is complete. He has already done everything he needed to do to forgive. But remember that, although God's action of forgiveness is complete, the outworking of forgiveness in the lives of humankind is not yet complete. The outworking of God's complete forgiveness continues in human experience.

For us, therefore, forgiveness is more about outworking than it is about an event. Because God's act of forgiveness is complete, we are now a forgiven people, and there is nothing else that God needs to do. We do not need to ask God for forgiveness; we already have it. But we do need to receive it, and we do need to let the reality of his forgiveness go on working and growing in us day-by-day. God has done everything that needed to be done for forgiveness to be real in people's lives. Therefore, stop focusing on trying to improve your own behavior. Stop trying to keep short accounts with a God who doesn't keep accounts. Stop focusing on other people's behavior and trying to get them to improve. Forgiveness is not about behavioral modification. It is about inner transformation through revelation. That is the testimony of the Scriptures.

Now I must move on to the testimony of my own experience and see if it agrees with the testimony of the Scriptures. In order to help me grow with God and deepen my experience of him and my love for him, he taught me how relationships with him and with other people work—especially in relation to forgiveness. If I was to continually experience forgiveness, I had to understand what sin was in God's eyes. I needed a practical understanding of sin so that I could avoid doing it. After all, a purely theological understanding of sin is of no use to the person who has only just encountered Christ for themselves. Here, then, is an understanding that a person can put into practice: sin is willful damage of relationships.

Now, here comes the amazing fact of my relationship with God: through all the years I have grown with God, he has never once mentioned my sin to me. He has never once wagged a finger in my face and pointed to this sin or that sin, and it is not as though he was short of material! Why has God not mentioned my sin to me? I initially thought that God was just being gentle and nice with me, but that didn't make sense. After all, sin must be dealt with. Over time, I realized why God never mentioned sin to me.

Since I was utterly and completely forgiven in the past perfect tense, how could God mention sin to me? My life needed to come into line with what God had already done in Christ. You see, God's relationship with me is love-based, not sin-based. And love—certainly not sin—needs to be the sole basis of our relationships with each other. The good news of the gospel is that we are totally and utterly forgiven in Christ, but that we do need to receive that reality and grow daily in it.

Now, let me be totally honest here. Telling someone that he is a filthy, rotten sinner and that he is going to hell unless he accepts Jesus, doesn't count as good news in my book. Does that sound like good news to you? It sure doesn't to me.

Showing and telling the wonderful love of God in actions and in words is good news. The revelation that one is utterly forgiven in Christ leads to inner transformation. I grew and matured in the love of God as he lavished it upon me. Forgiveness was not merely something I practiced; it became my way of life. Is the work of forgiveness in me complete? No. Am I the finished article? No, of course not.

In Christ, I have grown in the reality that my character is to be rooted in forgiveness. Therefore I have confidence in me. In Christ, I have grown in the reality that my relationships flow from forgiveness and that I touch others with forgiveness. Therefore I have confidence in God, who is constantly at work in me. This is about the practice of practical forgiveness, not a theory.

Let me share with you two important practicalities of forgiveness from my own life. First, I know I am forgiven because God never uses my past as a weapon against me in the present. Therefore, I never knowingly use the past as a weapon against anyone else in the present. Second, I know I am forgiven because God never took advantage of my weakness or injury. Therefore, I will never knowingly take advantage of anyone else's weakness or injury.

God has done everything that needed to be done for real forgiveness in people's lives. It only needs to be being received. Those who do not (or will not) receive the gift, cannot get the benefit of the gift. Therefore God has given to us the ministry and message of reconciliation. This is the practical foundation of forgiveness that enables us live forgiven lives, to be forgiven people, and to be forgiving people. But how do we practice the reality of forgiveness in our everyday relationships?

As far as forgiveness is concerned, we cannot "wipe the slate clean." That option is simply not open to us, because we are not capable of doing it. Our own lives tell us this. In our heads, we cannot help but remember what has gone before, what has happened to us, what experiences we have had. In our hearts, we cannot help but feel again the emotions of remembered suffering. Nevertheless, we do have a choice. Our reactions are in our own hands. The words with which you respond and the deeds with which you react are under your control.

"I said, 'I will guard my ways that I may not sin with my tongue'" (Psalm 39:1).

You can indeed muzzle your mouth so that you do not speak hastily, and you can choose not to count people's sins against them. But if the head cannot forget, then how do we show forgiveness? The answer is as simple as it is profound. You cannot forget, but you can remember no more. You always have a choice about how you react to people and to what they have done to you.

That does not mean that there should not be justice. But justice should be people-centered, not mere law enforcement. Revenge is self-centered, not people-centered. Judgment is God-centered, not self-centered. Loving your neighbor as yourself is a God-given, people-centered command. And before that commandment comes the God-centered command to love the Lord your God.

This is about practical forgiveness—the practice of forgiveness, not a theory. Any theory of forgiveness is based in the head, whereas the practice of forgiveness is based in the heart. For human beings, forgiveness is a work in progress, an outworking more than an event. Only God's act of forgiveness is complete. The outworking of God's forgiveness continues in human experience and must be grounded in a relationship understanding of Scripture. Therefore, stop focusing on your own behavior and trying to improve it. Stop focusing on others' behavior and trying to get them to improve.

Instead, let your heart receive the reality that you are fully forgiven, right here and now. Here is another thought. If God has completely and utterly forgiven me in Christ, shouldn't you do the same? For far too long the church has focused on "sinful" behavior and has condemned the sinner. God cannot do that, because he has already forgiven the sinner. The gospel is not that God will forgive the sinner. The gospel is that God has already forgiven the sinner. Only Christians who know the reality of being a forgiven people can bring that reality into the lives of other people. We cannot lead where we have never been ourselves. Christians who do not know the reality of being a forgiven people will live by the law of traditional evangelical forgiveness.

> Then Jesus said, "There was a man who had two sons. The younger of them said to his father, 'Father, give me the share of the property that will belong to me.' So he divided his property between them. A few days later the younger son gathered all he had and travelled to a distant country, and there he squandered his property in dissolute living. When he had spent everything, a severe famine took place throughout that country, and he began to be in need. So he went and hired himself out to one of the citizens of that country, who sent him to his fields to feed the pigs. He would gladly have filled himself with the pods that the pigs were eating; and no

one gave him anything. But when he came to himself he said, 'How many of my father's hired hands have bread enough and to spare, but here I am dying of hunger! I will get up and go to my father, and I will say to him, "Father, I have sinned against heaven and before you; I am no longer worthy to be called your son; treat me like one of your hired hands."' So he set off and went to his father. But while he was still far off, his father saw him and was filled with compassion; he ran and put his arms around him and kissed him. Then the son said to him, 'Father, I have sinned against heaven and before you; I am no longer worthy to be called your son.' But the father said to his slaves, 'Quickly, bring out a robe—the best one—and put it on him; put a ring on his finger and sandals on his feet. And get the fatted calf and kill it, and let us eat and celebrate; for this son of mine was dead and is alive again; he was lost and is found!' And they began to celebrate.

"Now his elder son was in the field; and when he came and approached the house, he heard music and dancing. He called one of the slaves and asked what was going on. He replied, 'Your brother has come, and your father has killed the fatted calf, because he has got him back safe and sound.' Then he became angry and refused to go in. His father came out and began to plead with him. But he answered his father, 'Listen! For all these years I have been working like a slave for you, and I have never disobeyed your command; yet you have never given me even a young goat so that I might celebrate with my friends. But when this son of yours came back, who has devoured your property with prostitutes, you killed the fatted calf for him!' Then the father said to him, 'Son, you are always with me, and all that is mine is yours. But we had to celebrate and rejoice, because this brother of yours was dead and has come to life; he was lost and has been found.'" (Luke 15:11–32)

Sin is the willful damage of relationships. This story that Jesus told deserves careful study. The man had two sons. This is not the story of the prodigal son; it is the story of two sons. They were both heirs, but the younger, immature, impatient son wanted to possess in inheritance now.

In verse 12, the younger son said to his father, "Father, give me my share of the property." He wanted his inheritance immediately, but he also called his father "Father."

Notice carefully the father's response (v. 12): "So he divided his property between them."

The younger son carried out his premeditated plan and cut loose from his father (v. 13). A few days later, the younger son gathered all that he had and traveled to a distant country. When the money ran out, the friends ran out. When famine struck, the younger son found himself in need for the first time in his life (v. 14). When he had spent everything, a severe famine took place throughout that country, and he began to be in need.

While in desperate need, he came to his senses and remembered who his father was (v. 17). But when he came to himself, he said, "How many of my father's hired hands have bread enough and to spare?"

So the younger son set off for home, rehearsing his speech as he went (vv. 18–19): "I will get up and go to my father, and I will say to him, 'Father, I have sinned against heaven and before you; I am no longer worthy to be called your son; treat me like one of your hired hands.'"

While the younger son was stumbling home in repentance, his father was running to him in joy (v. 20). But while he was still far off, his father saw him and was filled with compassion. He ran and put his arms around him and kissed him.

The younger son had a wrong concept of his father (v. 21), thinking he was no longer worthy to be called a son. But the parent-child relationship is based on worthiness-by-birth, not birth-by-worthiness. The younger son spoke from his wrong concept of his father, but the father spoke and acted from the love relationship that was formed through birth. Notice that the younger son's pride was broken by his father's love. He did not reject the father's gifts. He realized afresh who his father was and, therefore, who he was, and he forgave himself.

The older son questioned the celebration (v. 26). He called one of the slaves and asked what was going on. Unforgiveness will cause us to hate joy.

The older son reacted in self-centered anger (v. 28). He became angry and refused to go in. Unforgiveness makes "I" the center of the world.

The older son denied the father he claimed to love (v. 29). "Listen!" he said. "For all these years I have been working like a slave for you, and I have never disobeyed your command." Unforgiveness makes us self-righteous.

The older son revealed his thankless heart (v. 29). He said, "Yet you have never given me even a young goat so that I might celebrate with my friends." Unforgiveness makes us into liars.

The older son disclaimed his own brother (v. 30). He said, "But when this son of yours came back." Unforgiveness denies all responsibility.

The older son stirred up trouble (v. 30). He said, "But when this son of yours came back, who has devoured your property." Unforgiveness turns us into abominations.

The older son blackened reputation with gossip (v. 30). He said, "But when this son of yours came back, who has devoured your property with prostitutes." Unforgiveness will cause our imaginations to speculate. Unforgiveness is a cancer that eats away at every part of our being, consuming reason, sense, and love.

The father always spoke out of relationship, but the older son never called him "Father." The father could not give any more than he had already given. Relationship means giving, but the older son was working to earn the inheritance that his father had already given to him.

The father had his son back, and he was glad and celebrated. Forgiveness loves joy. If the father was glad, shouldn't the son be glad also? The father would not let the older brother cast off his responsibility: family is family.

Our Father's heart celebrates when dead sons and daughters become alive again, when lost children are found. The Father is focused on relationships: renewing, restoring, encouraging, and healing them.

The loving fatherhood that Jesus presented in this story sweeps away the image of strict fatherhood that the Jews strongly held. And the new covenant in Jesus has the same relationship focus. That is why the new covenant says, "Forgive us our debts, as we also have forgiven our debtors."

The new covenant in Jesus has a relationship focus, and if you have not or will not forgive others, then you are proving that you have not truly received God's forgiveness into yourself. If you haven't yet received God's forgiveness into yourself, then you are not yet ready to enter into this new covenant with God through Jesus.

We need to mature from a place where forgiveness is only a reaction in our lives, to a place where forgiveness is our proactive initiative, even with people we haven't met yet. We need to mature so that forgiveness isn't something we merely practice but is our whole way of life. Our character needs to be rooted in forgiveness. It needs to flow from forgiveness and touch others with forgiveness.

To that end, I will not knowingly use the past as a weapon in the present, and God will never use the past as a weapon in the present.

I will never knowingly take advantage of you, and God will never take advantage of you.

I will never knowingly exploit you, and God will never exploit you.

People who live this way are living the ministry of reconciliation, and they have a right to proclaim the message of reconciliation.

25

Trials and the Evil One

"Pray then in this way: Our Father in heaven, hallowed be your name. Your kingdom come. Your will be done, on earth as it is in heaven. Give us this day our daily bread. And forgive us our debts, as we also have forgiven our debtors. *And do not bring us to the time of trial, but rescue us from the evil one*" (Matthew 6:9–15).

Trial is not the same as temptation. And this is not referring to every little (or big) temptation to sin that we may face. The Greek word that the NIV translates as "temptation" can indeed be translated that way. Nevertheless, our modern popular idea of temptation is not what Jesus was referring to. Instead, the translation "trial," meaning "testing, proving," is much more appropriate. Our difficulty today is that the word *temptation* is almost always linked to sin. And it is almost always linked to our being tempted to sin every minute of the day and watching out that we do not give in to that temptation.

The covenant context here is not sin—being tempted to sin every minute of the day and watching out that we do not give in to that temptation. The context is about a trial, a testing, a proving. An engineer who has been involved in the design and manufacture of a new machine knows what it means to put the machine through a "trial." But here in the new covenant, it is a trial—a testing, a proving—that we should be careful to avoid whenever possible. For some examples of trials such as this, think of Job, Elijah in the wilderness, Jesus in the wilderness, Jesus in the garden of Gethsemane, Peter's denial of Jesus. We need to look at some of these times of trial and understand why they happened.

Elijah

> Ahab told Jezebel all that Elijah had done, and how he had killed all the prophets with the sword. Then Jezebel sent a messenger to Elijah, saying, "So may the gods do to me, and more also, if I do not make your life like the life of one of them by this time tomorrow." Then he was afraid; he got up and fled for his life, and came to Beer-sheba, which belongs to Judah; he left his servant there. But he himself went a day's journey into the wilderness, and came and sat down under a solitary broom tree. He asked that he might die: "It is enough; now, O LORD, take away my life, for I am no better than my ancestors." Then he lay down under the broom tree and fell asleep. Suddenly an angel touched him and said to him, "Get up and eat." He looked, and there at his head was a cake baked on hot stones, and a jar of water. He ate and drank, and lay down again. The angel of the LORD came a second time, touched him, and said, "Get up and eat, otherwise the journey will be too much for you." He got up, and ate and drank; then he went in the strength of that food forty days and forty nights to Horeb the mount of God. At that place he came to a cave, and spent the night there. Then the word of the LORD came to him, saying, "What are you doing here, Elijah?" He answered, "I have been very zealous for the LORD, the God of hosts; for the Israelites have forsaken your covenant, thrown down your altars, and killed your prophets with the sword. I alone am left, and they are seeking my life, to take it away." (1 Kings 19:1–10)

Why did Elijah's trial (testing, proving) happen? Because he ran away in fear for his life. And then he made claims: "I have been very zealous for the LORD, the God of hosts. I alone am left." But Elijah wasn't the only one left. And he ran because he was afraid for his life.

Jesus in the Wilderness

Then Jesus was led up by the Spirit into the wilderness to be tempted by the devil. He fasted forty days and forty nights, and afterwards he was famished. The tempter came and said to him, "If you are the Son of God, command these stones to become loaves of bread." But he answered, "It is written, 'One does not live by bread alone, but by every word that comes from the mouth of God.'" Then the devil took him to the holy city and placed him on the pinnacle of the temple, saying to him, "If you are the Son of God, throw yourself down; for it is written, 'He will command his angels concerning you,' and 'On their hands they will bear you up, so that you will not dash your foot against a stone.'" Jesus said to him, "Again it is written, 'Do not put the Lord your God to the test.'" Again, the devil took him to a very high mountain and showed him all the kingdoms of the world and their splendor; and he said to him, "All these I will give you, if you will fall down and worship me." Jesus said to him, "Away with you, Satan! for it is written, 'Worship the Lord your God, and serve only him.'" Then the devil left him, and suddenly angels came and waited on him. (Matthew 4:1–11)

Why did this trial (testing, proving) happen? Because the claim made by Jesus that he truly was God's Son had to be tried (tested, proved).

Jesus in Gethsemane

Then Jesus went with them to a place called Gethsemane; and he said to his disciples, "Sit here while I go over there and pray." He took with him Peter and the two sons of Zebedee, and began to be grieved and agitated. Then he said to them, "I am deeply grieved, even to death; remain here, and stay awake with me." And going a little farther, he threw himself on the ground and prayed, "My Father, if it is possible, let this cup pass from me; yet not what I want but what you want." Then he came to the disciples and found them sleeping; and he said to Peter, "So, could you not stay awake with me one hour? Stay awake and pray that you may not come into the time of trial; the spirit indeed is willing, but the flesh is weak." Again he went away for the second time and prayed, "My Father, if this cannot pass unless I drink it, your will be done." Again he came and found them sleeping, for their eyes were heavy. So leaving them again, he went away and prayed for the third time, saying the same words. Then he came to the disciples and said to them, "Are you still sleeping and taking your rest? See, the hour is at hand, and the Son of Man is betrayed into the hands of sinners. Get up, let us be going. See, my betrayer is at hand." (Matthew 26:36–46)

Why did this trial (testing, proving) happen? Because the claim that Jesus made—that he was on earth to do the will of the Father—had to be tested.

Peter

When they had sung the hymn, they went out to the Mount of Olives. And Jesus said to them, "You will all become deserters; for it is written, 'I will strike the shepherd, and the sheep will be scattered.' But after I am raised up, I will go before you to Galilee." Peter said to him, "Even though all become deserters, I will not." Jesus said to him, "Truly I tell you, this day, this very night, before the cock crows twice, you will deny me three times." But he said vehemently, "Even though I must die with you, I will not deny you." And all of them said the same. (Mark 14:26–31)

Peter said to him, "Even though I must die with you, I will not deny you." And so said all the disciples. (Matthew 26:35)

While Peter was below in the courtyard, one of the servant-girls of the high priest came by. When she saw Peter warming himself, she stared at him and said, "You also were with Jesus, the man from Nazareth." But he denied it, saying, "I do not know or understand what you are talking about." And he went out into the forecourt. Then the cock crowed. And the servant-girl, on seeing him, began again to say to the bystanders, "This man is one of them." But again he denied it. Then after a little while the bystanders again said to Peter, "Certainly you are one of them; for you are a Galilean." But he began to curse, and he swore an oath, "I do not know this man you are talking about." At that moment the cock crowed for the second time. Then Peter remembered that Jesus had said to him, "Before the cock crows twice, you will deny me three times." And he broke down and wept. (Mark 14:66–72)

Why did Peter fall so hard and so often? Why did his trials (testings, provings) happen? Peter fell badly because of the claims he made, and claims must always be tested. These were Peter's claims:

- Even if all fall away, *I never will.*
- Even if I have to die with you, *I will never disown you.*
- *I am ready* to go with you to prison and to death.

But Peter's bold claims contradicted Jesus, who had said, "You will all fall away." Peter's claims:

- sprang from immaturity
- were an attempt to prove that he was a "real man"
- showed that he was not aware of consequences

- disregarded Jesus' own words
- opposed Jesus
- deadened spiritual awareness
- made him certain to fall
- worsened the inevitable fall

Peter led his brothers in Christ astray. He caused them to fall also; because all of them had agreed with Peter that they would never disown Jesus, even though Jesus had just told them all otherwise.

"Then he came to the disciples and found them sleeping; and he said to Peter, "So, could you not stay awake with me one hour? Stay awake and *pray that you may not come into the time of trial*; the spirit indeed is willing, but the flesh is weak" (Matthew 26:40–41).

"And once more he came and found them sleeping, for their eyes were very heavy; and they did not know what to say to him" (Mark 14:40).

Peter's claims showed that he was looking from a human point of view when the soldiers came to arrest Jesus. "But one of those who stood near drew his sword and struck the slave of the high priest, cutting off his ear" (Mark 14:47). It was Peter who drew his sword and attacked the slave, and he did so to prove his loyalty—but in a human way of understanding.

Peter's claims led him to lie. "While Peter was below in the courtyard, one of the servant-girls of the high priest came by. When she saw Peter warming himself, she stared at him and said, 'You also were with Jesus, the man from Nazareth.' But he denied it, saying, 'I do not know or understand what you are talking about.' And he went out into the forecourt. Then the cock crowed. And the servant-girl, on seeing him, began again to say to the bystanders, 'This man is one of them.' But again he denied it. Then after a little while the bystanders again said to Peter, 'Certainly you are one of them; for you are a Galilean.' But he began to curse, and he swore an oath, 'I do not know this man you are talking about'" (Mark 14:66–71).

Peter's claims led him to despair. "At that moment the cock crowed for the second time. Then Peter remembered that Jesus had said to him, 'Before the cock crows twice, you will deny me three times.' And he broke down and wept" (Mark 14:72).

Claims will lead us into trial (testing, proving). Therefore, we must be very careful about making claims. And we must be very careful about drawing others into our claims. There is only one kind of claim that we should ever make.

> Jesus spoke to them, saying, "I am the light of the world. Whoever follows me will never walk in darkness but will have the light of life." Then the Pharisees said to him, "You are testifying on your own behalf; your testimony is not valid." Jesus answered, "Even if I testify on my own behalf, my testimony is valid because I know where I have come from and where I am going, but you do not know where I come from or where I am going" … They said to him, "Who are you?" … Jesus said to them, "Very truly, I tell you, before Abraham was, I am." (John 8:12–14, 25, 58)

What God has said is so, and we can safely claim it. Jesus could claim that God was his Father, because YHWH himself had called Jesus his Son. I may safely claim of myself only that which God has said about me. Great care and wisdom are needed here! Claims that are not based in the revelation of God are dangerous to your spiritual and physical health, and they are also dangerous to those who are influenced by you. Too many Christian's lives have been shipwrecked by claims. Those whose claims are based in the revelation of God himself can expect God to back them up, and he will! Peter fell because when his claims were tried (tested, proved), he was found wanting.

Jesus allowed Peter to make claims, but he didn't allow Peter to self-destruct. "Simon, Simon, listen! Satan has demanded to sift all of you like wheat, but I have prayed for you that your own faith may not fail; and you, when once you have turned back, strengthen your brothers" (Luke 22:31–32).

Jesus allowed Peter to lead others astray, but Jesus didn't lose anybody because of it. Jesus allowed all of his disciples to abandon him, but he remained in control. He allowed his disciples to lose all their authority, but Jesus lost none of his.

I am to do what I can do, and Jesus does what he can do. I don't try to do what Jesus can do, and Jesus won't do what I can do. I do not claim anything for myself. That is what it means to be "of no reputation." I claim only that which Jesus has claimed for me.

"We do this so that we may not be outwitted by Satan; for we are not ignorant of his designs" (2 Corinthians 2:11). Jesus never stepped outside the authority that was given to him by his Father. Jesus never claimed anything except that which his Father declared of him. The enemy of your soul wants you to make claims that are outside the authority of Jesus. If the Evil One succeeds, when the trial (test, proving) comes, you will go down with a bang, and he will then call God into question.

Part III

Christ-Centered Marriage

If we are to understand God's design for Christ-centered marriage, we need to understand these things:

- who God is
- who I am
- what a man is
- what a woman is

At some point in every person's life, he asks the all-important question: who am I? In the context of marriage, the answer to that question lies in exploring two other questions: What is a man? and What is a woman?

These are not questions of sexuality; they are questions of gender. And through gender, they are questions about relationships. To understand who and what we are at the very center of our beings, we need to understand something of who and what God is at the very center of his being.

"In the beginning when God created the heavens and the earth, the earth was a formless void and darkness covered the face of the deep, while a wind from God swept over the face of the waters" (Genesis 1:1–2). "In the beginning was the Word, and the Word was with God, and the Word was God. He was in the beginning with God" (John 1:1–3).

"Beginning—God." That is literally how the Scriptures begin. "Beginning—three persons." God is one God, but he is community. He is one God but three persons who are alike—different yet equal. God is three persons, yet one in nature, one in essence. All gender is found in God and originates in God. God himself is "like fellowshipping with like." And the three-in-one God expressed their creativity in the physical realm by filling the air, the sea, and the land.

"And God said, 'Let the waters bring forth swarms of living creatures, and let birds fly above the earth across the dome of the sky.' So God created the great sea monsters and every living creature that moves, of every kind, with which the waters swarm, and every winged bird of every kind. And God saw that it was good. God blessed them, saying, 'Be fruitful and multiply and fill the waters in the seas, and let birds multiply on the earth'" (Genesis 1:20–22).

Then came something special. Man was different from God. Man was different from every other creature on earth. When Adam, the first man, was created, he was created from the dust of the earth, as were all the mammals. But God breathed the breath of life only into his nostrils. When Adam was created, he was not only the first human being; he was the only human being. Obvious? Perhaps. God had breathed life into Adam in a way that he had not done with any other creature.

Adam was unique because he was God-aware—made for direct relationship with God—and so he was also self-aware. There were other created beings (angels) that were also God-aware and self-aware, but they weren't created from the dust of the earth as the first man was. But man could not enjoy like-for-like fellowship with anyone, because there was no one else like him. God wanted Adam to care for the creation, but Adam couldn't do it alone, because there was no one to give him like-for-like fellowship in the task.

> The LORD God took the man and put him in the garden of Eden to till it and keep it. And the LORD God commanded the man, "You may freely eat of every tree of the garden; but of the tree of the knowledge of good and evil you shall not eat, for in the day that you eat of it you shall die." Then the LORD God said, "It is not good that the man should be alone; I will make him a helper as his partner." So out of the ground the LORD

God formed every animal of the field and every bird of the air, and brought them to the man to see what he would call them; and whatever the man called every living creature, that was its name. The man gave names to all cattle, and to the birds of the air, and to every animal of the field; but for the man there was not found a helper as his partner. So the LORD God caused a deep sleep to fall upon the man, and he slept; then he took one of his ribs and closed up its place with flesh. And the rib that the LORD God had taken from the man he made into a woman and brought her to the man. Then the man said, "This at last is bone of my bones and flesh of my flesh; this one shall be called Woman, for out of Man this one was taken." Therefore a man leaves his father and his mother and clings to his wife, and they become one flesh. And the man and his wife were both naked, and were not ashamed. (Genesis 2:15–25)

Adam was to care for God's creation, but he couldn't do it alone. He needed a companion. So God brought every living creature to the first man for him to name, but not one of them did he call "companion." There was a foundational problem here, because God, in three persons, enjoyed fellowship like for like, but there was no other creature with whom Adam could enjoy that like-for-like fellowship. So God made woman—but not from the dust of the earth. She was made from part of Adam himself. She was like him. By taking part of man and making woman, God gave man like-for-like fellowship.

But there was another massive change in creation. No longer would new human beings be formed from the dust of the earth. Instead, sexuality was extended to human beings. Sexuality in humankind meant that new human beings would birthed by that which came out of man: woman.

Gender was found in God before sexuality was found in creation. Therefore, gender and sexuality are not the same thing. Men and women are (or should be) defined by their gender, not by their sexuality.

"Then God said, 'Let us make humankind in our image, according to our likeness; and let them have dominion over the fish of the sea, and over the birds of the air, and over the cattle, and over all the wild animals of the earth, and over every creeping thing that creeps upon the earth'" (Genesis 1:26).

The earth was filled with livestock, the air with birds, and the sea with fish. Humankind was to rule, to have dominion over all creation, but how were they to do it? Sit in an office and issue a decree? No! Man was to explore, because an explorer is what he is. And that is directly reflected in his sexuality.

Man is not content to know what is behind a door; he wants to see for himself. Man climbs mountains, goes to the poles, walks on the moon. Man acts first and thinks later (if he thinks at all!). Man takes risks purely for the thrill of it. Man courts danger. Man doesn't sit still. Man needs to know. Man needs to go. Man needs to show. This is how man was made. So, what of woman?

Woman is a companion. She was made to be with man. But notice that this has nothing to do with status. Neither is better than the other, nor is one more valuable than the other. This is about relationship, not status. Man and woman are different, but they are equal and complementary. Equality is not conformity. True equality recognizes differences between the genders but holds that these differences bind them together rather than push them apart. Consider these essential differences in the genders.

- Where man is about the destination, woman is about the journey.
- Where man is about achievement, woman is about the achieving.
- Where man is about knowledge, woman is about knowing.
- Where man is about having, woman is about holding.
- Where man is about doing, woman is about being.
- Where man is task-driven, woman is relationship-driven.
- Where man is competitive, woman is complementary.

Man and woman are equal. That should be written into every marriage vow. Man and woman can make a truly formidable team, but how does that team work? It works because man is the head of the relationship—but not the boss! It is critical to understand the concept of headship here. Headship equals responsibility. Headship responsibility should not be understood in the context of either blame or control; it has nothing to do with either of them. Blame and control came into humankind because of the fall, but they were not part of God's original design.

Consider the parents of a newborn baby and the responsibility that they have for the child. This responsibility has nothing to do with blame or control. The parents are personally responsible for that baby human being. Man has the responsibility for the health and well-being of the marriage relationship. When the relationship hits difficult times, it is the man's responsibility to put things right. In the context of marriage, man is responsible.

But this is not about control, blame, performance, or leadership. Rather, it has to do with covering and protection. Headship, then, is male, but headship and leadership are not the same thing. Therefore, important marriage leadership decisions should always be taken by both partners together—never by one alone. Man is explorer, woman is companion. This is not a statement about status. It is a statement of gender that defines the male-to-female marriage partnership. We must now consider what happened at the fall.

26

What Happened at the Fall?

Now the serpent was more crafty than any other wild animal that the LORD God had made. He said to the woman, "Did God say, 'You shall not eat from any tree in the garden'?" The woman said to the serpent, "We may eat of the fruit of the trees in the garden; but God said, 'You shall not eat of the fruit of the tree that is in the middle of the garden, nor shall you touch it, or you shall die.'" But the serpent said to the woman, "You will not die; for God knows that when you eat of it your eyes will be opened, and you will be like God, knowing good and evil." So when the woman saw that the tree was good for food, and that it was a delight to the eyes, and that the tree was to be desired to make one wise, she took of its fruit and ate; and she also gave some to her husband, who was with her, and he ate. Then the eyes of both were opened, and they knew that they were naked; and they sewed fig leaves together and made loincloths for themselves.

They heard the sound of the LORD God walking in the garden at the time of the evening breeze, and the man and his wife hid themselves from the presence of the LORD God among the trees of the garden. But the LORD God called to the man, and said to him, "Where are you?" He said, "I heard the sound of you in the garden, and I was afraid, because I was naked; and I hid myself." He said, "Who told you that you were naked? Have you eaten from the tree of which I commanded you not to eat?" The man said, "The woman whom you gave to be with me, she gave me fruit from the tree, and I ate." Then the LORD God said to the woman, "What is this that you have done?" The woman said, "The serpent tricked me, and I ate."

To the woman he said, "I will greatly increase your pangs in childbearing; in pain you shall bring forth children, yet your desire shall be for your husband, and he shall rule over you." And to the man he said, "Because you have listened to the voice of your wife, and have eaten of the tree about which I commanded you, 'You shall not eat of it,' cursed is the ground because of you; in toil you shall eat of it all the days of your life; thorns and thistles it shall bring forth for you; and you shall eat the plants of the field. By the sweat of your face you shall eat bread until you return to the ground, for out of it you were taken; you are dust, and to dust you shall return." (Genesis 3:1–13, 16–19)

The fall resulted in a number of explicit consequences, but there were also some implicit ones. The creation, God's handiwork, was very good, but the fall took that which was very good and twisted and corrupted it. The consequences of the fall were very far-reaching for the whole of creation. The woman eating some kind of forbidden fruit was not the original sin. The original sin happened before woman took the fruit. Notice what God said to the man: "Because you have listened to the voice of your wife, and have eaten of the tree about which I commanded you, 'You shall not eat of it,' cursed is the ground because of you." God never said that the ground was cursed because of woman. The man's sin was that, when the serpent deceived woman, he stood and watched it happen and did nothing to intervene.

"So when the woman saw that the tree was good for food, and that it was a delight to the eyes, and that the tree was to be desired to make one wise, she took of its fruit and ate; and she also gave some to her husband, *who was with her,* and he ate" (Genesis 3:6).

The man was with her when woman fell. Man stood and watched and did absolutely nothing to stop it as his wife was deceived by the serpent. Man abdicated his responsibility for his wife because he had already abdicated his own headship responsibility. That was the original sin. Man showed neither headship nor leadership at the fall. Man abdicated the responsibility of his own gender, and in so doing, he put a burden on the woman that she was never made to carry. Woman was fully equipped to handle leadership alongside her husband, but she was not equipped to handle the solo headship responsibility that was thrust upon her as she faced the serpent. Little wonder, then, that she was deceived.

Under the weight of the headship burden that she was never meant to carry, woman's leadership was flawed, because she was forced to make a decision alone that they should both have made—because the man had already abdicated his responsibility. In the garden, the man abdicated his headship responsibility. That was why he stood and watched as the serpent deceived his wife. What had already happened in the man so that he stood and watched his wife being deceived?

Consider this question: Why were the man and woman standing at that tree in the middle of the garden in the first place? It was the last place they wanted to be! But the man's heart was already dead, as he stood and watched his wife being deceived. The serpent had already done his work in man. Even though the man was standing there as his wife was dragged down by the serpent, the serpent knew that he would not intervene, because the first man had already given in to the serpent. That meant that the way was clear to deceive the woman, because serpent had already gotten to the man so that he would not intervene. The man abdicated his headship responsibility, because his heart was already dead, and the result was that he was now head-driven, not heart-driven. The cold-hearted man stood by and watched his wife crash and burn.

The head-driven man always looks to blame someone else. It was her fault. Because man abdicated his headship responsibility, their marriage partnership was wrecked before it really got off the starting blocks. Through his fall, man became self-centered and head-driven. The implicit consequence of the man being compromised by that serpent was that his heart was already dead when he stood and watched his wife being deceived. He was cold-hearted and head-driven. Let us consider self-centeredness.

Self-centeredness is the opposite of headship. While headship takes responsibility for another, self-centeredness denies responsibility for another.

Self-centeredness corrupts headship into dictatorship. Where headship lifts and blesses the wife, dictatorship oppresses and crushes the wife.

Self-centeredness corrupts leadership into control. Where leadership acts for the benefit of others, self-centeredness controls others for the benefit of self.

Self-centeredness loses respect through fear. Where self-sacrifice invests in others and produces the return of respect, self-centeredness rules through fear and forfeits all respect.

Self-centeredness is a most aggressive cancer that eats away at and destroys the heart of man. When God came into the garden after the fall, he called to man, "Where are you?" He did so because the original sin was his, not hers.

> To the woman he said, "I will greatly increase your pangs in childbearing; in pain you shall bring forth children, yet your desire shall be for your husband, and he shall rule over you." And to the man he said, "Because you have listened to the voice of your wife, and have eaten of the tree about which I commanded you, 'You shall not eat of it,' cursed is the ground because of you; in toil you shall eat of it all the days of your life; thorns and thistles it shall bring forth for you; and you shall eat the plants of the field. By the sweat of your face you shall eat bread until you return to the ground, for out of it you were taken; you are dust, and to dust you shall return." (Genesis 3:16–19)

To the woman God said, "Your desire will be for your husband, and he will rule over you." One effect of the fall was that man would control the woman rather than partner with her and thereby cause her to be unnaturally dependent upon him. Control causes dependency. Absolute control causes absolute dependency.

One effect of the fall upon men was to produce dictators. This is where, in a marriage relationship, the husband exerts total control over the wife and over every meaningful aspect of their lives, marriage, and family. Such men will probably believe that they are being the head of the family, when actually they are its dictator. In a marriage relationship that has a dictator husband, any or all of the following may be present.

- He will have total control of money.
- He will tightly control his wife's spending, yet he will spend freely to fulfill his own desires.
- He will tightly control his wife's time, yet he will treat all time as "his" time.
- He will control his wife's mobility, yet he will go where and when he likes.
- He will view his wife by what she does or does not do, rather than by who she is.
- He will constantly speak of what he does for the family, ignoring what he actually is.
- He will take sex from his wife instead of making love with her.
- He will give her nothing lasting or meaningful from sex, with the possible exception of children.

Dictators cause devastating damage to their wives, their children, and their marriage. God is not a dictator, and the image of man as seen in a dictator is far removed from the reality of God's character. Where a man is dictator, there is no marriage in Scriptural terms, because there is no partnership. Where a man is dictator, there is no love in Scriptural terms, because love does not insist on its own way. Where a man is dictator, there is no freedom in Scriptural terms, only slavery.

In families where children have a dictator father, boys grow up with no true role model of partnership, headship, love, leadership, or respect. And in the years that lie ahead, when such boys become men (physically), they will exert over their women exactly the same control they saw their fathers exerting over their mothers. The sins of the fathers will be visited upon their children and by their children.

The wife who lives with a dictator is absolutely dependent, because she is absolutely controlled. Dictators are extremely destructive. Physically, the dictator husband is a man, but inwardly he is a boy. Outside the marriage relationship, dictators will also exert control over anyone and everyone in order to get their own way. It was never meant to be that way. It still isn't meant to be that way. It does not have to be that way. But there is also another possibility.

This is where the man abdicates his headship responsibility and relationally abandons his wife so that she has to take up that headship responsibility herself. The wife will often take up that responsibility because "someone has to." So the family's direction becomes her responsibility. The children become her responsibility. The family's spiritual health becomes her responsibility. But she was never designed to take that responsibility alone.

The pressure of headship that she wasn't made to take will, sooner or later, burst out of her and cause terrible destruction to her and to the family. And when it happens, she will get the blame, and it will be seen as her fault. The abdicator husband may proclaim his innocence and say, "I never saw it coming." The tragedy is indeed that he was blind for so long. Physically, the abdicator husband is man, but inwardly he is a little boy.

Those abdicators who relationally abandon their wives and cause them to pick up the burden of headship are little boys who usually treat their wives as their mothers. Those dictators who twist headship into absolute control are boys who usually treat their wives as their servants.

27

For This Purpose

"The Son of God was revealed for this purpose, to destroy the works of the devil" (1 John 3:8).

The Devil's work needs to be undone. But what is the Devil's work? And where is it? The fall had a number of explicit consequences, but there were also a number of implicit consequences, as we have seen. The fall didn't just affect humankind; it impacted the whole of creation. For the woman, the direct result of the fall was that the man, who was himself no longer fit for headship, would rule over her.

"The man named his wife Eve, because she was the mother of all living" (Genesis 3:20). Adam named his wife. To name someone is to exert authority over them. To name someone is to exert ownership over them. Exerting authority or ownership over someone needs to be handled very carefully. It is dangerous for the one who is subjected to that power, but it is much more dangerous for the one who exerts that power over another. Think of names that are forced onto people—names like *Loser, Failure, Useless*, and so on.

> And the LORD God made garments of skins for the man and for his wife, and clothed them. Then the LORD God said, "See, the man has become like one of us, knowing good and evil; and now, he might reach out his hand and take also from the tree of life, and eat, and live forever"—therefore the LORD God sent *him* forth from the garden of Eden, to till the ground from

which he was taken. He drove out the *man*; and at the
east of the garden of Eden he placed the cherubim, and
a sword flaming and turning to guard the way to the
tree of life. (Genesis 3:21–24)

Woman paid a terribly heavy price for being deceived. Being of low
or nonexistent status in society is a part of that price. Woman was no
longer an equal companion to man. She had become an unequal slave.
Oh, the terrible damage that the first man did.

Through the fall, there is an inherent weakness in many women,
which needs a true headship covering for protection, and it causes
women no end of trouble. It is that she listened to the voice of the
deceiver and so became very vulnerable to that voice. Woman are often
vulnerable to the voice of doom and gloom, worst-case scenarios, what-
ifs, and worry.

For women, this is potentially a massive weakness that needs
headship covering in a marriage context. But husbands, beware! She
needs understanding, not patronizing. Despite woman's weakness with
the voice of doom and gloom, there is one part of a woman's character
that helps to cover this weakness, though it can also emphasize it.
Where man is task-driven, woman is relationship-driven.

The marriage dictator's inherent characteristic of being task-driven
can also be corrupted so that it is actually anti-relationship. This is when
men become unhealthily competitive with each other. The symptoms
involve winning at all costs and hating to come in second—sometimes
to a particular person but often to anyone.

This highlights a major difference between men and woman. Men
play games to win, but women play games for companionship. Oh that
men—and especially husbands—would learn that.

The man gave names to all cattle, and to the birds of
the air, and to every animal of the field; but for the
man there was not found a helper as his partner. So the
LORD God caused a deep sleep to fall upon the man,
and he slept; then he took one of his ribs and closed up
its place with flesh. And the rib that the LORD God

had taken from the man he made into a woman and brought her to the man. Then the man said, "This at last is bone of my bones and flesh of my flesh; this one shall be called Woman, for out of Man this one was taken." Therefore a man leaves his father and his mother and clings to his wife, and they become one flesh. And the man and his wife were both naked, and were not ashamed" (Genesis 2:20–25).

This is marriage within God's purpose. This is the order of things that was ordained by God before the fall. This is how it was meant to be. This is God's design for family. Children were meant to grow up in a family where the man and the wife were in true partnership, and the husband exercised true headship.

Therefore a man will leave his father and mother. This is not a geographical statement; it is a relationship statement. A man must:

- come out from the headship of his father
- learn to think and speak for himself
- learn to believe for himself
- come out from the intensity of being mothered
- learn to make decisions and so reap the consequences for himself
- learn the reality and responsibility of freewill independence

Before man does these things, he must first relationally leave his parents. Physical separation, leaving home, is not enough, and it is not even necessary. If this leaving does not happen before marriage, then the man will tend to abdicate his headship and thrust the burden on his wife.

A man is to be united to his wife. This statement is:

- a relationship statement, not a sexual one
- the establishing of a new partnership
- the establishing of a new headship

Being geographically joined to his wife is not enough. This cleaving cannot happen if the man has not done the leaving.

And they will become one flesh. This is a sexual statement. When all the preparation has been done and the foundations are in place, sexual intimacy can stand on a solid foundation of established relationship and partnership.

God ordained this order of things before the fall. The man must come out from the authority of his parents and learn in practice what it means to be in a new partnership of his own. Only then is he ready for sexual intimacy. The family is God's specially designed environment where children can grow up into healthy, well-balanced adults.

Especially important in a family environment is the father. So much hinges on him being a true role model for the whole family—but especially for sons and their own future marriages. Most boys who do not mature properly have been held back by the lack of a male role model. Immature men need a male role model who can help them grow up into the men that they can and should be.

The apostle Paul was well aware of this, and it deeply affected how he interpreted and responded to people's behavior. (See 1 Corinthians 3:1–10; 5:1–5.) Therefore, Paul did not respond to what was happening in the Corinthian church by having lots of people thrown out of the fellowship. He knew that what they actually needed was to grow up! Paul's response to them and their circumstances was that of a loving father (1 Corinthians 4:14–16).

Paul didn't warn them as an apostle, a pastor, or an overseer. He warned them as a father. This is spiritual parenting, and it is just as important as biological parenting—perhaps even more so. It is never too late for men who have never grown up inwardly to have a male role model to help them grow toward maturity, but there is ultimately only one role model who can actually give them that growth. They need to meet Jesus for themselves. And Jesus loves children! They need to meet Jesus with the help of a spiritual father. It is not enough for boys to merely believe in Jesus. They actually need to meet Jesus for themselves, and they need to go on meeting Jesus. That is the only way that boys grow up.

Wives need to be married to mature men, not to little boys or immature teenagers. If the husband does not grow up, the wife's growth will likewise be severely impaired. Husbands, if you want to know what you are like, look at your wife and children. The apostle Paul knew about fathering others, for he knew about being fathered by God and adopted as his son. Indeed, one theme that Paul majored on throughout his writings was our adoption as God's children. And everything Paul said and did was to bring people into full maturity in Christ. In relation to marriage, Paul's writing was based on the foundation that we have now discovered. Let us look at the path to maturity that Paul laid out for husbands.

> Husbands, love your wives, just as Christ loved the church and gave himself up for her, in order to make her holy by cleansing her with the washing of water by the word, so as to present the church to himself in splendor, without a spot or wrinkle or anything of the kind—yes, so that she may be holy and without blemish. In the same way, husbands should love their wives as they do their own bodies. He who loves his wife loves himself. For no one ever hates his own body, but he nourishes and tenderly cares for it, just as Christ does for the church, because we are members of his body. "For this reason a man will leave his father and mother and be joined to his wife, and the two will become one flesh." This is a great mystery, and I am applying it to Christ and the church. Each of you, however, should love his wife as himself. (Ephesians 5:25–33)

This cannot be understood academically, because the mind simply cannot handle it, but the heart of a man needs to engage with this. Husbands must love their wives as Christ loved the church and gave himself up for her. If they don't, they will never be truly fulfilled as husbands or fathers. This is no theory, unattainable ideal, or mere romantic words. This is to be an ongoing and growing daily reality.

Husband, in the daily reality of life, put your wife before yourself, before your ministry, before your job, before your own life. Leave behind your macho image, your macho ways, and your hard, controlling character—and come and die. Show your wife in reality that you live first and foremost for her, that you want the very best for her, that you want her to be the very best that she can be, that you put her first. As a husband, your true headship is to wash her with holy water, to present her radiant, without stain or wrinkle or blemish but rather as holy and blameless. As a husband, this is your responsibility, your headship.

Husbands, love your wives as your own bodies. Love your wives as you love yourselves. This is the responsibility of headship. True freedom is found in complete surrender to Jesus that finds expression in putting your wife first. The key to be being a Christlike husband is your own absolute surrender to Jesus Christ. This is not a one-off commitment; this is a daily covenant commitment for a lifetime.

Marriage is "like fellowshipping with like," being equals. But husbands and wives are equals only when husbands give themselves up for their wives. Then, and only then, do the husband and wife begin to be a true leadership team. Because men are usually head-driven, task-orientated, and issue-focused, and women are heart-driven, people-orientated, and person-focused, together they can cover all the angles. The strengths of one cover the weaknesses of the other. That is why they make a dynamic and powerful leadership team, even as they grow together.

This leadership team together takes all things into account when making a decision of significance and/or importance. Such a leadership team is powerful in the world for the kingdom of God, and so it is no wonder that marriage comes under severe attack from the enemy of our souls. The Enemy will do everything he can to prevent each husband and wife from reaching their full potential in Christ, because he greatly fears them. That is precisely why we must have Christ-centered marriages.

28

Growth and Healing

Some of us are married to a hurt and wounded person. My own wife married a hurt and wounded person. Some of us are married to a deeply hurt and wounded person. My wife married a deeply hurt and deeply wounded human being. There is, therefore, a difficult paradox at work here: relationships cause hurt and pain in us, but they also encourage growth and healing in us.

Relationships can hinder both growth and healing. Let us look now at the damage caused in people by unhealthy relationships.

The Tree of Death

Let us look at the tree of death.

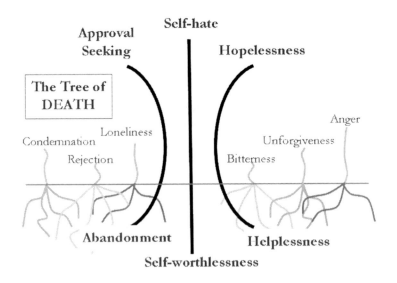

The roots of the tree of death are abandonment, self-worthlessness, and helplessness. The external branches growing from those roots are approval-seeking, self-hate, and hopelessness. We will briefly consider each of them. There are also weeds growing around the tree—many of them. They include condemnation, rejection, loneliness, bitterness, unforgiveness, and anger, though that is by no means a complete list.

Abandonment

Abandonment is primarily relational rather than physical. Relational abandonment can only come from people we have been close to, like family or close friends. People who have had a real and meaningful place in our hearts can hurt us deeply when they relationally abandon us, for whatever reason. Relational abandonment may be accompanied by physical abuse or neglect. Such abandonment can be real or only perceived—or both. This is internal.

Both God the Father and the Son knew abandonment. The Father was abandoned in the garden, Jesus was abandoned in another garden—and at the cross. The healing God was himself wounded. God knows what abandonment is like. He has been there.

Approval-Seeking

Approval-seeking verbalizes and externalises one's sense of abandonment. Approval-seeking is the constant desire to please people and thereby find acceptance through approval. It can take many forms, but the basic instinct is to win approval by saying or doing something. But approval-seeking never finds fulfilment; it always needs more. Approval-seeking is highly addictive for the one seeking approval, but this person usually ends up pushing people away instead of winning their approval or drawing them near. Thus it achieves exactly the opposite of what it is trying to do. A fiercely competitive spirit that hates to come in second (usually in men) is usually a clear sign of approval-seeking.

Self-Worthlessness

Self-worthlessness is imposed on us and rammed into us by family or close friends, and it can begin even before we are born. Childhood is especially important, as negative words and hurtful actions can penetrate very deep into the young heart. A sense of self-worthlessness is received and believed because of the person from whom it comes. Family and friends are often greatly trusted, and it makes the pain all the worse when that trust is shattered.

Self-worthlessness is received at a very deep level and becomes a foundational part of imposed identity. The failure of approval-seeking merely confirms the "truth" of self-worthlessness. Self-worthlessness believes that God does not and cannot have time for me—because I am worthless. Self-worthlessness blocks self-forgiveness. This is internal.

Self-Hate

Self-hate verbalizes and externalises one's sense of self-worthlessness. Self-hate deliberately deprives self. It denies justice to self. It harms self through neglect or willful injury. Self-hate feeds unforgiveness of self. Self-hate speaks only negatively of itself. In doing so, it is also speaking negatively of God, too. Self-hate blocks the growth of Christ in me.

Helplessness

A sense of helplessness says, "I was abandoned because I am worthless, and there is nothing I can do about it. I am powerless to change my situation. I must accept my lot and not complain about it, because being helpless is what being a Christian is all about, isn't it?"

Hopelessness

Helplessness verbalizes and externalises one's sense of hopelessness. Hopelessness says, "I am abandoned, worthless, and helpless, and there is nothing anyone can do about it. No one can change my situation. Anyway, I am not worth it, so you should not waste your time trying. The situation is hopeless. Trust me, I know. I've tried everything, so there's no point in you trying." Hopelessness speaks only negatively about itself.

Weeds

When the tree of death grows, it causes weeds to grow too. While those weeds are not as strong or dangerous as the tree itself, they can be problematic. As we said already, they include condemnation, rejection, loneliness, bitterness, unforgiveness, and anger—an incomplete list.

One of the Enemy's tricks is to get people to focus on pulling the weeds that are growing in the garden—while at the same time being totally blind to the massive tree that has become strong over time. If the garden is full of weeds, it is the tree of death that needs to be attacked first, and as a matter of urgency.

The Tree of Life

Acceptance

Acceptance comes from God through Jesus, but it is (hopefully) to be experienced through his people as they accept us. We are accepted by God for who and what we are, and change always begins (again and again) from there. Acceptance is totally relational and is relationally received. We cannot receive acceptance in isolation. We are utterly accepted into the Godhead. We will be with God, but we will not be God. As wholly as God does the knowing of us, we are to do the knowing of God. Acceptance is Christ-centered, not self-centered. (See Ephesians 1:3–6; Romans 5:6–8; 8:31–32.)

Approved

I am approved by God because I correctly handle the Word of truth (2 Timothy 2:15). I am approved by God, and so God's Word of truth does its work (Hebrews 4:12). I am approved by God, and the visible evidence of that is that people's lives are constantly being changed around me and through me. I do what I can do, and God does what he can do. I do what God asks me to do, and God does what I ask him to do. This is acceptance made known.

Self-Worth

God's redemptive act showed the value that he placed on each and every one of us (1 John 4:9–10). In that act of salvation, God showed his generosity to me (Ephesians 1:7–8). Jesus too showed his great love for me (John 14:1–4). He also showed his amazing generosity to me (John 15:15). The Holy Spirit is always in me and with me to show me who and what I am going to be in Christ.

Self-Love

Loving yourself is Christ-centered, not self-centered (Mark 12:28–31). You can only love your neighbor to the extent that you love yourself. What God has done for us is staggering (Colossians 2:9–10). Loving yourself allows you to grow into the fullness that God has for you. Self-love shows to others that your self-worth is Christ-centered, not self-centered.

Hope

Jesus loves me. Jesus loves *me*. Since Jesus loves me, I am worth it. In Jesus I trust; in Jesus I hope. I am changing, and my situation is changing (Ephesians 1:18). Hope is alive inside me. Hope is internal and it is the atmosphere in which faith breathes.

Hopeful

Jesus loves you. Jesus loves *you*. Since Jesus loves you, you are worth it. In Christ, you can. In you, Christ can. Your future rests on Christ and what he has done, not on you and what you can do (Philippians 1:4–6). My outward self is a hopeful self that speaks and acts in hopeful ways. Being hopeful reaches out to others with the hope of Christ and says, "Yes!" Being hopeful before others reaches out to the hopeless and helpless. Being hopeful gives hope real expression.

29

Languages of Love

We will now look at some languages of love that are central to the Christ-centered marriage relationship. I am aware that this subject has been explored elsewhere in other ways by other people, but I want to take it where I received it.

Marriage to a Spouse

Words are involved in how we speak to and about our partner. They can be words of love, affirmation, confirmation, and encouragement. Words reveal your heart and speak to your partner's heart. In the whole of creation, there is no power that can compare with the power of words. That power can be constructive or destructive. Let your words to and about your partner demonstrate absolute and unswerving loyalty to your partner.

Gifts can be purchased, made, invented, sung, and so on, and are given to an individual person. A gift should be given unconditionally, not for a purpose. A gift is an expression of relationship, not just something belonging to a special occasion, like a birthday, Christmas, and so forth.

Touch involves intimate and appropriate signs, not just sexuality. Touchless relationships are loveless relationships. Touch is the most important expression of relationship. A newborn baby needs touch above everything else. So do you. Touch is precious and should always be appropriate.

Time is a gift that allows our partners to be themselves. Those who will not give quality time to their partners, cannot keep that time for themselves. The gift of time is most precious, and we discover this when we give it as a gift.

Deeds include acts of kindness that are partner-centered. Deeds done for us show how valuable we are to our partners. Deeds can say "I love you and I accept you" in a way that words never can. Deeds are love made known.

Extended Languages are other ways of expressing love and affection within your marriage, which do not fit neatly into one of the above languages. Your partner must be the sole beneficiary of your extended languages. Never give to someone outside of marriage that which belongs to your partner inside marriage. Here are some ways you can make it absolutely clear to your partner that he or she is the only beneficiary of that love and affection.

1. Maintain an open heart before your partner. Secret loves devastate marriages.
2. Maintain an open diary before your partner. Secret meetings destroy trust.
3. Agree on and stick to your spending guidelines. Excessive spending wounds your partner.
4. As far as it depends upon you, do what you said you would do. Keep your word!
5. As far as it depends upon you, maintain your timekeeping. Don't be late!
6. Maintain absolute transparency in your relationships with people of the opposite gender.
7. Give the highest value to the ultimate commitment.

Marriage to the Lamb

In considering marriage, we must now think about the forthcoming marriage of Jesus to his church and the way he relates to his bride, whom he is preparing for that day.

Words are used by Jesus to speak to and about us. He uses words of love, affirmation, confirmation, and encouragement. Words reveal his heart—and speak to our hearts. In the whole of creation, there is no power that can compare with the power of words. Jesus is God's Word. That power is constructive and makes it possible for us to emulate him. Let his words about you demonstrate his absolute and unswerving loyalty to you.

Gifts are given to us personally and unconditionally. Jesus freely gave himself for his bride. God the Father freely gave all he had for you and me. These are not free gifts, but very expensive gifts freely given.

Touch is not that of sexuality but of intimate and appropriate signs of the deepest love. Touch is the most important expression of relationship. How often we wait for a word from God, while he is standing silent with arms open wide to receive us! A newborn baby needs touch above everything else. So do you. Touch is precious.

Time is a quality gift from God to me, an opportunity for me to be myself. Why does God want to spend quality time with me? Because he loves me and time is a most precious gift. The preciousness of time is discovered when it is given to me by God himself.

Deeds include acts of kindness that are Christ-centered. Deeds done for me show me the value the Saviour has for me. Deeds say "I love you and I accept you" in a way that words never can. Deeds are love made known.

30

The Marriage Leadership Team

Headship and leadership are not the same thing. Headship is male, but leadership is not gender specific. What is leadership? Did you know that the word *leader* does not appear in the new covenant Scriptures? Did you know that the word *leaders* only appears in the new covenant Scriptures three times? Two of those references to leaders are in the closing remarks in Hebrews. Did you know that the word *leadership* only appears in the new covenant Scriptures twice? That brings me to a stark realization.

The concept of leadership as we know it today is an entirely human construct that is unknown in the new covenant Scriptures. There is nothing wrong with our concept of leadership, but it is not a Scriptural concept. One must therefore ask if it is a godly concept.

The foundation of human leadership rests on the appointment of leaders who are perceived to have the right qualifications needed to do the job, to fulfil the role. Our human concept of leadership is necessary for everyday life, but it has no Scriptural foundation. Leadership is not gender specific, and single-gender leadership teams are imbalanced, incomplete, and ineffective.

Since leadership is an entirely human construct, we cannot define leadership from the new covenant Scriptures. Since almost everybody in life could be called a leader for one reason or another, we need a definition of leadership that brings a real meaning to that word. What is leader?

A leader takes others where he himself has been before. He cannot lead somewhere he has never been. Man is explorer and woman is companion, and together they make a formidable leadership team. The explorer and his companion are made to lead. Marriage needs to have a complete leadership team, because:

- hearts forgive, and heads keep score—and every marriage leadership team needs both.
- hearts include, and heads exclude—and every marriage leadership team needs both.
- hearts live, and heads learn—and every marriage leadership team needs both.
- hearts value people for who they are, and heads value people for what can be gained from them—and every marriage leadership team needs both.
- hearts give, and heads take—and every marriage leadership team needs both.

The marriage leadership team was designed to showcase stable, committed, loving, and dynamic marriage-team leadership to the world around us—and to give an example worth following to those who are themselves heading toward marriage. By definition, single parents are functioning at a huge disadvantage, and Christian marriages within church were designed to help and support those disadvantaged and hurting people. The church was designed to be the world's resource center of fathers and mothers, grandfathers and grandmothers, and brothers and sisters for all those who need them. Is it any wonder that the enemy of God crusades so hard against marriage?

The marriage leadership team is a leadership team of equals who complement each other. The well-being of their relationship is the responsibility of the head of the marriage, the husband. The husband is responsible before God for the well-being of their relationship. In leadership terms, they are completely equal. We will return to the subject of leadership later.

Part IV

Christ-Centered Prayer

If YHWH is the preexistent God, if Jesus is the Alpha and Omega, if the Holy Spirit is the agent who created everything—then prayer begins and ends with God. Prayer is God's work, not mine or yours or anybody else's. We do not originate prayer, and it does not belong to us. Furthermore, mature prayer is unknown to us until we learn it. With regard to prayer, we have to learn that we have a lot to learn.

"Those who abide in me and I in them bear much fruit, because apart from me you can do nothing" (John 15:5).

Do we really believe that Jesus meant that? If we can do nothing separated or parted from Jesus, that includes prayer. When we first come to Christ, it may be hard for us to face up to our utter helplessness, because we are so used to living independent lives and looking after ourselves. At that time, we may well have seen Christ as merely a good addition to our lives. But utter helplessness is the way of fruitfulness. Still, we don't do utter helplessness very well. Fruitfulness in prayer is about developing a relationship through prayer. It is not primarily about an abundance of words or about getting things done.

"It is the spirit that gives life; the flesh is useless" (John 6:63). Our natural selves are incapable of mature prayer. Learning mature prayer is, by definition, stepping outside our comfort zone. Prayer confined within our comfort zone quickly becomes a repetitive chore. Learning mature prayer means leaving behind that which we know in order to discover that which we cannot even imagine.

"The Advocate, the Holy Spirit, whom the Father will send in my name, will teach you everything, and remind you of all that I have said to you" (John 14:26).

If the Holy Spirit will teach us everything, then that includes prayer. Listening to Jesus is a vital part of learning mature prayer. Being led by the Holy Spirit is a huge learning curve for those who value their independence and self-sufficiency. Independent people struggle with being utterly dependent, but if we would explore mature prayer, then we must make ourselves utterly dependent upon the Holy Spirit of God to continually lead us into a deeper experience of prayer. We must make ourselves utterly dependent upon him, with the assurance that the Holy Spirit is not with us to chastise, criticize, or condemn but to lovingly lead us into all things that are ours in Christ. How do we do all of this? By personally meeting Jesus continually.

"Likewise the Spirit helps us in our weakness; for we do not know how to pray as we ought, but that very Spirit intercedes with sighs too deep for words" (Romans 8:26).

In ourselves, we are so incapable of mature prayer that the Spirit must intercede in us and through us. True prayer comes from deep within us. It is much more than just our heads speaking words. This alone should cause us to be careful in our exploration and learning of prayer so that we do not miss or disregard anything—especially that which we do not currently recognize as prayer.

"When you are praying, do not heap up empty phrases as the Gentiles do; for they think that they will be heard because of their many words. Do not be like them, for your Father knows what you need before you ask him" (Matthew 6:7–8).

Words are so very easy—and they are so very easily empty. Empty words do not prayer make, no matter how many words there are. How do we recognize empty words and phrases? What are they? Empty words and phrases come from the mouths of people who do not let God work his change inside them. Jesus was not rebuking the Pharisees because of the quantity of their words but because those words were empty. Words that flow from a heart that will not change are empty words. Therefore, we need to realize that mere words are, on their own, the shallowest form of prayer.

Beloved reader, we are so easily like children. Children constantly ask for things. (It is, of course, true that constantly asking for things is part of what it means to be a child.) But children who constantly ask for things are seeking benefit without cost, whether they realize it or not. We need to grow up in prayer and grow out of constantly asking for things from God. If prayer for us is only about constantly asking God for things, then we are merely seeking benefit without cost. It is so easy to pray for others with words, and it so often costs us nothing. True prayer always costs, because it always begins with "Change my heart, Lord." Those words may not always be spoken, but you can be absolutely certain that the changing of your own self is the only starting point of true prayer. True prayer is always about relationships, never about results.

"Consequently Jesus is able for all time to save those who approach God through him, since he always lives to make intercession for them" (Hebrews 7:25). Jesus's ability to intercede for us came at great personal cost to both himself and his Father. True prayer never seeks benefit without cost.

"This is my Son, the Beloved; with him I am well pleased; listen to him!" (Matthew 17:5).

True prayer begins not with us talking to God but rather with us listening to God. It begins not with us giving to God but rather with us receiving from God. It begins not with us giving ourselves to God but rather with us receiving God himself. True prayer, then, is based in the heart, not in the head. Pray without ceasing, and use words only when absolutely necessary. Such mature prayer needs to be learned through a repeated pleading with God to change our own selves on the inside.

"I pray that the God of our Lord Jesus Christ, the Father of glory, may give you a spirit of wisdom and revelation as you come to know him" (Ephesians 1:17).

If we are to know God better and better in order to exercise ever deeper prayer, then we need the Holy Spirit of wisdom and revelation. Our own spirits need to be open to receiving revelation—and the wisdom to understand and know what to do with that revelation. God is a God of revelation who loves to make himself known, but he does not make himself known unconditionally.

"All things have been handed over to me by my Father; and no one knows the Son except the Father, and no one knows the Father except the Son and anyone to whom the Son chooses to reveal him" (Matthew 11:27).

How does Jesus choose whom he will reveal the Father to? God's hand stretches all the way to us, but he will not force-feed us. God is a God of revelation, not secrecy. He wants to be known. But the exploration of knowing God involves the exploration of knowing ourselves. That is why true prayer always involves change for us. We cannot truly pray and yet stay the same. If we pray and stay the same, it isn't prayer. Speaking words of prayer for others while we are unwilling for God to change us only proves that what we speak is not true prayer.

The first and most important principle of prayer is this: prayer changes the person praying. Prayer changes us. Is change what we really want? We can say very easily that we are willing to change. But change equals cost.

Whenever God comes near to us, change is imminent, and therefore cost is imminent. There is always a cost to be paid for change. Is change what we really want?

"No one can come to me unless drawn by the Father who sent me" (John 6:44).

Relationship lies at the heart of prayer. Prayer is not learned from a distance. Drawing people to himself is the primary activity of a God of love. "Submit yourselves therefore to God. Resist the devil, and he will flee from you. Draw near to God, and he will draw near to you" (James 4:7–8).

Prayer is discovering that God's heart is for you. Prayer is not an attempt to establish a relationship with God; it is the expression of a real and growing relationship. We can only truly pray with the God we truly know. How we know God determines how we pray. As we grow in Christ and Christ grows in us, so should we grow in our maturity in prayer. If we are not growing in our maturity in prayer, then we are unwilling for our own selves to change. Maturity in character brings maturity in prayer. Maturity in prayer is not the same as quantity of prayer. A constant growth to maturity is critically important for us as the people of God. We need to understand the paths of growth if we are to mature in prayer.

31

Paths of Growth

The gifts [Christ] gave were that some would be apostles, some prophets, some evangelists, some pastors and teachers, to equip the saints for the work of ministry, for building up the body of Christ, until all of us come to the unity of the faith and of the knowledge of the Son of God, to maturity, to the measure of the full stature of Christ. We must no longer be children, tossed to and fro and blown about by every wind of doctrine, by people's trickery, by their craftiness in deceitful scheming. But speaking the truth in love, we must grow up in every way into him who is the head, into Christ, from whom the whole body, joined and knit together by every ligament with which it is equipped, as each part is working properly, promotes the body's growth in building itself up in love. (Ephesians 4:11–16)

Paul was writing here about paths of growth, but he was not being specific about what those paths look like because he was writing to a multi-cultural society that was under Roman rule. Paul was also aware of the huge cultural differences between Jewish society and European societies. We are going to consider what those paths of growth look like for us—or rather, what they should look like.

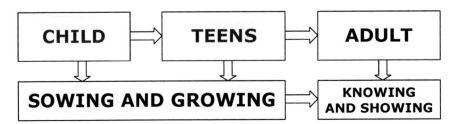

I am well aware that, even before birth, every person is being shaped and formed by what goes on around them. Childhood and teen years are phases through which every individual must pass, in both the physical and inner person. These two phases are key learning periods during which children and teenagers learn deeply from what is modeled to them. Such modeling—and learning—can be positive or negative, good or bad.

While learning never ceases in adulthood, it is clearly different from that of the childhood and teen years that precede it. Those earlier periods are times of great sowing into the individual and—hopefully—great growing, as the individual is profoundly influenced for good or bad, and most often a mixture of both.

Unfortunately, physical adulthood does not always mean inner adulthood, adulthood in character, or adulthood in spirit. A great many people grow up hurt, damaged, and broken, and that severely impairs their ability to mature into adulthood. Their bodies may be adult, but their inner selves may be far from it. Therefore, we need to be very sensitive to a person's level of growth, aware of the state they are in. For what we see is not always what we get.

Adulthood, then, should be a good time of experiencing life from a mature perspective, seeing the world through eyes of maturity, and positively influencing children and teenagers. It should be a time of growing in interpersonal relationships from a mature, wise, and discerning point of view. Adulthood is also a time of showing: living in maturity, wisdom, and discernment, all of which have been enriched and enabled through the childhood and teen years. That is the human design and hope, though it doesn't always work out that way. One of the primary reasons that it does not work out ideally is that our society has removed the words *knowing and showing* from our vocabulary and has substituted the word achievement. Thus the flowchart has been adjusted.

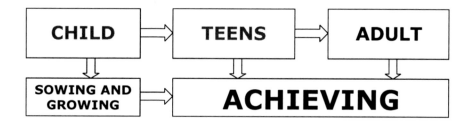

In our understanding of the way things ought to be, there is a much more important, significant, and urgent understanding to gain. Our society has gone beyond even this significant change. It has actually extended achieving into childhood itself. Children today are increasingly expected to be little adults who act, think, and speak as adults do. Children today are increasingly missing out on childhood. That is true not just here but in many other cultures and situations as well. You only have to think of child soldiers in some parts of the world, and child reality TV shows in others. So we now return to our flowchart, in which I suggest a radical, if simple, way of seeing things.

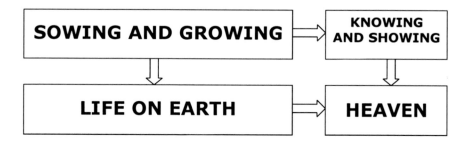

I am suggesting here that earthly life is primarily meant to be a time of sowing and growing, and that it is one huge learning and growing experience. I am further suggesting that it is not the main event. Whatever the heavenly life is going to be like, it will be the supreme time of knowing, a time of seeing from a mature, wise, and discerning point of view, a time of face-to-face knowing. The heavenly life will also be a time of showing: living outwardly in maturity, wisdom, and discernment in the heavenly life, which will have been enriched and enabled through the years of life on earth.

But there is more. We all too easily think that the earthly life is the main event and that the heavenly life is just a nice little add-on that we Christians get. That kind of thinking borders on the ridiculous. How can we as Christians—who only have a poor, dim, out-of-focus view of things—possibly believe that earthly life is the main event? We miss the fact that the heavenly life that is to come is actually the main event and that it is being profoundly influenced by the earthly life we now live. Therefore, we need to face up to the self-evident fact that the earthly life is merely preparation for the heavenly life to come. We must always remember that the heavenly life to come is the main event so that we don't take ourselves too seriously in the earthly life we now share. We will be fully participating in that main event that is to come, for then we will see face-to-face, seeing things as they really are. Then we will truly know what the earthly life was about.

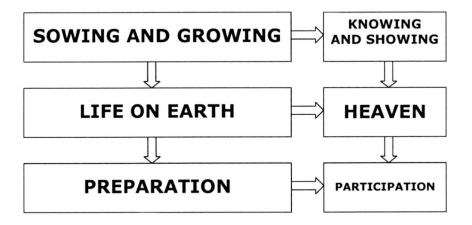

Life on earth is a time of preparation, of sowing and growing, while our heavenly life will be a time of participation, of knowing and showing. Life on earth is not an end in itself. It is the testing and proving ground for the life to come. It is crucial that we realize the significance and importance of this preparation time here on earth, because the kingdom of heaven runs contrary to our earthly experience. And all of this is especially true when it comes to prayer.

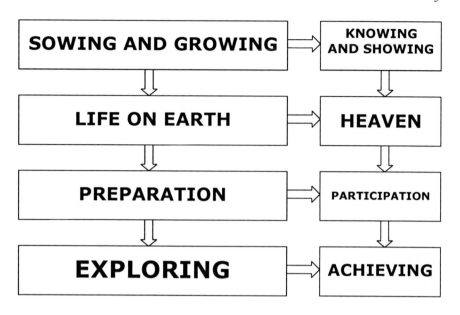

At the human level of family, careers, and so on, we all too easily put the emphasis on achievement of any kind. I believe that the primary focus of this short, earthly life is to explore, not achieve. I therefore contend that achieving is primarily for the heavenly life, not the earthly life. Yet so much of what is said and written about prayer is about achieving—results—when it should be about exploring relationships. Prayer is concerned with the primary exploration of our relationship with God. Too often we view prayer as a way of getting things done instead of getting to know God through exploring him. Prayer is also making ourselves known to God through his exploration of us. Prayer makes us known. But that knowing comes from exploring relationship, not from knowing facts and figures about someone.

"When I was a child, I spoke like a child, I thought like a child, I reasoned like a child; when I became an adult, I put an end to childish ways. For now we see in a mirror, dimly, but then we will see face to face. Now I know only in part; then I will know fully, even as I have been fully known" (1 Corinthians 13:11–12).

If now, as earthly adults, we see only dimly as in a mirror, then when we were children, we didn't really see at all, even though we thought we did. Before Christ was in us, we didn't see at all, even though we thought we did. Now that Christ is in us, we see only dimly as in a dark mirror. If we can only see dimly, then we cannot possibly achieve anything meaningful. That revelation, that realization is crucial for us, because we must put away the idea that we can now see clearly and understand fully. If we believe that we can see and understand clearly here and now, then we will never realize that the primary purpose of prayer is to help us to know God and to love him. If we believe that we can see and understand clearly here and now, then we will never properly explore the secrets of prayer. Children see prayer as a way of getting things done. We must grow up.

The way of learning prayer is through self-denial and the recognition that we must constantly be changing if we are to know God better. We cannot carry on believing that we have prayer—and God—all worked out. We may well tell God that we want everything that he has for us. We may well tell God that we are willing for him to work in power through us. And we may well be utterly sincere. But until we realize that the starting point of real prayer is our own personal cost, our words to God will go unheeded. Therefore, since the way of learning prayer involves essential, internal change, it most certainly involves the power of God at work deep inside us.

32

Power of God

The same day some Sadducees came to Jesus, saying
there is no resurrection; and they asked him a question,
saying, "Teacher, Moses said, 'If a man dies childless,
his brother shall marry the widow, and raise up children
for his brother.' Now there were seven brothers among
us; the first married, and died childless, leaving the
widow to his brother. The second did the same, so also
the third, down to the seventh. Last of all, the woman
herself died. In the resurrection, then, whose wife of the
seven will she be? For all of them had married her."

Jesus answered them, "You are wrong, because you
know neither the scriptures nor the power of God. For
in the resurrection they neither marry nor are given in
marriage, but are like angels in heaven. And as for the
resurrection of the dead, have you not read what was said
to you by God, 'I am the God of Abraham, the God of
Isaac, and the God of Jacob'? He is God not of the dead,
but of the living." And when the crowd heard it, they
were astounded at his teaching. (Matthew 22:23–33)

The Sadducees were trying to argue with Jesus and force him into
conceding that there could not be a resurrection from the dead. The
Sadducees were a Pentateuch people, and that was where their theology
was based. Since resurrection from the dead is a theology based on

other parts of the old covenant Scriptures, the Sadducees did not accept resurrection from the dead as a true theology. They would not have been at all pleased to hear this rabbi telling them that they didn't know the Scriptures or the power of God.

As we have seen already, the power of God effects change in people's lives from the inside out, transforming inwardly those who welcome God to work in their lives. The Jewish religious leaders did not have their own inner change on their agenda. That was why they did not know the power of God. They expected Jesus to conform to their idea of what a rabbi should be like. The thought that they themselves needed to change inside never even entered their heads or their hearts. The moment that you get serious about exploring prayer, you are getting serious about wanting to change. Inner change is impossible except for the power of the Spirit of the living God. A person's inner being can be depressed, oppressed, suppressed, and any other "pressed" you can think of, but the inner person cannot be changed except by the power of the Spirit of the living God. There is no other way to inner change.

People can be manipulated and coerced into behavioral modification. Children frequently are. But behavioral modification and inner change are not the same thing. I say again that the inner person cannot be changed except by the power of the Spirit of the living God. But God is not a power station. He doesn't send his power along cables of prayer or channels of Scripture reading. He comes himself. And the Holy Spirit comes because he has work to do to effect change in each and every one of us. The power of the Holy Spirit is:

- an examining power
- a personal power
- a realizing power
- a transforming power
- a purifying power

If we are to mature in prayer, we must have the power of the Holy Spirit at work inside us. In the kingdom of God there is no such thing as benefit without cost. And for us, as God's children, real prayer begins with personal cost.

"Very truly, *I* tell you, the one who believes in *me* will also do the works that *I* do and, in fact, will do greater works than these, because *I* am going to the Father. *I* will do whatever you ask in *my* name, so that the Father may be glorified in the Son. If in *my* name you ask *me* for anything, *I* will do it" (John 14:12–14).

Jesus is not speaking about works here; he is speaking about himself. What Jesus said here is conditional. It is not an open promise. The promise is for those who personally stick to believing Jesus, not those who merely study his teaching or even try to live by it. Mature prayer is for those who personally stick to Jesus himself.

Jesus spoke of what it is like to stick to him. "Come to me, all you that are weary and are carrying heavy burdens, and I will give you rest. Take my yoke upon you, and learn from me; for I am gentle and humble in heart, and you will find rest for your souls. For my yoke is easy, and my burden is light (Matthew 11:28–30).

Jesus is not speaking about rest here but about himself. Mature prayer is learned from Jesus. Anybody who spent any time at all around Jesus was challenged to allow the Spirit of God to change him inside. The challenge is that of knowing the power of the Holy Spirit at work in us wherever we are, at any given time of day or night. The challenge is to welcome the Holy Spirit in us to do his work, moment-by-moment, hour-by-hour, day-by-day, using whomever and whatever he wills. If the power of the Holy Spirit is constantly at work in us, then we can pray at all times. Where the power of the Holy Spirit is at work, there is prayer. Now let's look at a well-known example of the power of God at work.

Immediately Jesus made the disciples get into the boat and go on ahead to the other side, while he dismissed the crowds. And after he had dismissed the crowds, he went up the mountain by himself to pray. When evening came, he was there alone, but by this time the boat, battered by the waves, was far from the land, for the wind was against them. And early in the morning Jesus came walking toward them on the sea. But when the disciples saw him walking on the sea, they were terrified, saying, "It is a ghost!" And they cried out in fear. But immediately Jesus spoke to them and said, "Take heart, it is I; do not be afraid." Peter answered him, "Lord, if it is you, command me to come to you on the water." He said, "Come." So Peter got out of the boat, started walking on the water, and came toward Jesus. But when he noticed the strong wind, he became frightened, and beginning to sink, he cried out, "Lord, save me!" Jesus immediately reached out his hand and caught him, saying to him, "You of little faith, why did you doubt?" When they got into the boat, the wind ceased. And those in the boat worshipped him, saying, "Truly you are the Son of God." (Matthew 14:22–33)

Having fed thousands of hungry people through the disciples, Jesus needed and wanted to be alone. The disciples didn't make it to the other side of the lake before Jesus went to them across the water. They were terrified by the sight of Jesus on the water, but he reassured them that it was he. The very presence of Jesus provoked a response of prayer from Peter. Peter's response was quite remarkable, because it centered on the identity of the person walking on the lake, not the miraculous event unfolding in front of him. Jesus' response was also remarkable, given that he might have thought Peter was just being stupid in the way that he reacted to Jesus' walking on the water. Peter's response in prayer then needed a response in action. Peter got out of the boat.

When Peter got close to Jesus, he looked down and saw the wind whipping up the water at his feet. Peter's fear of the impossible circumstances overcame the faith that had brought him to Jesus, and he began to sink. Jesus was close enough to Peter that he had only to reach out his hand and catch him. Jesus told Peter that he had trusted in the person of Jesus to get out of the boat in the first place but that he had lost sight of Jesus when he looked at the water beneath them. It was only when both Jesus and Peter got back into the boat that the wind died down. Furthermore, when Jesus and Peter got back into the boat, only then did those who were in the boat worship Jesus. This event began when Jesus sent the disciples across the lake without him. But Jesus didn't relationally leave them alone, and he physically went out to them. While the disciples were frightened to receive Jesus, Peter wanted to be with Jesus more than he wanted the safety of the boat. This brings me to an important principle of prayer:

Prayer does not bring Jesus at our beck and call; prayer moves us to be with Jesus.

The higher part of prayer is not to bring Jesus to us, but to move us to be where Jesus is. We want Jesus in our world, but Jesus wants us in his world. The disciples in the boat had a story to tell, but Peter had an encounter with Jesus through the power of the Holy Spirit. Peter had an experience to remember. That experience of deep, inner change through the power of God at work in him stood Peter in good stead.

"For we did not follow cleverly devised myths when we made known to you the power and coming of our Lord Jesus Christ, but we had been eyewitnesses of his majesty" (2 Peter 1:16).

The power of the Holy Spirit at work deep inside will transform us. Therefore, the experience of encountering Jesus will transform our prayer life, because the experience of encountering Jesus will transform us! If Jesus really wants to work in us for our own good, will he not eagerly respond to his people when they ask him to change their hearts?

Peter didn't talk about the many miracles that he had seen and known, but he spoke often of the power of God at work inside him. Grow in the reality that your life is now hidden with Christ in God. When God looks at you, he sees:

- his own DNA rewriting you into his likeness
- his own signature woven through the fabric of your being
- his family likeness growing in you, day-by-day
- his purpose being fulfilled in you, encounter-by-encounter

33

Scriptures

The Scriptures need to be read with your heart, not your head, because God's truth is made known in relationships, not in individualism. The Scriptures tell us far more about God's heart than they tell us about his mind. Read the Scriptures under the direct heart influence of the Holy Spirit. Look out for what God is feeling before you look for what he is saying. Let the Spirit be the lens through which you read the Scriptures. It is the Spirit's work to guide you into all truth. The deepest truths of God are often hidden in the best-known verses of Scripture. And if we assume we know what the Scriptures say, then we will miss the deeper meanings. Therefore, read the Scriptures with openness and you will receive.

As far as it is humanly possible, assume nothing, because assumption is the mother of deception. As far it is humanly possible, receive everything God wants to give you, and do not let your prejudices get in the way.

When reading the Scriptures, actively consider the relationship between our curiosity and God's secrets. Also consider the relationship between Jesus and the parables he told. Read the Scriptures with two questions in your heart and on your lips: *how* and *why*.

When you read the Scriptures, it is very important to consider what the Scriptures say, but it is equally important to realize what the Scriptures do not say. The Spirit of God must lead us in our exploration of the Scriptures, because such an exploration is not about logic. If the Scriptures are not inspired by the Spirit of God to you personally, then they are just good literature.

"You search the scriptures because you think that in them you have eternal life; and it is they that testify on my behalf. Yet you refuse to come to me to have life" (John 5:39–40).

Explore what Jesus said here, but also explore what he did not say. Also, consider what the Scriptures say of themselves. "All scripture is inspired by God and is useful for teaching, for reproof, for correction, and for training in righteousness, so that everyone who belongs to God may be proficient, equipped for every good work" (2 Timothy 3:16–17).

Also consider what the Scriptures do not say of themselves. When you read the Scriptures, consider the fourfold usefulness of Scripture that Paul highlighted.

- The teaching of the Scriptures is to show us through historical narrative what the character of God is like and what the character of people is like.
- The reproof of the Scriptures is to reveal Jesus the Christ and to make him known.
- The correction of the Scriptures tells us that we must come to Jesus to have life.
- The training of the Scriptures is such that we actually change, day-by-day and by degree of glory into degree of glory to be like our Father in heaven.

The revealing of Jesus is to be the daily experience of prayer. The more you know the Scriptures, the more you will see that they call you to meet Jesus personally and to know him and love him. The Scriptures find their fulfilment in the context of a love relationship with Jesus the Christ. When you understand that, you are beginning to understand the Scriptures. The teaching of the Scriptures is to show us through historical narrative what the character of God is like, and what the character of people is like. They must be understood alongside each other, not in isolation from each other. Through the Scriptures, God wants you to know what he is like, so that you will be encouraged to draw near to him. And the focus of that knowing, the lens and fulcrum of that knowing—everything about that knowing—is Jesus himself.

"Long ago God spoke to our ancestors in many and various ways by the prophets, but in these last days he has spoken to us by a Son, whom he appointed heir of all things, through whom he also created the worlds. He is the reflection of God's glory and the exact imprint of God's very being, and he sustains all things by his powerful word. When he had made purification for sins, he sat down at the right hand of the Majesty on high" (Hebrews 1:1–3).

Meditation on just these three verses will reap great reward. Explore the Scriptures through the Gospels. Read about Jesus and see how he related to people and how they related to him. When you read the Scriptures, you will need your imagination. Don't leave it behind, reject it, or neglect it. Reading the Scriptures without your imagination will produce only rules and regulations. We need to rediscover the value of reflection and meditation, because they are essential components of prayer.

"Finally, beloved, whatever is true, whatever is honorable, whatever is just, whatever is pure, whatever is pleasing, whatever is commendable, if there is any excellence and if there is anything worthy of praise, think about these things" (Philippians 4:8).

The earth is the Lord's and everything in it. What the Lord made is good and is worthy of thinking on. Every day and in every way, God communicates with us, if we will only have listening ears, open hearts, and teachable spirits.

"Think over what I say, for the Lord will give you understanding in all things" (2 Timothy 2:7).

34

Meditation

Everybody meditates. The only question is what everybody meditates on—shopping, football, work, family, money, house, or car. Worry is a (negative) form of meditation. Scriptural meditation is one of the most powerful forms of prayer and yet one of the most neglected, because the word meditation itself tends to get bad press. When we treat the Scriptures as a textbook or, even worse, as a collection of proof-texts, then we are doing the Scriptures a dreadful injustice. When we do not take time to think, reflect, or meditate upon the Scriptures, we rob the Scriptures of much of their power. I will say, then, that Scriptural meditation:

- needs to be learned, practiced, and developed, and it takes time and effort.
- involves the will. It needs determination.
- involves revelation and your imagination.
- is worth every moment of time, effort, and practice invested.
- reaches the parts that prayer ministry can never reach.
- gives us valuable insight and wisdom.
- is gold that is personally discovered, rather than being secondhand.
- gives us the raw material of which visions and dreams are made.
- reveals to us what God wants to show us at that time.
- greatly sharpens insight.

- enables us to personally meet with God.
- has many forms and variations. There is no "right" way to meditate.

Select a well-known passage of Scripture from the Gospels that tells a story about how Jesus interacted with different people. Well-known stories are good to use, but assume nothing. Read the story through slowly a few times, and perhaps take into account other details of the same story from other gospels. Read the stories carefully, and let your curiosity get the better of you. That is what is meant to happen. Find the parts that arouse your curiosity and ask the questions *how* and *why*. Ask questions and explore. Don't just answer the questions quickly and simply from your head knowledge. Choose a central, but not crucial, character from the story, one that is unnamed. Let your imagination see the event unfolding from your character's point of view. Take the opportunity to speak to Jesus personally. Let him have the opportunity to speak to you personally. After the meditation—or even during it—write the experience down.

> O LORD, our Sovereign, how majestic is your name in all the earth! You have set your glory above the heavens. Out of the mouths of babes and infants you have founded a bulwark because of your foes, to silence the enemy and the avenger. When I look at your heavens, the work of your fingers, the moon and the stars that you have established; what are human beings that you are mindful of them, mortals that you care for them? Yet you have made them a little lower than God, and crowned them with glory and honor. You have given them dominion over the works of your hands; you have put all things under their feet, all sheep and oxen, and also the beasts of the field, the birds of the air, and the fish of the sea, whatever passes along the paths of the seas. O LORD, our Sovereign, how majestic is your name in all the earth! (Psalm 8)

Look at the sky, the land, and flowers—all that God has made—and let God draw near to you through this psalm. Consider the sun. It is one of billions of suns in our galaxy, and there are billions of galaxies.

> Now when Jesus heard this, he withdrew from there in a boat to a deserted place by himself. But when the crowds heard it, they followed him on foot from the towns. When he went ashore, he saw a great crowd; and he had compassion for them and cured their sick. When it was evening, the disciples came to him and said, "This is a deserted place, and the hour is now late; send the crowds away so that they may go into the villages and buy food for themselves." Jesus said to them, "They need not go away; you give them something to eat." They replied, "We have nothing here but five loaves and two fish." And he said, "Bring them here to me." Then he ordered the crowds to sit down on the grass. And he said to his disciples, "Make them sit down in groups of about fifty each. Then he ordered them to get all the people to sit down in groups on the green grass. So they sat down in groups of hundreds and of fifties. Taking the five loaves and the two fish, he looked up to heaven, and blessed and broke the loaves, and gave them to the disciples, and the disciples gave them to the crowds. And all ate and were filled; and they took up what was left over of the broken pieces, twelve baskets full. And those who ate were about five thousand men, besides women and children. (Matthew 14:13–21; Luke 9:14; Mark 6:40)

How do you get people to sit down in groups of hundreds and fifties? Why have people sit down in groups of hundreds and fifties?

> Six days later, Jesus took with him Peter and James and his brother John and led them up a high mountain, by themselves. And he was transfigured before them,

and his face shone like the sun, and his clothes became dazzling white. Suddenly there appeared to them Moses and Elijah, talking with him. Then Peter said to Jesus, "Lord, it is good for us to be here; if you wish, I will make three dwellings here, one for you, one for Moses, and one for Elijah." While he was still speaking, suddenly a bright cloud overshadowed them, and from the cloud a voice said, "This is my Son, the Beloved; with him I am well pleased; listen to him!" When the disciples heard this, they fell to the ground and were overcome by fear. But Jesus came and touched them, saying, "Get up and do not be afraid." And when they looked up, they saw no one except Jesus himself alone. (Matthew 17:1–8).

"Listen to him." Why did the Father say that?

One day Peter and John were going up to the temple at the hour of prayer, at three o'clock in the afternoon. And a man lame from birth was being carried in. People would lay him daily at the gate of the temple called the Beautiful Gate so that he could ask for alms from those entering the temple. When he saw Peter and John about to go into the temple, he asked them for alms. Peter looked intently at him, as did John, and said, "Look at us." And he fixed his attention on them, expecting to receive something from them. But Peter said, "I have no silver or gold, but what I have I give you; in the name of Jesus Christ of Nazareth, stand up and walk." And he took him by the right hand and raised him up; and immediately his feet and ankles were made strong. Jumping up, he stood and began to walk, and he entered the temple with them, walking and leaping and praising God. All the people saw him walking and praising God, and they recognized him as the one who used to sit and ask for alms at the Beautiful Gate of the temple;

and they were filled with wonder and amazement at what had happened to him. (Acts 3:1–10)

Why did Peter and John look intently at the man? Why did they get the man to look at them?

> Paul, an apostle of Christ Jesus by the will of God, and Timothy our brother, to the saints and faithful brothers and sisters in Christ in Colossae: Grace to you and peace from God our Father. In our prayers for you we always thank God, the Father of our Lord Jesus Christ, for we have heard of your faith in Christ Jesus and of the love that you have for all the saints, because of the hope laid up for you in heaven. You have heard of this hope before in the word of the truth, the gospel that has come to you. Just as it is bearing fruit and growing in the whole world, so it has been bearing fruit among yourselves from the day you heard it and truly comprehended the grace of God. This you learned from Epaphras, our beloved fellow servant. He is a faithful minister of Christ on your behalf, and he has made known to us your love in the Spirit. For this reason, since the day we heard it, we have not ceased praying for you. (Colossians 1:1–2)

Whose idea was it for Paul to belong to God? What did Paul send to the believers at Colossae? Did Paul start off by fault-finding with the Christians at Colosse? Was Paul a team player? (Read these few verses and see how many times Paul says "we" or "us" rather than "I.")

35

Voice of God

A personal study of the Scriptures—and of the accounts of the lives of God's people that are recorded there—leads me to the firm conclusion that hearing God's actual voice is the exception rather than the rule. Major characters of the old covenant Scriptures, such as Abraham, Moses, and Elijah, only rarely heard the voice of God, even though they lived very long lives, and there are very few recorded accounts of God speaking to them.

Even a study of the life of Jesus himself shows that the Son of God himself only rarely heard the actual voice of God his Father, and some of those occasions were when his Father was really speaking to the crowds around Jesus, rather than to Jesus himself. Christians tend to spend a lot of time asking God what he wants to say. We keep telling him that we need a word from him. What we actually need to do first is to truly receive, believe, and realize what God has already said to us through his Word, Jesus the Christ.

Receive "The Word" Himself

The vast bulk of what God wants to say to us has already been said in the person of the Word of God himself: Jesus, who is the Christ. Think about what God has already said in and through Christ. If my reading of the Scriptures is accurate, actually hearing God's voice speaking to us individually is really quite rare. Therefore, we should not expect to hear the voice of God every ten minutes and feel like failures when we don't. It is, however, certainly true that God does speak to us personally from time to time. In my experience, when God spoke to me personally, it was to reassure me, to build me up, and to draw me nearer to himself. It was to bring this frightened child closer to his daddy. As I matured in Christ, God spoke through his direct voice in ever-decreasing frequency. The deeper the relationship, the less words are needed.

Check the Word(s)

If we believe that we really have heard the voice of God speaking personally to us, then:

- we ought to write down what we believe God has said to us
- we ought to use friends we trust to test and check the word(s)
- we ought to see if what God has said is repeated or added to over a time period
- we ought to determine if what we believe God is saying is consistent within itself
- the important next question is: what do we do with it?

Use the Word(s)

How we use the word(s) that God has spoken to us is critically important. Standing on a soapbox and publicly declaring "Thus says the Lord ..." is unlikely to win us much credibility from anybody. There are simply far too many gods saying far too many things in our world today—and far too many people proclaiming them. If God has spoken to you, be careful of what you say and how you say it. Discern whether you need to say anything at all about it publicly. By all means, share what God has said to you with you someone you trust who can help you to discern and apply what God is saying to you. God does speak directly to his people on occasion, and we will now examine how to discern that the voice we hear is God's and not another's. If the voice you heard turns out not to be God's voice, it doesn't really matter whose voice it actually is. It should not be given godly authority.

> Ahab told Jezebel all that Elijah had done, and how he had killed all the prophets with the sword. Then Jezebel sent a messenger to Elijah, saying, "So may the gods

do to me, and more also, if I do not make your life like the life of one of them by this time tomorrow." Then he was afraid; he got up and fled for his life, and came to Beer-sheba, which belongs to Judah; he left his servant there.

But he himself went a day's journey into the wilderness, and came and sat down under a solitary broom tree. He asked that he might die: "It is enough; now, O LORD, take away my life, for I am no better than my ancestors." Then he lay down under the broom tree and fell asleep. Suddenly an angel touched him and said to him, "Get up and eat." He looked, and there at his head was a cake baked on hot stones, and a jar of water. He ate and drank, and lay down again. The angel of the LORD came a second time, touched him, and said, "Get up and eat, otherwise the journey will be too much for you." He got up, and ate and drank; then he went in the strength of that food forty days and forty nights to Horeb the mount of God. At that place he came to a cave, and spent the night there.

Then the word of the LORD came to him, saying, "What are you doing here, Elijah?" He answered, "I have been very zealous for the LORD, the God of hosts; for the Israelites have forsaken your covenant, thrown down your altars, and killed your prophets with the sword. I alone am left, and they are seeking my life, to take it away."

He said, "Go out and stand on the mountain before the LORD, for the LORD is about to pass by." Now there was a great wind, so strong that it was splitting mountains and breaking rocks in pieces before the LORD, but the LORD was not in the wind; and after the wind an earthquake, but the LORD was not in the earthquake; and after the earthquake a fire, but the LORD was not in the fire; and after the fire a sound of sheer silence. When Elijah heard it, he wrapped his face in his mantle and went out and stood at the entrance of the cave. Then there came a voice to him that said, "What are you doing here, Elijah?" (1 Kings 19:1–13)

This account of Elijah running away in panic from Jezebel is a good place to examine the characteristics of God's voice.

Know God's Voice

The first and most important characteristic of God's voice is that it was heard in utter silence. There must be no inner background noise if we are to hear God speaking. There must be no other voices if we are to hear the voice of God. God will not compete with all the other voices that demand to be heard. There is often far too much turmoil and noise inside our hearts for us to hear the voice of God. Because the voice of God speaks to our hearts, not our heads. Therefore our hearts need to be at peace if we are to hear the voice of God. Elijah was at the end of himself, and that exhausted silence was God's opportunity. Sometimes we can be so exhausted that there is nothing left inside us anymore, and it can be in that moment of inner quiet that God speaks to us.

"The word is near you, on your lips and in your heart (that is, the word of faith that we proclaim); because if you confess with your lips that Jesus is Lord and believe in your heart that God raised him from the dead, you will be saved. For one believes with the heart and so is justified, and one confesses with the mouth and so is saved" (Romans 10:8–10).

The mind did not even get a mention there. The state of our hearts determines whether we will hear the voice of God or not. A divided heart with many voices speaking will struggle to hear the voice of God but, even if it hears, it will find it almost impossible to discern it. This is about holiness, separation and otherness, being set apart to God. If you are not willing to be ridiculed by other Christians, don't explore prayer.

The second characteristic of God's voice is that there is no need for him to shout, and he will not do so. A gentle whisper is what will be heard. Examine the Scriptures and you will discover that God never shouted. Examine the Scriptures and you will discover that Jesus never shouted. The Scriptures do exhort God's people to shout, and although Jesus sometimes spoke in a loud voice, he never shouted.

The third characteristic of God's voice is that there is no need for God to explain his personal words to us. We know exactly what he means.

Test God's Voice

The first test of God's voice is that the Scripture is always in line with God. It is a mistake to think that it should be the other way around. God does not have to align himself with (our interpretation of) Scripture. It is the Scriptures that are aligned with God, and they should never be used to test the authenticity of God himself. But the Scriptures should be used to test the authenticity of what God says. Test God's words by all means, but do not test God!

The second test of God's voice is that God's words are always consistent with themselves, but it may be a while before we realize that! God does not say one thing and then say an opposing thing ten minutes later.

The third test of God's voice is that God's words are life and they lead to life. God's words will encourage, strengthen, reveal, challenge, and uplift, even when we are disobedient or frightened. On the two occasions that the angel came to Elijah, what was the first thing that happened? The angel touched him. I love the account of the transfiguration, where Peter, James, and John were prone on their faces, terrified, and Jesus came and tenderly touched them before he spoke to them. God's words usually touch us before they speak to us. They are always spoken to bring us closer to God and closer to each other, never to drive us away from God or each other.

The fourth test of God's voice is that God's words glorify himself in and through Christ—and no one else. God's words never inflate our own egos or glorify us.

Recognize God's Voice

Write down what God says to you. If you are not totally sure it was God's voice you heard, scrap it. Don't keep it. But persevere and don't give up. You may hear individually from Father, Son, and Holy Spirit.

In your daily life, be sensitive to the urge to draw aside and listen to God—and obey it! Too busy? We will always make time for that which is important to us. God's words may well have a self-contained relevance that is soon obvious, but more often than not they will be part of a bigger picture, one that:

- helps us to know that we are growing the right way
- encourages us to persevere in the way we are growing
- corrects us when we grow in unhelpful or damaging ways
- gives us direction, not destination
- guides us into maturity, presence, praise, and worship

Remember that God's words are never divorced from his character and love. God's words never drive us away from him, though we may well run away from God in fear and panic as we react to God's words. God's words always draw us near to him. They never drive us away. Our reaction may be to run away, but that reflects on the state of our hearts more than on the word(s) that God speaks. God is love, and love is patient and kind, but God will not be soft with us or pander to us.

"As surely as God is faithful, our word to you has not been 'Yes and No.' For the Son of God, Jesus Christ, whom we proclaimed among you, Silvanus and Timothy and I, was not 'Yes and No'; but in him it is always 'Yes.' For in him every one of God's promises is a 'Yes.' For this reason it is through him that we say the 'Amen,' to the glory of God" (2 Corinthians 1:18–20).

True prayer always finds a yes from God. As God's beloved children, we need to grow into the maturity in prayer that enables us to find God's yes.

36

Praise

Praise is essentially corporate; worship is essentially individual. Praise is plural; it's something we do. Worship is singular; it's something I do. (As a general rule, that is how you distinguish praise songs from worship songs.) Modern Christian songs can often blur this distinction, as do songs that mix the singular and the plural, but it is a useful starting point.

"He is your praise; he is your God, who has done for you these great and awesome things that your own eyes have seen" (Deuteronomy 10:21).

The *your* here is plural. But what if God hasn't done great and awesome things for us? What if our eyes haven't actually seen anything of God's power and deeds? What if we don't actually need God? What if we're doing all right, thank you very much? If we do not need God and we're doing fine as we are, then praise will be nothing more than communal singing to us. But praise is not primarily about music or songs. Praise is much more about the hearts of those who praise God in any way they choose to do so. And praise is ultimately entirely about the person of God himself. He himself is your praise. So what is praise, and what does it do?

Praise Has the Focus on God

Praise focuses on God by recognizing his:

* being (what he is: love, eternal, spirit, etc.)
* character (what he is like: loving, forgiving, tender, firm, fair, etc.)

- deeds (what he does: deeds of power, etc.)

Praise always has the focus on God, never on the one(s) praising. Praise acknowledges the mighty, living God and declares his mighty loving deeds. That recognition itself sparks further praise.

> Sing to the LORD, all the earth. Tell of his salvation from day to day. Declare his glory among the nations, his marvelous works among all the peoples. For great is the LORD, and greatly to be praised; he is to be revered above all gods. For all the gods of the peoples are idols, but the LORD made the heavens. Honor and majesty are before him; strength and joy are in his place.
>
> Ascribe to the LORD, O families of the peoples, ascribe to the LORD glory and strength. Ascribe to the LORD the glory due his name; bring an offering, and come before him. Worship the LORD in holy splendor; tremble before him, all the earth. The world is firmly established; it shall never be moved. Let the heavens be glad, and let the earth rejoice, and let them say among the nations, "The LORD is king!" Let the sea roar, and all that fills it; let the field exult, and everything in it. Then shall the trees of the forest sing for joy before the LORD, for he comes to judge the earth. O give thanks to the LORD, for he is good; for his steadfast love endures forever.
>
> Say also: "Save us, O God of our salvation, and gather and rescue us from among the nations, that we may give thanks to your holy name, and glory in your praise. Blessed be the LORD, the God of Israel, from everlasting to everlasting." Then all the people said "Amen!" and praised the LORD. (1 Chronicles 16:23–36)

Praise is corporate. It is about God's people and his love demonstrated in their midst. Praise is corporate, but it is also personal. Our praise of

God is relative to our image of God, to what we know of him personally. Our personal, corporate image of God—what we all know of him personally—is relative to what he has done for us personally.

Praise Is Holistic and Involves Our Whole Being

Praise is actually good for us, because it involves our whole being, not just our mouths. Praise involves our hearts, our minds, our bodies, and our wills. Praise rejoices in the wondrous God and his works of power for us. But what if God hasn't done great and awesome things for us personally? In that case, help is at hand. If God has not done anything for you personally:

- read about those for whom he has done great things
- listen to those for whom God has done great things

The history of God's people tells you that God is worthy to be praised!

Praise Sees the Bigger Picture

We need to see a bigger picture than just our own individual lives here and now. We need to see a bigger picture than just the life of our local fellowship here and now. That is one reason why the Scriptures are useful; they help us to see the bigger picture that we would not otherwise see. Praise helps us to be open to receiving that bigger picture. Praise comes from our whole being and flows out to the God who loves and cares for his people. Praise is like a mighty river that comes from deep inside us. If our rivers aren't flowing, they need to be unblocked. It is an act of will to let that river flow. Let me give you a Scriptural example.

"Because your steadfast love is better than life, my lips *will* praise you. So I *will* bless you as long as I live; I *will* lift up my hands and I *will* call on your name" (Psalm 63:3–4).

Praise is primarily an act of the will, not a reaction to emotion. Praise doesn't begin with emotion, though it should stir emotion up. Praise is for any time!

Praise Polarizes

"To the leader: according to the Deer of the Dawn. A Psalm of David. My God, my God, why have you forsaken me? Why are you so far from helping me, from the words of my groaning? O my God, I cry by day, but you do not answer; and by night, but find no rest. Yet you are holy, enthroned on the praises of Israel" (Psalm 22:1–3).

It is easy to misunderstand verse three because of our predominantly Greek mind-set, believing that Israel's praise in some way enthrones God. It is easy to further believe that God is in some way enthroned by our praises. (Indeed, I have heard this verse interpreted that way many times.) But neither Israel's praise nor our praise changes God's status one iota. God has always been enthroned, God is always enthroned, and God will always be enthroned. God is not enthroned by the praises of his people. He is *revealed* as enthroned by the praises of his people. Praise brings revelation of the always-enthroned God. This revelation has very important consequences. When the always-enthroned God is revealed in our midst, the Enemy takes flight. When the Enemy takes flight, the works of the Enemy are undone, canceled, nullified.

> David danced before the LORD with all his might; David was girded with a linen ephod. So David and all the house of Israel brought up the ark of the LORD with shouting, and with the sound of the trumpet. As the ark of the LORD came into the city of David, Michal daughter of Saul looked out of the window, and saw King David leaping and dancing before the LORD; and she despised him in her heart ... David returned to bless his household. But Michal the daughter of Saul came out to meet David, and said, "How the king of Israel honored himself today, uncovering himself today before the eyes of his servants' maids, as any vulgar fellow might shamelessly uncover himself!" David said to Michal, "It was before the LORD, who chose me in place of your father and all his household, to appoint me as prince over Israel, the people of the LORD, that I have danced before the LORD. I will make myself

yet more contemptible than this, and I will be abased in my own eyes; but by the maids of whom you have spoken, by them I shall be held in honor." (2 Samuel 6:14–16, 20–22)

People who despise praise open themselves up to the very grave risk of opposing God's anointed people. Do not despise or criticize how someone else praises God. Praise either kills pride or exposes pride. Praise changes us, not God. Praise dethrones self a little more by revealing that God is on the throne. Praise has the focus on God and takes the focus off ourselves. Praise reveals a little more of God as he really is. Therefore, when we come to praise God together, we should expect to receive revelation about the authority of God, as we see that he is forever enthroned on high.

37

Worship

Praise is essentially corporate. Worship is essentially individual. *Corporate* refers to the body of Christ, and that is where two are three (or more) are gathered. It does not only mean gathered meetings such as church services. The primary purpose of praise is to bring each one of us into a worship experience with God in the midst of the gathered company, whether it be two or three, or two or three thousand. We must now understand what worship really is:

Worship is a personal, unique submission before a holy God.

As human beings, we were created to worship. We have a built-in need to worship. Everybody worships something or somebody. That which we worship, we submit to. That which we worship controls us and defines us. Tell me what you worship, and I will tell you what you are. The enemy of our souls will not try to stop us from worshipping. But he will do everything he can to stop us from worshipping Jesus. The enemy of our souls is happy with virtually whatever we worship, so long as it isn't Jesus.

In worship, you personally meet with the holy God on your own. Even in the midst of a crowd, you are alone with God. And every worship meeting where you meet with God will transform you. Consider Abram.

"When Abram was ninety-nine years old, the LORD appeared to Abram" (Genesis 17:1). "The LORD appeared to Abraham by the oaks of Mamre" (Genesis 18:1).

Worship changed the man: Abram became Abraham. Why? Because

of Abram's response when God appeared to him: "Then Abram fell on his face" (Genesis 17:3).

Abram's response to the appearing of the Lord before him was personal, unique submission. Such personal, unique submission always causes change in the inner being of those who meet with God. And so the relationship with God grows.

"After these things God tested Abraham. He said to him, 'Abraham!' And he said, 'Here I am'" (Genesis 22:1). Abraham didn't need to try and identify who it was that called him. Abraham knew the voice of the Lord. When God called, Abraham worshipped.

Now let's consider Moses.

> Moses was keeping the flock of his father-in-law Jethro, the priest of Midian; he led his flock beyond the wilderness, and came to Horeb, the mountain of God. There the angel of the LORD appeared to him in a flame of fire out of a bush; he looked, and the bush was blazing, yet it was not consumed. Then Moses said, "I must turn aside and look at this great sight, and see why the bush is not burned up." When the LORD saw that he had turned aside to see, God called to him out of the bush, "Moses, Moses!" And he said, "Here I am." Then he said, "Come no closer! Remove the sandals from your feet, for the place on which you are standing is holy ground." He said further, "I am the God of your father, the God of Abraham, the God of Isaac, and the God of Jacob." And Moses hid his face, for he was afraid to look at God. (Exodus 3:1–6)

Moses was going about his daily life when God called him. Moses saw something that didn't make sense; it was illogical. God called Moses personally, by name. This was a worship encounter.

Worship is always on God's terms. God revealed himself as the God of history. This awesome God reveals himself to ordinary people who will worship him in their ordinary, daily lives. In church or in a prayer meeting, do we seek to have a worship encounter with the awesome God? If we do not seek to have a worship encounter with the living God, then we probably will not have one. When worship is experienced, it transforms our concept and practice of prayer. If there is not a personal, unique submission before a holy God, then it isn't true worship. True worship always transforms. If worship doesn't change you, it isn't worship.

Let's look at some characteristics of worship.

"I appeal to you therefore, brothers and sisters, by the mercies of God, to present your bodies as a living sacrifice, holy and acceptable to God, which is your spiritual worship" (Romans 12:1).

Don't limit your worship to a particular building or to a certain time. Don't restrict your worship to a particular type or method. Don't limit your worship to only a part of you or your time.

"For in him all the fullness of God was pleased to dwell ... For in him the whole fullness of deity dwells bodily, and you have come to fullness in him" (Colossians 1:19; 2:9–10).

Worship in fullness!

Do you not know that you are God's temple and that God's Spirit dwells in you? ... Now the Lord is the Spirit, and where the Spirit of the Lord is, there is freedom" (1 Corinthians 3:16; 2 Corinthians 3:17).

The true Holy of Holies is in each of us. There is no restriction to our worship.

> Six days later, Jesus took with him Peter and James and his brother John and led them up a high mountain, by themselves. And he was transfigured before them, and his face shone like the sun, and his clothes became dazzling white. Suddenly there appeared to them Moses and Elijah, talking with him. Then Peter said to Jesus, "Lord, it is good for us to be here; if you wish, I will make three dwellings here, one for you, one for Moses, and one for Elijah." While he was still speaking, suddenly a bright cloud overshadowed them, and from the cloud a voice said, "This is my Son, the Beloved; with him I am well pleased; listen to him!" When the disciples heard this, they fell to the ground and were

overcome by fear. But Jesus came and touched them, saying, "Get up and do not be afraid." And when they looked up, they saw no one except Jesus himself alone. (Matthew 17:1–8)

The experience of personal, unique submission changed Peter, James, and John. Has Jesus ever led you up a high mountain? Have you ever led someone else up a high mountain? Has the experience of real worship changed you? Did you have someone else with you to share in this transformation? Has the experience of real worship changed that person who was with you? Take someone with you when you worship the Lord.

Peter wanted that moment on the mountain to last forever, even though he was terrified. Jesus touched them. They heard the Father. But they saw only Jesus. Worship enables us to know Jesus personally. Worship enables Jesus to share his heart and mind and will with us. If we worship consistently, worship stops being an event and becomes a lifestyle. Here, then, is the key.

- Wholeness is the destination.
- Healing is the journey.
- Worship is the way.
- Prayer is the experience.

If your experience of prayer is not continually deepening, then your relationship with God is not continually deepening either. Pentecost was a worship experience. Worship led up to Pentecost. Pentecost was worship. Worship followed after Pentecost. Worship sprang from worship. That worship touched three thousand people! And a worshipping community is an outreaching community.

38

Visions and Dreams

When I speak here and now about visions and dreams, I am always speaking about visions and dreams that are from God, not from any other source. A dream is a vision during sleep. Everybody has visions and dreams that come through their imagination, but where do those visions and dreams come from? What or who is the source of those visions and dreams? Visions and dreams that are from God will involve our imaginations, but our imaginations cannot help us very much in that regard unless they are free to roam and explore under God's direction.

We also need to be open to receive from God if we are to have visions and dreams that have real significance for us. That also means remembering visions and dreams, which is not always easy. The real and immediate significance of a vision or dream from God may well be that it challenges our prejudices and causes us to change—or else our hearts will harden.

A classic example of that is found in Acts 10, where Cornelius and then Peter had challenging visions of great personal significance for each of them that resulted in important consequences for a great many people. The critical thing for Cornelius and Peter was not how the visions came about nor how they developed. The critical thing was that the source was God, not anyone or anything else. Visions and dreams from God will usually have immediate implications for those receiving them, but they normally have a longer-term significance too.

"The vision of Isaiah son of Amoz, which he saw concerning Judah and Jerusalem in the days of Uzziah, Jotham, Ahaz, and Hezekiah, kings of Judah" (Isaiah 1:1).

Isaiah's ministry under God only began somewhere around the last year of King Uzziah's reign. That would place the beginning of his ministry at about 640 BC. The reign of the four kings mentioned here covers a hundred years. Therefore, although Isaiah's vision had an immediate significance for Isaiah because he had received it from God, it was actually a long-term vision spanning many decades. The events of the vision and prophecy, which were still to come, extended far beyond Isaiah's own lifetime—and even the lifetime of the prophetic community that Isaiah was a part of.

> In the year that King Uzziah died, I saw the Lord sitting on a throne, high and lofty; and the hem of his robe filled the temple. Seraphs were in attendance above him; each had six wings: with two they covered their faces, and with two they covered their feet, and with two they flew. And one called to another and said: "Holy, holy, holy is the LORD of hosts; the whole earth is full of his glory." The pivots on the thresholds shook at the voices of those who called, and the house filled with smoke. And I said: "Woe is me! I am lost, for I am a man of unclean lips, and I live among a people of unclean lips; yet my eyes have seen the King, the LORD of hosts!" Then one of the seraphs flew to me, holding a live coal that had been taken from the altar with a pair of tongs. The seraph touched my mouth with it and said: "Now that this has touched your lips, your guilt has departed and your sin is blotted out." Then I heard the voice of the Lord saying, "Whom shall I send, and who will go for us?" And I said, "Here am I; send me!" (Isaiah 6:1–8)

Visions are rarely "stand-alone." They are usually connected with other things and so are part of a longer-term process of events in history. This strikes at the heart of those who want instant results from God. The number of visions and dreams experienced by God's people is directly related to the significance of the event(s) those visions and dreams are about. The more significant the event, the more visions and dreams about it. And the most significant event in history, the incarnation, has the most visions and dreams recorded about it. The visions that Isaiah was given were part of a long-term revelation to the nation(s).

Therefore, we should not expect to have visions and dreams from God every ten minutes of every day. And we should be careful around those people who claim to have a vision from God every ten minutes. Especially those who insist on sharing those visions with us, and through which they themselves—not Jesus—get the glory.

Visions from God will inevitably involve revelation, change, and purpose. These three things are intertwined and cannot be separated, and I separate them here only to aid understanding as we look at Isaiah's vision in Isaiah 6:1–8.

Isaiah's vision began with the Lord enthroned, and the vision was itself worship. "I saw the Lord sitting on a throne, high and lofty" (v. 1).

There was no room in the temple for anything that did not belong to God. "The hem of his robe filled the temple" (v. 1).

The majesty of God highlighted first the poverty of the person who saw the vision. "Woe is me!" (v. 5).

Isaiah was painfully aware of his own shortcomings and sin. "I am lost, for I am a man of unclean lips" (v. 5).

Isaiah knew that his people were far from God. "I live among a people of unclean lips" (v. 5).

Isaiah's eyes had seen the Lord, and his vision changed his vision. "Yet my eyes have seen the King, the LORD of hosts!" (v. 5).

From this experience of worship, Isaiah received the commission of compassion. "Then I heard the voice of the Lord saying, 'Whom shall I send, and who will go for us?'" (v. 8).

Visions from God are spiritual realities that are manifested through the workings of human imagination in order to cause us to change and become more like God so that his purposes might be fulfilled even through ordinary people like you and me. Since our imagination is used by the Spirit of God in our receiving of visions and dreams, what we consistently feed into our hearts and minds has a huge impact on our ability to receive and remember visions and dreams. For people like us who live in a sophisticated and intelligent, Greek-inspired society, visions—and especially dreams—easily fall under suspicion. But God has historically used dreams to speak to people—and not just to his own people. Take time to read about and consider how God used dreams to speak to Jacob (Genesis 31:11), Joseph (Genesis 37:5), Gideon (Judges 7:15), Solomon (1 Kings 3:5), and Joseph (Matthew 1:20).

And there are many others. It is one thing to have a vision or a dream. It is quite another thing to discern how to handle it. Therefore, interpretation of visions and dreams is of great importance and depends on further revelation from God, not on logic.

> But you, mortal, hear what I say to you; do not be rebellious like that rebellious house; open your mouth and eat what I give you. I looked, and a hand was stretched out to me, and a written scroll was in it. He spread it before me; it had writing on the front and on the back, and written on it were words of lamentation and mourning and woe. He said to me, O mortal, eat what is offered to you; eat this scroll, and go, speak to the house of Israel. So I opened my mouth, and he gave me the scroll to eat. He said to me, Mortal, eat this scroll that I give you and fill your stomach with it. Then I ate it; and in my mouth it was as sweet as honey. (Ezekiel 2:8–3:3)

Where is the logic in what Ezekiel received? Understanding may come. Interpretation must come. Receiving from God is the key. Discerning the source is critical. God's hand stretches all the way to us, but he will not force-feed us. (I wonder what the scroll was that God gave Ezekiel to eat—words of lament and mourning and woe. Lamentations?) Ezekiel received the vision from God, but in that vision he received something else from God. Because visions and dreams usually have long-term significance, write them down! Think what we would be missing from the Scriptures if visions and dreams had not been written down for us.

Now let us take a closer look at some visions and dreams that we now know were related to the incarnation. We begin by looking further at the vision of Isaiah.

"For a child has been born for us, a son given to us; authority rests upon his shoulders; and he is named Wonderful Counselor, Mighty God, Everlasting Father, Prince of Peace. His authority shall grow continually, and there shall be endless peace for the throne of David and his kingdom. He will establish and uphold it with justice and with righteousness from this time onward and forevermore" (Isaiah 9:6–7).

These are famous words, but Isaiah was not given words. Isaiah was given a vision, which he described in words when he wrote it down. It is very hard to reduce to words something you have seen that has had a great impact on you. For example, describe in words the birth of your first baby. Think of how Isaiah must have struggled with the next vision we read about now.

> See, my servant shall prosper; he shall be exalted and lifted up, and shall be very high. Just as there were many who were astonished at him—so marred was his appearance, beyond human semblance, and his form beyond that of mortals so he shall startle many nations; kings shall shut their mouths because of him; for that which had not been told them they shall see, and that which they had not heard they shall contemplate. Who has believed what we have heard? And to whom has the arm of the LORD been revealed? For he grew up before him like a young plant, and like a root out of dry ground; he had no form or majesty that we should look at him, nothing in his appearance that we should desire him. He was despised and rejected by others; a man of suffering and acquainted with infirmity; and as one from whom others hide their faces he was despised, and we held him of no account.
>
> Surely he has borne our infirmities and carried our diseases; yet we accounted him stricken, struck down by God, and afflicted. But he was wounded for our transgressions, crushed for our iniquities; upon him was the

punishment that made us whole, and by his bruises we are healed. All we like sheep have gone astray; we have all turned to our own way, and the LORD has laid on him the iniquity of us all.

He was oppressed, and he was afflicted, yet he did not open his mouth; like a lamb that is led to the slaughter, and like a sheep that before its shearers is silent, so he did not open his mouth. By a perversion of justice he was taken away. Who could have imagined his future? For he was cut off from the land of the living, stricken for the transgression of my people. They made his grave with the wicked and his tomb with the rich, although he had done no violence, and there was no deceit in his mouth.

Yet it was the will of the LORD to crush him with pain. When you make his life an offering for sin, he shall see his offspring, and shall prolong his days; through him the will of the LORD shall prosper. Out of his anguish he shall see light; he shall find satisfaction through his knowledge. The righteous one, my servant, shall make many righteous, and he shall bear their iniquities. Therefore I will allot him a portion with the great, and he shall divide the spoil with the strong; because he poured out himself to death, and was numbered with the transgressors; yet he bore the sin of many, and made intercession for the transgressors. (Isaiah 52:13–53:12)

We know that these words found their ultimate fulfilment in Christ. How Isaiah must have struggled to put the revelation he received into words. God is seen in a vision and speaks to his servant. That servant sees and hears things that will not find their ultimate fulfilment for hundreds of years. That servant must have looked for the fulfilment of the vision and the prophecies over the years of his own life, but he never found them. Did that servant wonder if God had slipped up? Or, far more likely, did that servant come to doubt that he had really heard from God? If he did doubt, I am sure he wasn't the only one.

Then you spoke in a vision to your faithful one, and said: "I have set the crown on one who is mighty, I have exalted one chosen from the people. I have found my servant David; with my holy oil I have anointed him; my hand shall always remain with him; my arm also shall strengthen him. The enemy shall not outwit him, the wicked shall not humble him. I will crush his foes before him and strike down those who hate him. My faithfulness and steadfast love shall be with him; and in my name his horn shall be exalted. I will set his hand on the sea and his right hand on the rivers. He shall cry to me, "You are my Father, my God, and the Rock of my salvation!" I will make him the firstborn, the highest of the kings of the earth. Forever I will keep my steadfast love for him, and my covenant with him will stand firm. I will establish his line forever, and his throne as long as the heavens endure. (Psalm 89:19–29)

You hear words if a book is read aloud, but this faithful one saw a vision in which God spoke. We now know that these visions and dreams were ultimately to find their fulfilment in Jesus. Because of that, all these visions and dreams were part of God's long-term work on earth. They were not concerned with short-term results. That is hard, because we naturally want to know what our visions and dreams are about. We naturally want to see the fulfillment of that which we have been given. So how strange must it have been for people in the old covenant to encounter Jesus but not know who he really was? Think about how Jesus appeared to people in the encounters recorded in the old covenant.

Take, for example, Daniel. "As I watched in the night visions, I saw one like a human being coming with the clouds of heaven. And he came to the Ancient One and was presented before him. To him was given dominion and glory and kingship, that all peoples, nations, and languages should serve him. His dominion is an everlasting dominion that shall not pass away, and his kingship is one that shall never be destroyed" (Daniel 7:13–14).

Daniel was watching in the night visions—in dreams. Do we watch in the night? Do we expect to have dreams from God? Do we expect to have important dreams from God? I wonder what people would have thought about Daniel's dreams in his day?

And of course we know about the birth of Jesus himself.

> Now the birth of Jesus the Messiah took place in this way. When his mother Mary had been engaged to Joseph, but before they lived together, she was found to be with child from the Holy Spirit. Her husband Joseph, being a righteous man and unwilling to expose her to public disgrace, planned to dismiss her quietly. But just when he had resolved to do this, an angel of the Lord appeared to him in a dream and said, "Joseph, son of David, do not be afraid to take Mary as your wife, for the child conceived in her is from the Holy Spirit. She will bear a son, and you are to name him Jesus, for he will save his people from their sins." All this took place to fulfill what had been spoken by the Lord through the prophet: "Look, the virgin shall conceive and bear a son, and they shall name him Emmanuel," which means, "God is with us." When Joseph awoke from sleep, he did as the angel of the Lord commanded him; he took her as his wife, but had no marital relations with her until she had borne a son; and he named him Jesus. (Matthew 1:18–25)

A dream turned Joseph around and saved Mary from disgrace. A dream! Critical events in history rested on a dream! Would we let the rest of our lives rest on a dream? Yet the incarnation itself was realized through visions and dreams.

Consider the astrologers who knew that something special was going on. "And having been warned in a dream not to return to Herod, [the astrologers] left for their own country by another road" (Matthew 2:12). God even gave visions and dreams surrounding the incarnation to people who did not even know or follow him. How weird is that?

Consider Joseph again and the events immediately after the birth of

Jesus. "Now after they had left, an angel of the Lord appeared to Joseph in a dream and said, 'Get up, take the child and his mother, and flee to Egypt, and remain there until I tell you; for Herod is about to search for the child, to destroy him' ... When Herod died, an angel of the Lord suddenly appeared in a dream to Joseph in Egypt and said, 'Get up, take the child and his mother, and go to the land of Israel, for those who were seeking the child's life are dead' ... And after being warned in a dream, [Joseph] went away to the district of Galilee" (Matthew 2:13, 19–20, 22).

How can it be that so much critical history rests on visions and dreams? Would you trust your entire future to a dream? Let me ask a different question. How can it be that so much of the Christian church has written off visions and dreams as being the sole purview of drug addicts and occultists? The incarnation is surrounded by visions and dreams. For example:

- an angel appeared to Zechariah the priest (Luke 1:5–20)
- an angel appeared to Jesus' mother, Mary (Luke 1:26–38)
- an angel appeared to shepherds (Luke 2:8–14)

All of this clearly tells us something.

- God takes visions and dreams far more seriously that we do.
- Prayer is totally illogical. (Would you change the whole direction of your life because of a vision? Would you trust your future career to a dream?)
- God is much more active through human imagination than he is through merely speaking words.
- God wants to communicate with the whole of our being, not just one part of us.
- We normally use our imaginations in almost anything that takes our fancy—except God.

But God does communicate in dreams and visions today, because God hasn't changed. Visions and dreams that we experience mean that God is on the move in a specific way. If we want to see what God is doing so that we can join with him in doing it, then we need to take visions and dreams seriously. We need to share our visions and dreams in order to build up a bigger picture of what God is doing and is going to do in our midst. So don't keep visions and dreams to yourself. Share them carefully and with wisdom.

Visions and dreams experienced mean that we are involved in what God is doing. If we are receiving visions and dreams, we should expect more! But we should not expect instant results. Expect to be history-makers! We sing about that often enough. Believe it! Visions and dreams will help you to deepen your relationship with God and so lead you into more mature and deeper prayer.

39

Presence

"Those who love me will keep my word, and my Father will love them, and we will come to them and make our home with them" (John 14:23).

Prayer is at first the most natural and inbuilt part of every human being. I will say it again. At the beginning of human life, prayer is the most natural and inbuilt part of every human being. Every one of us instinctively knew how to pray long before we even knew that there was a God to pray to! Most of us quickly unlearned that kind of instinctive prayer and grew out of it, but all too often we did not grow into mature prayer.

What is mature prayer? It is Christ-centered prayer. If we do not grow into mature, Christ-centered prayer, it creates a vacuum in our Christian lives that is rapidly filled by religious rules and regulations—especially concerning prayer. I want to see that changed to the way it should be. Our understanding of prayer is going to be shown to us by a baby.

Picture a newborn baby. This newborn baby is going teach us about the beginnings of prayer that were built by God into every one of us. Consider that the baby cannot talk. It can barely see. It hears only confusion. The baby does not understand anything of what it sees or hears. It does not even understand that it does not understand. It cannot think or imagine anything. And the baby is utterly helpless. It cannot feed, clothe, or clean itself. The baby does not even know that it needs these things.

There are, of course, a great many things that the baby does not know. Indeed, it does not even know that it does not know them, because the baby is not yet self-aware. But there is one thing that the baby does know instinctively: presence. Everything within the baby wants presence. The baby needs presence. For the baby, presence is made manifest by touch, which is inherent in presence. Presence brings the touch that feeds, cleans, and comforts the baby.

The baby already knows perfectly well how to get the presence that he wants and needs. It doesn't need to think about it, because it can't think. It does not need to learn how to get the presence that it wants and needs, because the prayer that brings that presence is built into him. The baby cries. Its cries may mean that it is hungry, uncomfortable, dirty, lonely, or bored. Its cries may mean many different things. The baby's mother will soon learn what the different cries mean, and she will respond accordingly.

What the baby needs is presence, but what the baby wants is awareness of that presence. The baby may well have presence without being aware of that presence, but when it realizes that it is no longer aware of presence, it panics—and cries. The baby's emotional response to its perceived needs make its very real needs known. The baby cries, not because it does not have presence but because it is not aware of that presence. The mother's known presence and touch meet the baby's wants and needs. Of course, all of you mothers already know this. So how does this apply to us?

God's presence is promised to his people. Jesus himself promised his presence to his disciples down through the centuries. For Christians, God's presence brings the touch that feeds us, cleans us, comforts us, and so on. Within every human being is the means to get the presence that we need, but many of us have repressed and silenced our emotions for many and varied reasons. Yet our emotions were designed to be our automatic responses to our realized need(s). The answer to that realized need is God's presence. As Christians, what we need is presence; what we have is presence.

But like the baby, though we have that presence, we may not be aware of it. We cry to God (sometimes) because we are not aware of his presence, and therefore we assume that he is not present. So we panic.

We panic because we think that God is not present with us, when in fact he is present with us. We are simply not aware of his presence. When we panic, God often may graciously make himself known. Our emotions have achieved their purpose, and we are aware of the presence of God. But what if we have repressed emotions? What if, instead of panicking, we simply withdraw into ourselves or lock ourselves up emotionally? What then?

Theology is absolutely right to say that God is always with us. Jesus certainly meant what he said when he told us that he would always be with us. But Jesus never said that we would always be aware of his presence. The issue for us, then, is not presence, but awareness of presence—just like the baby. As Christians, we need to relearn how we can be aware of God's presence with us—as individuals and as a group. We tend to more easily believe that God is with us when we are in a large group, because the faith level rises as the numbers increase. We need to learn and practice the awareness of the presence of God. How do we do that? Awareness of presence comes through invitation and welcome. It really is as simple as that. Long before the baby can think, speak, or understand, it knows how to invite and welcome. It simply makes its need known by crying. The baby's invitation is hard to ignore, as its emotional response makes its need known. The baby prays instinctively.

Long before we have maturity as Christians, we also know how to invite and welcome. But knowing how to do it is very different from actually doing it! Let us invite and welcome Jesus to make his presence known to us. We must let go of our inhibitions and our sophistication. Our emotions were designed to make us invite God to be with us at a time when we are aware of real need. All too often, when we are aware of real need, we run from God and from each other. Yet God longs to make his home in each of us—not just to live in us but to actually make his home in us. This is truth that is easily taken for granted. Let the revelation break upon you even now that it is YHWH himself who makes his home in you because of Jesus. The God who always was, always is, and always will be, is making his home in you. The God who created everything in heaven and on earth is making his home in you. The God who sustains everything by his power is making his home in you. YHWH himself is making his home in you.

"Those who love me will keep my word, and my Father will love them, and we will come to them and make our home with them" (John 14:23).

The problem for many Christians is that, while they know this verse, they don't believe it. They don't live it, thereby proving that they don't believe it. They have the theory of what Jesus said but not the reality. The test of a mature love relationship with God is that the Father and Son have made their home in you. If your love relationship with God is not yet mature, then the Father and Son are making their home in you. Abiding presence—and the fruit of that presence—is a sign of maturity. The more like Christ we are, the more at-home God is in us.

Prayer works to change us day-by-day in order that God may make his home in us day-by-day. This revelation realized in us will radically transform our prayer lives. We will stop praying to the God who is somewhere out there, and we will pray with the God who is in us. Mature prayer is Christ-centered prayer. The Holy Spirit works tirelessly to bring us to that point, because it is where true prayer begins. Mature Christ-centered prayer is not a final destination but only the beginning of the deeper part of the journey.

If our prayer lives are routine, mundane, and unchanging, we are not short of words but of revelation. If we aren't being transformed by prayer, then we aren't praying.

40

Intercession

What is intercession? Intercession is "standing in the gap." It means literally standing in the gap between a person and his own damage or destruction. Intercession involves taking someone's place in the battle for his heart and soul. It means paying a cost so that someone else doesn't have to pay. Intercession literally pays someone else's cost.

Intercession is rare, because it is very costly for the one who intercedes. Intercession has literally cost some people their lives, just as it cost Jesus his life. God the Father intervened at the incarnation; God the Son interceded at the incarnation. Intercession costs some people their lifestyles, because their own plans, ideas, and hopes simply disappear from sight.

Intercession has taken on the popular meaning of simply praying for others with words. By itself, prayer for others with words isn't intercession. It is merely praying for others with words alone, good though that is. Praying often with words alone for someone is not intercession, though it may lead to intercession further down the road. Intercession very rarely involves words at all, though it frequently involves groans, cries, screams, sighs, and gasps.

Intercession never seeks benefit without cost. True prayer begins with personal cost. Intercession begins with great personal cost. Intercession will continually pay that great cost, because it always seeks cost without benefit. This is such an important principle that I want to highlight it again. True prayer never seeks benefit without cost, but true intercession always seeks cost without benefit. Jesus came to earth to stand in the gap. He sought only cost without benefit, without any guarantee of success. Praying with words alone for others usually costs us nothing. That which costs nothing is worth nothing.

Let us now consider the intercession of Aaron that he undertook at the instruction of Moses.

> On the next day, however, the whole congregation of the Israelites rebelled against Moses and against Aaron, saying, "You have killed the people of the LORD." And when the congregation had assembled against them, Moses and Aaron turned toward the tent of meeting; the cloud had covered it and the glory of the LORD appeared. Then Moses and Aaron came to the front of the tent of meeting, and the LORD spoke to Moses, saying, "Get away from this congregation, so that I may consume them in a moment." And they fell on their faces. Moses said to Aaron, "Take your censer, put fire on it from the altar and lay incense on it, and carry it quickly to the congregation and make atonement for them. For wrath has gone out from the LORD; the plague has begun." So Aaron took it as Moses had ordered, and ran into the middle of the assembly, where the plague had already begun among the people. He put on the incense, and made atonement for the people. *He stood between the dead and the living; and the plague was stopped.* Those who died by the plague were fourteen thousand seven hundred, besides those who died in the affair of Korah. When the plague was stopped, Aaron returned to Moses at the entrance of the tent of meeting. (Numbers 16:41–50)

Aaron took the very real risk that his intercession would cost him his life, because it could easily have happened. Standing in the gap for someone should never be undertaken lightly, because it may cost you your life —or at the very least, your lifestyle. The Spirit of God who is in us may use anyone to intercede at any time, in any way, and for any purpose. But he will only use in intercession those who know and understand for themselves the very real cost of intercession. There is one realization, one revelation that we must receive, believe, and understand so that we do not slip into unhelpful assumption. It is this:

There are only two intercessors: Jesus and the Holy Spirit.

Some people are used by God in intercession, but that does not make them intercessors. Some people are used a lot by God in intercession, but that does not make them intercessors. For intercession, the Spirit of God will use whom he wills, when he wills, where he wills, how he wills, for whatever reason he wills. He alone has responsibility for the results of that intercession, because he intercedes for the saints according to God's will, not the saints' will.

"Likewise the Spirit helps us in our weakness; for we do not know how to pray as we ought, but that very Spirit intercedes with sighs too deep for words. And God, who searches the heart, knows what is the mind of the Spirit, because the Spirit intercedes for the saints according to the will of God" (Romans 8:26–27).

Paul speaks here of weakness, not sinfulness or unworthiness. The Spirit helps us in our weakness. Intercession is for the weak; the strong needn't apply. Paul speaks of ignorance, not unwillingness. We do not know how to pray as we ought. Intercession is for the ignorant; the clever needn't apply. Our theology, doctrine, experience, ideas, and beliefs will never lead us into intercession. Only the Spirit of God will do that. We cannot simply decide to do intercession. The Christian who is still living in independence or self-dependence, who has not entered into the new covenant with God through Christ, cannot be used in intercession—though, of course, he can pray with words for others. I will highlight the danger again. Praying with words alone for others usually costs us nothing. That which costs nothing is worth nothing.

Carrying someone in your heart is where intercession begins. Carrying someone in your heart is not the same as worrying about them. Parents—especially mothers—know what it is to carry their children in their hearts. Carrying someone in your heart is not the same as intercession, but it is where intercession begins. The reason mothers carry their children in their hearts is because they gave birth to them. The reason the Holy Spirit carries each of us in his heart is because he gave birth to us. But carrying someone in your heart will not automatically lead to intercession.

Intercession is not about words at all. It is about the reality of standing in the gap before God in place of others. And standing in the gap is spiritual work, not human activity. Intercession is not for the fainthearted or the uncovenanted. Intercession is very costly. It cost Jesus his life. Those who truly intercede don't speak lightly or often about their intercession. Those people who really do intercede will rarely, if ever, talk about their experiences. Those people who truly know what it is to intercede will rarely be seen or heard, because intercession happens in the secret place and is very rarely public. Intercession involves cost that is very difficult to bear in private, but it would be almost impossible to bear it in public. Intercession usually involves:

- identification
- revelation
- battle
- struggle
- waiting
- outworking
- victory

Those who would intercede must:

- know God
- be available
- persevere
- be set aside as holy
- be compassionate
- be of no reputation
- be faithful

I must say again that intercession is not for the fainthearted. Standing in the gap for others is very costly. Intercession always involves personal cost for those who intercede. Let's look at some people whose journey to intercession is touched on in the Scriptures.

"And I said: 'Woe is me! I am lost, for I am a man of unclean lips, and I live among a people of unclean lips'" (Isaiah 6:5).

"Let us lie down in our shame, and let our dishonor cover us; for we have sinned against the LORD our God, we and our ancestors, from our youth even to this day; and we have not obeyed the voice of the LORD our God" (Jeremiah 3:25).

"He said to me, 'O mortal, stand up on your feet, and I will speak with you.' And when he spoke to me, a spirit entered into me and set me on my feet; and I heard him speaking to me. He said to me, 'Mortal, I am sending you to the people of Israel, to a nation of rebels who have rebelled against me; they and their ancestors have transgressed against me to this very day'" (Ezekiel 2:1–3).

"When the LORD first spoke through Hosea, the LORD said to Hosea, 'Go, take for yourself a wife of whoredom and have children of whoredom, for the land commits great whoredom by forsaking the LORD'" (Hosea 1:2).

Intercession properly realized is first about identification. It then leads down the road toward standing in the gap. Identification may be for a person or persons known or unknown, and you may never know who you are interceding for. (Knowing who you are interceding for can actually hinder you, because it then profoundly affects your relationship with them.) Identification can have very serious consequences for those who intercede. Standing in the gap is real, not theoretical. Intercession is personal identification with another person and their circumstances, as their burdens are laid on you by the Holy Spirit. Their struggle becomes your struggle, their battle becomes your battle, and their pain becomes your pain.

In this way, the Holy Spirit can share with the body of Christ the battle that one individual on his own cannot cope with. Revelation from God is critical for those who would intercede. Without that revelation, all you can do is carry the person(s) in your heart, valuable though that is. Revelation is not about learning facts about another human being. It is about knowing God's heart, God's mind, and—sometimes—God's will. Without revelation, identification cannot happen, as the two are closely linked and critically important. Intercession may lead to action or direct involvement by the one interceding, but the battle is always the Lord's. "Thus says the LORD to you: 'Do not fear or be dismayed at this great multitude; for the battle is not yours but God's'" (2 Chronicles 20:15).

God leads the one who will intercede onto the battlefield, where they will stand in the gap for someone else. This is no intellectual exercise. It has nothing to do with mere words. It is usually more of a marathon than a single event. Intercession knows no time limit. It has nothing whatsoever to do with instant results. Those who would intercede must be led by the Spirit in how to react or how to stand—actually, in how to do anything. Therefore, don't be surprised by anything! Intercession will often not make logical sense.

> Thus said the LORD to me, "Go and buy yourself a linen loincloth, and put it on your loins, but do not dip it in water." So I bought a loincloth according to the word of the LORD, and put it on my loins. And the word of the LORD came to me a second time, saying, "Take the loincloth that you bought and are wearing, and go now to the Euphrates, and hide it there in a cleft of the rock." So I went, and hid it by the Euphrates, as the LORD commanded me. And after many days the LORD said to me, "Go now to the Euphrates, and take from there the loincloth that I commanded you to hide there." Then I went to the Euphrates, and dug, and I took the loincloth from the place where I had hidden it. But now the loincloth was ruined; it was good for nothing. (Jeremiah 13:1–7)

To intercede on someone else's behalf is to be, in reality, the body of Christ for that person, suffering with and on behalf of another and paying the cost of intercession. But if it really is your will to be used by God in intercession, you must keep on keeping on! The waiting period during intercession can be very difficult, as there is no guarantee of ever knowing how things will turn out. Waiting in intercession may lead to a clear outworking—or it may not.

You may never know what actually happened as a result of your intercession. Intercession is welcoming the battle for someone else's heart or life to take place in you, with no guarantee of the outcome. You may never know what actually happened as a result of your intercession.

There is no guarantee of victory—whatever we may think that victory should look like. But the most dangerous part of intercession is victory. In the context of intercession, what is victory? Victory is God's will being done. Victory is not our will being done. The victory in intercession is not our victory; it is God's victory. Unless you are of no reputation, victory will destroy your intercession.

You may be faced with unbelief, especially in yourself. Intercession changes the person who is interceding. If you would intercede, you may well be faced with opposition, and you may well be misunderstood, misrepresented, and mistreated. This is especially true where intercession is followed by action and/or involvement. They threw mud at the Master; they'll throw mud at you.

But now I must give a very serious warning: "I will do whatever you ask in my name, so that the Father may be glorified in the Son. If in my name you ask me for anything, I will do it" (John 14:13–14).

The object of intercession is that the Son may bring glory to the Father—never to the one who intercedes. Because of that, intercession rarely happens in public. Those who take the glory of God to themselves are taking the very real risk of losing their lives in the doing. Jesus was often on his own with his Father, and we know very little of what happened during those times. Only in Gethsemane did we get a glimpse of the cost of Jesus' intercession. "Consequently he is able for all time to save those who approach God through him, since he always lives to make intercession for them" (Hebrews 7:25).

Salvation is continually experienced by continually approaching God through Jesus, who continually intercedes for us. Jesus continually intercedes for us and draws us to the Father. Jesus' ability to intercede for us came at great personal cost to himself and to his Father—a cost that both Father and Son joyfully paid. Intercession never seeks benefit without cost. Intercession seeks to pay a deep cost that others may benefit without those others even knowing it. Therefore, blessed are the anonymous.

"Those who go out weeping, bearing the seed for sowing, shall come home with shouts of joy, carrying their sheaves" (Psalm 126:5–6). But in the meantime, the way of intercession is a hard way. The people who are most effective in intercession keep a low profile. The people who are most effective in intercession are of no reputation. Popularity, fame, and reputation tend to destroy effectiveness in intercession. When God is at work through us, all our instincts cry out to us to puff out our chests, raise our shoulders, and voice our own praise. But these instincts will cause us to fall into barrenness. Blessed are the anonymous, for they shall be fruitful.

"Now to him who by the power at work within us is able to accomplish abundantly far more than all we can ask or imagine, to him be glory in the church and in Christ Jesus to all generations, forever and ever. Amen" (Ephesians 3:20–21).

Intercession: Verses for Further Study

- Identification (Lamentations 2:11–12, 16, 20; 3:1–18, 40–42; Ezekiel 2:1–3; 3:1–3; Hosea 1:2; John 1:1–2, 14; Hebrews 2:14, 17–18; 4:15; 7:25)
- Revelation (Isaiah 6:9–10; Jeremiah 3:19–20, 22; 4:18–20; 6:10–11; 8:18–19, 21–22; 13:15, 17; Matthew 23:3–37; John 13:1–5; 16:8–15)
- Battle (Ecclesiastes 5:1–2; Matthew 10:1; Luke 10:19; Matthew 8:5–10, 13; 17:20; 21:31; 22; Mark 1:12–13; 14:32–34; 15:34; Hebrews 2:9, 14–15, 18; 7:25)
- Struggle (Isaiah 6:9–12; 8:1; Jeremiah 2:1; 7:1–3; Ezekiel 3:22–24; 4:1; Mark 7:32–33; 8:22–23; 1 Peter 4:11)
- Waiting (Proverbs 19:21; Mark 5:22–24, 35–40; John 9:1, 6–7; 11:1, 3, 14–17)
- Outworking (Isaiah 66:1–2; Mark 5:39–43; John 9:7–14; 11:38–44)
- Victory (Psalm 18:30–36; Isaiah 14:26–27; 46:5, 8–10; Matthew 9:18–19; Luke 5:17–26; Matthew 10:1; Luke 13:10–13; Acts 14:8–10)

41

Tabernacle

The tabernacle in the Old Testament was a portable structure through which the Jewish people met with God and in which the priests fulfilled their duties. It had an inner holy place that was separated by a curtain (veil) from the innermost holy place, the Holy of Holies. The veil shielded the most holy place and protected the people from what was inside: the very manifest presence of God.

In Jesus' day there was no portable structure but rather an actual temple that had been originally built by King Solomon. This temple also had a veil that shielded the most holy place. At Jesus' crucifixion, a remarkable thing happened to that veil that shielded the Holy of Holies. "Then Jesus cried again with a loud voice and breathed his last. At that moment the curtain of the temple was torn in two, from top to bottom" (Matthew 27:50–51).

The detail here is important, not incidental, for it marked a pivotal moment in history. Important to the understanding of what happened here is the remembrance of the fact that the tabernacle was built exactly according to God's specifications. Therefore, understanding the way the curtain was hung at the Holy of Holies is extremely important to realizing the significance of what happened there. Unlike the curtains we know today that are hung with hooks on poles or tracks and so held along their top length, the temple curtain was only held in each top corner and pulled taut. Thus, when the veil was split in two from top to bottom, the halves of the curtain fell to each side and the way was completely opened up.

The curtain was not torn to let us in to worship in the most holy place. The curtain was torn to show us that God no longer lived there. The tabernacle was finished, but God did not simply disappear from the Holy of Holies or abandon the tabernacle. God did not simply write off his people and walk away from them. Rather, there was something here that could only be known if the way to the Holy of Holies was opened up. What happened in the temple declared that the old covenant was superceded forever. The tabernacle—the temple in Jesus' day—was finished for all time. It was not merely being replaced by a new and improved model. The shadow tabernacle had faded away, for the real tabernacle had come.

"But when Christ came as a high priest of the good things that have come, then through the greater and perfect tent (not made with hands, that is, not of this creation), he entered once for all into the Holy Place … For Christ did not enter a sanctuary made by human hands, a mere copy of the true one, but he entered into heaven itself" (Hebrews 9:11–12, 24).

Jesus himself, in his own humanity, was the dwelling of God. Jesus went through the tabernacle. He did not stay in it, deny it, or go around it. He did not bypass it, abolish it, or destroy it. He actually went through it—and into heaven itself. By going through the tabernacle, Jesus was not dismissing it or setting it aside; he was fulfilling it. This understanding is of huge importance for Jewish Christians. Jesus' action in going through the tabernacle was testimony that the tabernacle was finished forever—not because it was destroyed in any way but because it had fulfilled its purpose. The tabernacle was no longer needed. The God of the tabernacle was now living among his people, walking face-to-face with them. Having gone through the tabernacle into heaven itself, Jesus made it possible for the true tabernacle to be filled with the very presence of God.

So where is that tabernacle now? Where is that temple now? Where is that Holy of Holies now? Where is that sanctuary now? Where is that place that is not made with human hands? Where is that place that is the real and lasting tabernacle?

"Do you not know that *your body* is a temple of the Holy Spirit within *you*, which *you* have from God, and that *you* are not your own?" (1 Corinthians 6:19).

We are:

- the tabernacle
- the temple
- the Holy of Holies
- the sanctuary
- the place not made with human hands
- the real and lasting place

That is the wonder of what God has done through Christ. Under the old covenant, God was living within the tabernacle; under the new covenant, God tabernacles within the living. Since God himself has decreed that we are the new and living tabernacle, don't let your life tell a different story. Since God has decreed that we are the new and living tabernacle, our experience of prayer should be transformed in the light of that decree. We do not pray to a God who is "out there." We pray with the God who dwells in us. Prayer needs to stop being mere words flowing from the mouth of a human being. It needs to be received by each of us for what it actually is: revelation from the mouth of the living God of heaven and earth. Your Father in heaven is telling you who you are, not me.

"For in Christ all the fullness of God was pleased to dwell... For in him the whole fullness of deity dwells bodily, and you have come to fullness in him" (Colossians 1:19; 2:9–10).

Redeemed humankind is the living tabernacle—the living temple—in which the whole manifest presence of God dwells forevermore. God is constantly drawing us toward that reality. Because we have fullness in and through Christ, we now have everything we need in us! That revelation must transform our prayer life! God doesn't just send a little bit of himself to live in us. The utter fullness of God himself dwells in us.

"Do you not know that you are God's temple and that God's Spirit dwells in you? For God's temple is holy, and you are that temple" (1 Corinthians 3:16–17).

We need to realize who and what we are. We need revelation to break upon us. We do not pray to a God "out there somewhere." We commune with the God who is in us in fullness. We need, then, to truly grasp what it means to pray with God instead of to God. "Christ in you, the hope of glory" (Colossians 1:27).

This is the overriding reality to which God is drawing us: Christ in us is everything. He is our everything. That revelation must have a huge impact on how we pray. It should stop us from praying to God and help us to pray with God. Praying with God needs to become a reality for us, not just a neat form of words. So what does it mean to pray with God? To answer that, we need to reflect back on our exploration of intercession and understand by revelation how the Spirit of God intercedes in us and through us.

"Likewise the Spirit helps us in our weakness; for we do not know how to pray as we ought, but that very Spirit intercedes with sighs too deep for words. And God, who searches the heart, knows what is the mind of the Spirit, because the Spirit intercedes for the saints according to the will of God" (Romans 8:26–27).

Praying with God involves knowing the will of God, and that means walking in close intimacy with the Spirit of God. Paul spoke of weakness, not sinfulness or unworthiness, and the Spirit helps us in our weakness. True prayer never flows from strength; it flows from weakness. Paul spoke of ignorance, not unwillingness. We do not know how to pray as we ought, but true prayer never flows from understanding. It flows from helplessness.

Our problem as adults is that we tend to think that we know all there is to know about prayer. We think that we have God all worked out. We say that we don't have God all worked out, but we often live as if we do. True prayer flows from the ongoing, daily knowing of the Holy Spirit himself, not from any head knowledge or understanding that we may have. And true prayer certainly never flows from prejudice or from tradition.

God is the God of the new thing, not of the way that things have always been done. And the ongoing, daily knowing of the Holy Spirit himself is the way of seeking cost without benefit. As adult human beings, seeking cost without benefit is precisely opposite of the way that we are used to living, even as Christians. As adult human beings, seeking cost without benefit is the way of self-sacrifice, which isn't very popular, but self-sacrifice is the only way to the true tabernacle of God's presence in fullness in us. I really do wonder if God wants to hear fewer words and see more self-sacrifice.

By turning Christianity into a simple acceptance of beliefs that do precious little to change our hearts or transform our lives, we have also turned prayer into a simple shopping list of requests that no self-respecting God would ever refuse. But true prayer always seeks cost without benefit.

> I appeal to you therefore, brothers and sisters, by the mercies of God, to present your bodies as a living sacrifice, holy and acceptable to God, which is your spiritual worship. Do not be conformed to this world, but be transformed by the renewing of your minds, so that you may discern what is the will of God—what is good and acceptable and perfect. For by the grace given to me I say to everyone among you not to think of yourself more highly than you ought to think, but to think with sober judgment, each according to the measure of faith that God has assigned. For as in one body we have many members, and not all the members have the same function, so we, who are many, are one body in Christ, and individually we are members one of another. We have gifts that differ according to the grace given to us: prophecy, in proportion to faith; ministry, in ministering; the teacher, in teaching; the exhorter, in exhortation; the giver, in generosity; the leader, in diligence; the compassionate, in cheerfulness. (Romans 12:1–8).

We can only present our bodies as living sacrifices by the mercies of God. Are we truly willing to die? A living sacrifice takes its identity from the one to whom it sacrifices itself. Are we truly willing to die? A living sacrifice cannot think of itself more highly than it ought to. Are we truly willing to die? A living sacrifice will only think of and measure itself according to the measure of faith that God has assigned. The measure of faith that God assigns is dependent upon our rate of transformation. The more transformed we are, the more God assigns faith. Faith is not something that we can muster up. A living sacrifice is not something that we can muster up. Are we truly willing to die? A living sacrifice will use gifts that are given to us according to God's grace. Are we truly willing to die?

Christ went through the tabernacle by way of total self-sacrifice. If we are to realize our true identity as the tabernacle of God, we need to go the way of total self-sacrifice. If we want to learn true prayer, then we must learn self-sacrifice. It was Jesus' self-sacrifice that made us the temple of God. It is our own self-sacrifice that will make this temple fit for his purpose.

Part V

Christ-Centered Leaders

"Then God said, 'Let us make humankind in our image, according to our likeness; and let them have dominion over the fish of the sea, and over the birds of the air, and over the cattle, and over all the wild animals of the earth, and over every creeping thing that creeps upon the earth'" (Genesis 1:26).

Let us return now to the subject of leadership and recap where we have already been for a short time. The earth was filled with livestock, the air was filled with birds, and the sea was filled with fish. Creation was ready for humankind. Humankind was to have dominion over all creation, but how were they to do it—sit in an office and issue a decree? No, man was to go and explore, because an explorer is what he is. Consider each of the following points about how the males of humankind are wired:

- Man is not content to be told what is behind a door. He will go and see for himself.
- Man climbs mountains, goes to the poles, and walks on the moon.
- Man acts first and (maybe) thinks later.
- Man takes risks for the fun of it.
- Man does extreme sports.
- Man deliberately courts danger.
- Man doesn't sit still.
- Man needs to know.

- Man needs to go.
- Man needs to show.
- Man needs to compete.
- Man needs to win.

So, what is a woman? She is helper, a companion. She was made to be with man. It is how she is wired. This is not at all about status. This is all about relationship. Man and woman are different but equal. They are different but complementary. Consider the following points about the females of humankind:

- Where man is about the destination, woman is about the journey.
- Where man is about the achievement, woman is about the achieving.
- Where man is about the knowledge, woman is about the knowing.
- Where man is about the having, woman is about the holding.
- Where man is about the doing, woman is about the being.
- Where man is task-driven, woman is relationship-driven.
- Where man is competitive, woman is complementary.
- Where man is solo, woman is community.

Man and woman are complementary. Together they make a truly formidable leadership team, but how does that team work? Husband is the head of the marriage relationship, but man is not the head of woman!

Headship = responsibility + covering + protection

Headship responsibility should not be understood in the context of blame or control. It has nothing to do with them. Blame and control came into humankind because of the fall, but they were not part of God's original design. Consider the parents of a newborn baby and the responsibility that they have for the child. That responsibility has nothing to do with blame or control. It is the responsibility for the protection, well-being, and development of that person.

Husband has the responsibility for the protection, well-being, and development of his wife and their relationship. When the relationship hits difficult times, it is the husband's responsibility to put things right as quickly as possible. In the context of marriage, the husband is responsible. Therefore, headship is male, but headship and leadership are not the same thing. It is a serious, though common, error to believe that headship and leadership are one and the same thing. Headship is male, but leadership is not gender specific, because men and women were both made in the image of God. Either man or woman can lead—or both—but the headship responsibility in marriage is man's alone. But we must ask: what is leadership? And why do a man and a woman make such a complete leadership team?

Love relationships flow from the heart, not from the head. Love is something that the heart knows, but the head does not understand it. And every leadership team needs both men and women, because

- Hearts forgive, but heads keep score.
- Hearts include, but heads exclude.
- Hearts live, but heads learn.
- Hearts learn life, but heads learn the lessons of life.
- Hearts value people for who they are, but heads value that which can be gained from people.

Every leadership team needs both men and women. Leadership teams need to be balanced, and single-gender leadership teams are about as imbalanced as you can get. But what is leadership?

Leadership is taking someone else where you have been before. You cannot lead where you have never been. Leading is not the same as merely walking ahead of the pack. Leadership is not passive. You are not a leader just because people happen to be behind you. If you drive on a narrow country road at twenty miles per hour, there will be a big queue of vehicles behind you, but that doesn't make you a leader; it makes you a blockage.

Did you know that the word *leader* does not appear in the new covenant Scriptures? Did you know that the word *leaders* only appears three times? Two of those occurrences are at the end of Hebrews. Did you know that the word *leadership* only appears twice in the new covenant Scriptures? Leadership, by that name, is not a concept found in the new covenant Scriptures. Do we use the word leader because we are frightened of words like apostle and prophet?

Leadership, as we know it, is an entirely human construct, and it is not gender specific. Any leadership that is restricted only to males is imbalanced, incomplete, and ineffective. Many of the passages written by the apostle Paul that have caused so much controversy were written in the specific context of headship, not leadership. (See 1 Corinthians 7:1; 11:2; 14:26; Ephesians 5:22; Colossians 3:18; 1 Timothy 2:1; and Galatians 3:26–28.)

The appointing of "leaders" is an entirely human construct, because it rests in the qualifications of the one being appointed. Now let us move on to the concept that is found all the way through all the Sciptures.

42

Callings

God's call to be an apostle (or any other calling) does not rest in the qualifications of the one being called. It rests in the qualifications of the one doing the calling. Furthermore, apostleship (or any other calling) is a God-given calling.

"And God has appointed in the church first apostles, second prophets, third teachers; then deeds of power, then gifts of healing, forms of assistance, forms of leadership, various kinds of tongues" (1 Corinthians 12:28).

"The gifts [Christ] gave were that some would be apostles, some prophets, some evangelists, some pastors and teachers, to equip the saints for the work of ministry, for building up the body of Christ" (Ephesians 4:11–12).

When reading the new covenant Scriptures, we need to remember that Jewish culture, like many others (including the Roman Empire that ruled the Jews), gave a very low place to women. That is a direct result of the fall. We need also to remember that much of what Paul wrote was in the context of headship, not leadership. Paul recognized that people received callings from God, and that both men and women were called by God. Indeed, one of Paul's lists of apostles included a woman. Jesus called only men because that was all the culture of the day allowed him to do. This was also Paul's background, but, while standing firm over headship, Paul welcomed men and women into leadership, because God was calling both men and women. Paul extended leadership to women in the European churches in a way he could never have done among Jewish believers.

"I urge Euodia and I urge Syntyche to be of the same mind in the Lord. Yes, and I ask you also, my loyal companion, help these women, *for they have struggled beside me* in the work of the gospel, together with Clement and *the rest of my coworkers*, whose names are in the book of life" (Philippians 4:2–3). In the culture in which Paul wrote, he was here equating women as coworkers with himself and thereby declaring them to be apostles too. Coworkers are equal.

In the context of leadership, Paul was open to men and women, and any honest examination of the new covenant Scriptures will come to that same conclusion. But we must understand the difference between headship and leadership—that headship is a Scriptural concept but leadership is a human concept. God calls apostles, but people appoint leaders. God calls people, and therefore they lead. People appoint leaders because there are jobs that need to be done. The early church wasn't a community that gathered once or twice a week; it was a network of house-churches. Those whom God called became house-church leaders, and the local church met and was based in their homes. Many of these church leaders and significant people were women.

"Give my greetings to the brothers and sisters in Laodicea, *and to Nympha and the church in her house*" (Colossians 4:15).

Nympha would have exercised leadership over men, but she would not have exercised headship over her husband if she was married. Men need to put aside their prejudices once and for all and give women the place in leadership that they should have. For far too long, leadership theology has been based on men's interpretation of the new covenant Scriptures from English translations only, and it is not possible to examine Scripture with integrity unless the original new covenant Greek is explored carefully. There are plenty of scholars who have done that work; we only need to take the time to read the scholars instead of building theological houses of cards on English translations only—and very often only on one verse. It is a serious error to build theology on English translations alone, and it is an even more serious error to build theologies on one English verse. Why do such serious errors continue to be made?

I must give a word of caution here. The calling of God on our lives is not revealed by our use of the gifts of the Spirit. It is revealed by the growth of the fruit of the Holy Spirit in our lives.

"Abide in me as I abide in you. Just as the branch cannot bear fruit by itself unless it abides in the vine, neither can you unless you abide in me. I am the vine, you are the branches. Those who abide in me and I in them bear much fruit, because apart from me you can do nothing" (John 15:4–5).

The fruit of the Spirit is not a gift. It is the result of time, growth, and maturity in abiding. The fruit of the Holy Spirit is not a flower. Flowers are decorative; fruit is functional. Flowers are pleasure giving; fruit is life giving. Therefore, I declare it in this way:

Fruit + grace + time = calling

While a discussion on spiritual gifts lies beyond the scope of this book, I will make one point here. Spiritual gifts do not cause division. Misuse of spiritual gifts causes division. It is not enough to know spiritual gifts or to use them. We need to know how to use them, and all that entails.

Jesus called his disciples, taught them, trained them, appointed them, anointed them, and then sent them out, and you cannot short-circuit that process! Many short-circuits make for much misunderstanding. Maturity is shown by a life of worship. Spiritual gifts and their use are no indication of maturity. It is what you are that shows maturity, not what you do. Spiritual gifts are good, important, and desirable, but it is the person you are that counts—because the person you are determines the things that you do.

43

Authority and Power

Do not confuse power with authority. Power is the dynamic ability to effect change. Authority is the delegated right to use power. In Matthew 28, Jesus said that all authority was given to him, not all power.

We were made to live lives of freedom. As human beings, we need to be set free to live lives of freedom. We need to be set free from that which binds us, restricts us, and clings to us. We need to be set free for the things that God has for us. "For freedom Christ has set us free" (Galatians 5:1).

Authority sets us free from. Power sets us free for. The freedom of power is founded and based upon the freedom of authority. The freedom of authority shows us who we are. The freedom of power shows us what to do. This brings us to something God impressed upon me personally many years ago: Jesus gives his authority to those who personally trust him; but he only gives his power to those he can personally trust.

"At that time Jesus said, 'I thank you, Father, Lord of heaven and earth, because you have hidden these things from the wise and the intelligent and have revealed them to infants; yes, Father, for such was your gracious will. All things have been handed over to me by my Father; and no one knows the Son except the Father, and no one knows the Father except the Son and anyone to whom the Son chooses to reveal him" (Matthew 11:25–27).

How does the Son decide on those to whom the Father will be revealed?

44

Jesus

Let's now consider the way that Jesus showed leadership, and how the apostle Paul developed that leadership in order to take it to the Gentiles.

> Let the same mind be in you that was in Christ Jesus, who, though he was in the form of God, did not regard equality with God as something to be exploited, but emptied himself, taking the form of a slave, being born in human likeness. And being found in human form, he humbled himself and became obedient to the point of death—even death on a cross. Therefore God also highly exalted him and gave him the name that is above every name, so that at the name of Jesus every knee should bend, in heaven and on earth and under the earth, and every tongue should confess that Jesus Christ is Lord, to the glory of God the Father. (Philippians 2:5–11)

> He is the image of the invisible God, the firstborn of all creation; for in him all things in heaven and on earth were created, things visible and invisible, whether thrones or dominions or rulers or powers—all things have been created through him and for him. He himself is before all things, and in him all things hold together.

He is the head of the body, the church; he is the beginning, the firstborn from the dead, so that he might come to have first place in everything. For in him all the fullness of God was pleased to dwell, and through him God was pleased to reconcile to himself all things, whether on earth or in heaven, by making peace through the blood of his cross. (Colossians 1:15–20)

For in him the whole fullness of deity dwells bodily, and you have come to fullness in him, who is the head of every ruler and authority. In him also you were circumcised with a spiritual circumcision, by putting off the body of the flesh in the circumcision of Christ; when you were buried with him in baptism, you were also raised with him through faith in the power of God, who raised him from the dead. And when you were dead in trespasses and the uncircumcision of your flesh, God made you alive together with him, when he forgave us all our trespasses, erasing the record that stood against us with its legal demands. He set this aside, nailing it to the cross. He disarmed the rulers and authorities and made a public example of them, triumphing over them in it. (Colossians 2:9–15)

From now on, therefore, we regard no one from a human point of view; even though we once knew Christ from a human point of view, we know him no longer in that way. So if anyone is in Christ, there is a new creation: everything old has passed away; see, everything has become new! All this is from God, who reconciled us to himself through Christ, and has given us the ministry of reconciliation; that is, in Christ God was reconciling the world to himself, not counting their trespasses against them, and entrusting the message of reconciliation to us. So we are ambassadors for Christ, since God is making his appeal through us; we entreat you on behalf of Christ, be reconciled to God. For our sake he made him to be sin who knew no sin, so that in him we might become the righteousness of God. (2 Corinthians 5:16–21)

After he had washed their feet, had put on his robe, and had returned to the table, he said to them, "Do you know what I have done to you? You call me Teacher and Lord—and you are right, for that is what I am. So if I, your Lord and Teacher, have washed your feet, you also ought to wash one another's feet. For I have set you an example, that you also should do as I have done to you. Very truly, I tell you, servants are not greater than their master, nor are messengers greater than the one who sent them. If you know these things, you are blessed if you do them. (John 13:12–17)

Then Jesus summoned his twelve disciples and gave them authority over unclean spirits, to cast them out, and to cure every disease and every sickness. These are the names of the twelve apostles: first, Simon, also known as Peter, and his brother Andrew; James son of Zebedee, and his brother John; Philip and Bartholomew; Thomas and Matthew the tax collector; James son of Alphaeus, and Thaddaeus; Simon the Cananaean, and Judas Iscariot, the one who betrayed him. These twelve Jesus sent out with the following instructions: "Go nowhere among the Gentiles, and enter no town of the Samaritans, but go rather to the lost sheep of the house of Israel. As you go, proclaim the good news, 'The kingdom of heaven has come near.' Cure the sick, raise the dead, cleanse the lepers, cast out demons. You received without payment; give without payment. Take no gold, or silver, or copper in your belts, no bag for your journey, or two tunics, or sandals, or a staff; for laborers deserve their food." (Matthew 10:1–10)

> Now when Jesus had finished instructing his twelve disciples, he went on from there to teach and proclaim his message in their cities. When John heard in prison what the Messiah was doing, he sent word by his disciples and said to him, "Are you the one who is to come, or are we to wait for another?" Jesus answered them, "Go and tell John what you hear and see: the blind receive their sight, the lame walk, the lepers are cleansed, the deaf hear, the dead are raised, and the poor have good news brought to them. And blessed is anyone who takes no offence at me." (Matthew 11:1–6)

Jesus gives his authority to those who personally trust him, but he only gives his power to those he can personally trust. Jesus gives his authority to those who personally trust him, and that is why he gave his authority even to Judas Iscariot. Authority is to be used, but it is not about status, ego, control, fame, money, or decoration. Maturity is shown not by the fact that you have Christ's authority, but by the way that you use it. Notice how Jesus said to use his authority.

- Cure the sick, raise the dead, and cleanse the lepers. Come against the *fruit* of the Enemy.
- Cast out demons. Come against the *person* of the Enemy.

Notice also the covenant basis for his disciples: you received without payment; give without payment.

As leaders, how we give is determined by how we receive. What if we haven't received anything? What if we have received very little? Do we as leaders freely receive through a yielded heart? As leaders, our maturity in Christ is shown by how we use Christ's authority. The evidence that the kingdom of God has come near is the Holy Spirit at work in people's lives. Blessed is the person who does not fall away on account of Jesus, but many of God's people do exactly that. Blessed is the person who does not take offence at Jesus, but many of God's people do exactly that. We will always have amongst us:

- those who have not but who are ready to receive the one who has it all
- those who cannot but who are ready to receive him who can do all
- those who are not but who are ready to receive him who is all

The covenant basis of life in Christ not only reveals his love and grace, but it also brings things into the light. The proud will not receive anything. The greedy will not refuse anything. Only the poor will receive the giver himself. Jesus said, "Blessed is anyone who takes no offence at me." The religious people wanted a sign from Jesus, but the people received Jesus himself. Are we, as leaders, willing to receive Jesus himself? Or only what he can do for us? Is life really all about Jesus, or is it all about ourselves? As leaders, do we have faith in Jesus himself or only in the things of Jesus?

Once while Jesus was standing beside the lake of Gennesaret, and the crowd was pressing in on him to hear the word of God, he saw two boats there at the shore of the lake; the fishermen had gone out of them and were washing their nets. He got into one of the boats, the one belonging to Simon, and asked him to put out a little way from the shore. Then he sat down and taught the crowds from the boat. When he had finished speaking, he said to Simon, "Put out into the deep water and let down your nets for a catch." Simon answered, "Master, we have worked all night long but have caught nothing. Yet if you say so, I will let down the nets." When they had done this, they caught so many fish that their nets were beginning to break. So they signaled their partners in the other boat to come and help them. And they came and filled both boats, so that they began to sink. But when Simon Peter saw it, he fell down at Jesus' knees, saying, "Go away from me, Lord, for I am a sinful man!" For he and all who were with him were amazed at the catch of fish that they had taken; and so also were James and John, sons of Zebedee, who were

> partners with Simon. Then Jesus said to Simon, "Do
> not be afraid; from now on you will be catching people."
> When they had brought their boats to shore, they left
> everything and followed him. (Luke 5:1–11)

There is a great deal that we can learn from Peter and his interaction with Jesus. Peter responded, "Master, we have worked all night long but have caught nothing" (v. 5). Peter didn't understand Jesus' words to him. He didn't believe or even like Jesus' words to him. He certainly had no faith in Jesus' word to him. Yet he obeyed Jesus. Why? Because Peter's faith was not in the words that Jesus spoke but in Jesus who spoke the words. "Yet if you say so, I will (v. 5). Peter had learned something that very many Christians have still to learn.

Faith in the words spoken leads to evaluation of the words spoken. Evaluation becomes opinion and opinion keeps a person from getting out of the boat. The mind assesses the risk of walking on water and puts the brakes on. But faith in the God who speaks leads to revelation from God. Revelation becomes worship, and worship walks on water and therefore leads to Jesus. Your personal worship leads you to meet Jesus personally, for your personal worship is your personal submission to the Lord Jesus Christ. Being with Jesus reveals more of him to you and more of you to him. Being with Jesus makes you more like him.

The quality of your leadership depends upon your character. The quality of your character depends upon your being with Jesus (or not). Leadership is not primarily about doing; it is first and foremost about being. Leadership is about who we are. The leader's primary responsibility is to be with Jesus. When we know Jesus, we can get to know his ways and his strategy. There were two boats at the water's edge. Why did Jesus choose Simon Peter's boat? Because Jesus knew that the Holy Spirit was at work in Simon Peter at that time. So Jesus strategically created the moment of revelation to which Simon Peter responded. Know Jesus; know his ways; know his strategy. To know the leader of character is to be a leader of character.

> But Peter, standing with the eleven, raised his voice
> and addressed them… Now when they heard this, they

were cut to the heart and said to Peter and to the other apostles, "Brothers, what should we do?" Peter said to them, "Repent, and be baptized every one of you in the name of Jesus Christ so that your sins may be forgiven; and you will receive the gift of the Holy Spirit. For the promise is for you, for your children, and for all who are far away, everyone whom the Lord our God calls to him." And he testified with many other arguments and exhorted them, saying, "Save yourselves from this corrupt generation." So those who welcomed his message were baptized, and that day about three thousand persons were added. They devoted themselves to the apostles' teaching and fellowship, to the breaking of bread and the prayers. Awe came upon everyone, because many wonders and signs were being done by the apostles. All who believed were together and had all things in common; they would sell their possessions and goods and distribute the proceeds to all, as any had need. Day by day, as they spent much time together in the temple, they broke bread at home and ate their food with glad and generous hearts, praising God and having the goodwill of all the people. And day by day the Lord added to their number those who were being saved. (Acts 2:14, 37–47)

Peter stood with the eleven, a leadership growing in their callings and walking in them. The crowd were cut to the heart by Peter's message as the Holy Spirit worked in them. Yet they asked Peter and the other apostles, "Brothers, what should we do?" Identification preceded commitment. Three thousand people were swept into the kingdom, and notice carefully what those three thousand did. They devoted themselves to the apostles' teaching and fellowship, to the breaking of bread and the prayers (v. 42). Notice something else too. Many wonders and signs were being done by the apostles (v. 43). It was not a charismatic free-for-all.

People's lives were being changed and transformed by the power of the Holy Spirit who was at work in people through his leaders. Leaders must be people of vision. That is why they were all in one place. Vision needs to be focused into purpose. Purpose in action brings the presence of God. The presence of God finds expression through the power of God. Power changes and transforms people's lives as they know Jesus and make him known. A leader's primary need is to know Jesus himself, to know him continuously and intimately. Leaders who know Jesus well know themselves well.

> Let the same mind be in you that was in Christ Jesus, who, though he was in the form of God, did not regard equality with God as something to be exploited, but emptied himself, taking the form of a slave, being born in human likeness. And being found in human form, he humbled himself and became obedient to the point of death—even death on a cross. Therefore God also highly exalted him and gave him the name that is above every name, so that at the name of Jesus every knee should bend, in heaven and on earth and under the earth, and every tongue should confess that Jesus Christ is Lord, to the glory of God the Father. (Philippians 2:5–11)

Never forget that the one who emptied himself and became the servant of all is now the exalted Lord of all. There is a direct relationship between the lives we live here on earth and the kind of lives that we will live in the life to come. Therefore God also highly exalted him. And Jesus spoke of this direct relationship again and again. Do not exalt yourself. The cost is too high.

> For it is as if a man, going on a journey, summoned his slaves and entrusted his property to them; to one he gave five talents, to another two, to another one, to each according to his ability. Then he went away. The one who had received the five talents went off at once and traded with them, and made five more talents. In the same way, the one who had the two talents made two more talents. But the one who had received the one talent

went off and dug a hole in the ground and hid his master's money. After a long time the master of those slaves came and settled accounts with them. Then the one who had received the five talents came forward, bringing five more talents, saying, "Master, you handed over to me five talents; see, I have made five more talents." His master said to him, "Well done, good and trustworthy slave; you have been trustworthy in a few things, I will put you in charge of many things; enter into the joy of your master." And the one with the two talents also came forward, saying, "Master, you handed over to me two talents; see, I have made two more talents." His master said to him, "Well done, good and trustworthy slave; you have been trustworthy in a few things, I will put you in charge of many things; enter into the joy of your master." Then the one who had received the one talent also came forward, saying, "Master, I knew that you were a harsh man, reaping where you did not sow, and gathering where you did not scatter seed; so I was afraid, and I went and hid your talent in the ground. Here you have what is yours." But his master replied, "You wicked and lazy slave! You knew, did you, that I reap where I did not sow, and gather where I did not scatter? Then you ought to have invested my money with the bankers, and on my return I would have received what was my own with interest. So take the talent from him, and give it to the one with the ten talents. For to all those who have, more will be given, and they will have an abundance; but from those who have nothing, even what they have will be taken away. As for this worthless slave, throw him into the outer darkness, where there will be weeping and gnashing of teeth." (Matthew 25:14–30)

What each person did with what they were given had a profound effect on what they were given at the end. Your calling is not just for this life but for the life to come. Now has eternal significance for the not yet.

> His divine power has given us everything needed for life and godliness, through the knowledge of him who called us by his own glory and goodness. Thus he has given us, through these things, his precious and very great promises, so that through them you may escape from the corruption that is in the world because of lust, and may become participants of the divine nature. For this very reason, you must make every effort to support your faith with goodness, and goodness with knowledge, and knowledge with self-control, and self-control with endurance, and endurance with godliness, and godliness with mutual affection, and mutual affection with love. For if these things are yours and are increasing among you, they keep you from being ineffective and unfruitful in the knowledge of our Lord Jesus Christ. For anyone who lacks these things is nearsighted and blind, and is forgetful of the cleansing of past sins. Therefore, brothers and sisters, be all the more eager to confirm your call and election, for if you do this, you will never stumble. For in this way, entry into the eternal kingdom of our Lord and Savior Jesus Christ will be richly provided for you. (2 Peter 1:3–11)

Everything we need for life and godliness comes through Jesus in the power of the Spirit. Yet our participation is required (vv. 5–7). You must make every effort to support your faith with goodness, goodness with knowledge, knowledge with self-control, self-control with endurance, endurance with godliness, godliness with mutual affection, and mutual affection with love—for your own good. This is the growth into maturity. "For if these things are yours and are increasing among you, they keep you from being ineffective and unfruitful in the knowledge of our Lord Jesus Christ" (v. 8). Your welcome into the kingdom depends upon making your calling and election sure.

"It is done! I am the Alpha and the Omega, the beginning and the end. To the thirsty I will give water as a gift from the spring of the water of life. Those who conquer will inherit these things, and I will be their God and they will be my children ... See, I am coming soon; my reward is with me, to repay according to everyone's work ... Blessed are those who wash their robes, so that they will have the right to the tree of life and may enter the city by the gates" (Revelation 21:6–7; 22:12, 14).

Understand the importance of knowing your calling and fulfilling it. People's lives are in your hands. Therefore, be!

45

Called to Be

For just as the body is one and has many members, and all the members of the body, though many, are one body, so it is with Christ. For in the one Spirit we were all baptized into one body—Jews or Greeks, slaves or free—and we were all made to drink of one Spirit.

Indeed, the body does not consist of one member but of many. If the foot would say, "Because I am not a hand, I do not belong to the body," that would not make it any less a part of the body. And if the ear would say, "Because I am not an eye, I do not belong to the body," that would not make it any less a part of the body. If the whole body were an eye, where would the hearing be? If the whole body were hearing, where would the sense of smell be? But as it is, God arranged the members in the body, each one of them, as he chose. If all were a single member, where would the body be? As it is, there are many members, yet one body. The eye cannot say to the hand, "I have no need of you," nor again the head to the feet, "I have no need of you." On the contrary, the members of the body that seem to be weaker are indispensable, and those members of the body that we think less honorable we clothe with greater honor, and our less respectable members are treated with greater respect; whereas our more respectable members do not need this. But God has so arranged the body, giving the greater honor to the inferior member, that there may be no dissension within the body, but the members may have the same care for one another. If one member suffers, all suffer together with it; if one member is honored, all rejoice together with it.

Now you are the body of Christ and individually members of it. And God has appointed in the church first apostles, second prophets, third teachers; then deeds of power, then gifts of healing, forms of assistance, forms of leadership, various kinds of tongues. Are all apostles? Are all prophets? Are all teachers? Do all work miracles? Do all possess gifts of healing? Do all speak in tongues? Do all interpret? But strive for the greater gifts. (1 Corinthians 12:12–31)

I therefore, the prisoner in the Lord, beg you to lead a life worthy of the calling to which you have been called, with all humility and gentleness, with patience, bearing with one another in love, making every effort to maintain the unity of the Spirit in the bond of peace. There is one body and one Spirit, just as you were called to the one hope of your calling, one Lord, one faith, one baptism, one God and Father of all, who is above all and through all and in all.

But each of us was given grace according to the measure of Christ's gift. Therefore it is said, "When he ascended on high he made captivity itself a captive; he gave gifts to his people." (When it says, "He ascended," what does it mean but that he had also descended into the lower parts of the earth? He who descended is the same one who ascended far above all the heavens, so that he might fill all things.) The gifts he gave were that some would be apostles, some prophets, some evangelists, some pastors and teachers, to equip the saints for the work of ministry, for building up the body of

> Christ, until all of us come to the unity of the faith and of the knowledge of the Son of God, to maturity, to the measure of the full stature of Christ. We must no longer be children, tossed to and fro and blown about by every wind of doctrine, by people's trickery, by their craftiness in deceitful scheming. But speaking the truth in love, we must grow up in every way into him who is the head, into Christ, from whom the whole body, joined and knit together by every ligament with which it is equipped, as each part is working properly, promotes the body's growth in building itself up in love. (Ephesians 4:1–16)

The gifts referred to here are not gifts such as prophecy or tongues (which are the gifts of the Spirit) but rather the gifts of the Father and Son, which are the people themselves. We are called to be, and that has nothing to do with pride, status, power, control, position, title, career or job. It has to do with God's call, our response, and the growth and fulfillment of that call. God's call is never revoked, but neither does it stand still, and it may remain unfulfilled.

Since God's call is not about pride, status, power, control, position, title, career or job, we need a new way to think about the passages we have just read. That new way is this: these passages do not present a mathematical formula or a pyramid authority structure. Rather, they are flowcharts. The key to understanding these flowcharts is this: "But strive for the greater gifts": (1 Corinthians 12:31).

But we need to remember that the appointing of "leaders" is an entirely human construct, because it rests in the qualifications of the one being appointed.

"Consider your own call, brothers and sisters: not many of you were wise by human standards, not many were powerful, not many were of noble birth. But God chose what is foolish in the world to shame the wise; God chose what is weak in the world to shame the strong; God chose what is low and despised in the world, things that are not, to reduce to nothing things that are, so that no one might boast in the presence of God" (1 Corinthians 1:26–29).

We also need to remember that God's call to be an apostle (or any other calling) does not rest in the qualifications of the one being called. It rests in the qualifications of the one doing the calling. Maturity leads to the higher callings; that is the flow of the flowchart. God's best for us will lead us to our highest calling. Pride, and that which flows from pride, will immediately block the flow of the flowchart and cause us to turn it back into a mathematical formula or pyramid authority structure. A mathematical formula or pyramid authority structure can be grasped, but a flow cannot. Before God sends out an apostle, he sets him apart as holy; and before he sets him apart, he calls him. That call needs to be answered, not by a decision but by a lifelong, total commitment to Christ. God calls a person and then sets him apart before sending him out. That is discipleship based in calling.

We cannot short-circuit this process. Calling-based discipleship that is preparing us for our service must run its full course. Many short circuits make for much misunderstanding. Failure to properly engage with the reality of God's callings leads to chaotic, self-centered leadership that is on a course of self-destruction. Where a church fails to properly engage with the reality of God's callings, the chaotic and self-centered leadership that self-destructs will surely contribute to the nation being set adrift on a sea of apathy. Where church leadership is detached from reality, the nation will be detached from reality. The nation will pay a heavy price for a church leadership that has failed to properly engage with the reality of God's callings. God's calling does not rest in the qualifications of the one being called. It rests in the qualifications of the one doing the calling. These are the essential keys to understanding.

> Now the boy Samuel was ministering to the LORD under Eli. The word of the LORD was rare in those days; visions were not widespread. At that time Eli, whose eyesight had begun to grow dim so that he could not see, was lying down in his room; the lamp of God had not yet gone out, and Samuel was lying down in the temple of the LORD, where the ark of God was. Then the LORD called, "Samuel! Samuel!" and he said,

"Here I am!" and ran to Eli, and said, "Here I am, for you called me." But he said, "I did not call; lie down again." So he went and lay down. The LORD called again, "Samuel!" Samuel got up and went to Eli, and said, "Here I am, for you called me." But he said, "I did not call, my son; lie down again." Now Samuel did not yet know the LORD, and the word of the LORD had not yet been revealed to him. The LORD called Samuel again, a third time. And he got up and went to Eli, and said, "Here I am, for you called me." Then Eli perceived that the LORD was calling the boy. Therefore Eli said to Samuel, "Go, lie down; and if he calls you, you shall say, 'Speak, LORD, for your servant is listening.'" So Samuel went and lay down in his place. Now the LORD came and stood there, calling as before, "Samuel! Samuel!" And Samuel said, "Speak, for your servant is listening." (1 Samuel 3:1–10)

God's powerful and heavy word to Israel was going to come through a boy—a boy who did not even know the Lord! Samuel had absolutely no doubt about the call. His only uncertainty lay in who was doing the calling. As leaders, we need to stop looking exclusively to the obvious people for new leaders and draw near to the God who calls us—to see whom he is calling. Samuel worshiped; he met God personally. And moment-by-moment worship lived out daily will lead us into maturity and into God's highest calling for us. God's call can be relied on, because the God who calls can be relied on.

"God is not a human being, that he should lie, or a mortal, that he should change his mind. Has he promised, and will he not do it? Has he spoken, and will he not fulfill it?" (Numbers 23:19).

"The human mind may devise many plans, but it is the purpose of the LORD that will be established" (Proverbs 19:21).

"No wisdom, no understanding, no counsel, can avail against the LORD" (Proverbs 21:30).

"The LORD of hosts has sworn: As I have designed, so shall it be; and as I have planned, so shall it come to pass ... For the LORD of hosts has planned, and who will annul it? His hand is stretched out, and who will turn it back?" (Isaiah 14:24, 27).

As leaders, are we living out our callings and growing in them, or are we leading in spite of our callings? Did God show you your calling many years ago and it is still not fulfilled? Do you look back with regret because the promises that God gave to you are still unfulfilled? Did God once ask you to do something that you have not yet done to this day? Have you received God's calling, only to let it slip away? How many people have heard the call of God and assumed that it was to happen immediately instead of their being discipled for that calling? Anything that lasts for only a lifetime and gets in the way of that which lasts for eternity is too expensive.

"Better is the end of a thing than its beginning; the patient in spirit are better than the proud in spirit" (Ecclesiastes 7:8).

"Jesus said, 'My food is to do the will of him who sent me and to complete his work'" (John 4:34).

"But I do not count my life of any value to myself, if only I may finish my course and the ministry that I received from the Lord Jesus" (Acts 20:24).

"According to the grace of God given to me, like a skilled master builder I laid a foundation, and someone else is building on it. Each builder must choose with care how to build on it" (1 Corinthians 3:10, 14). If what has been built on the foundation survives, the builder will receive a reward.

"Now I would remind you, brothers and sisters, of the good news that I proclaimed to you, which you in turn received, in which also you stand, through which also you are being saved, if you hold firmly to the message that I proclaimed to you—unless you have come to believe in vain" (1 Corinthians 15:1–2).

"I have fought the good fight, I have finished the race, I have kept the faith. From now on there is reserved for me the crown of righteousness, which the Lord, the righteous judge, will give me on that day, and not only to me but also to all who have longed for his appearing" (2 Timothy 4:7–8).

There is some value in starting something, but there is much more value in finishing what has been started. Agree with God now that you will let God finish what he once started in you. In the kingdom of God, leadership should always spring from calling, not the other way around. When we speak about leadership, there are three dangerous words to be wary of: *I*, *me*, and *mine*. Self-centered leadership is very dangerous to all concerned.

Control without accountability will inevitably lead to destruction. True accountability is not about deeds or work, but about who we really are deep inside. Leadership without calling will inevitably lead to control without accountability. For the sake of God's people and the world at large, leadership in the kingdom of God must be Christ-centered. The calling of God on our lives is not revealed by what we do but by the growth of the fruit of the Holy Spirit in our lives. And the growth of the Holy Spirit's fruit produces the character of Christ in us.

"Abide in me as I abide in you. Just as the branch cannot bear fruit by itself unless it abides in the vine, neither can you unless you abide in me. I am the vine, you are the branches. Those who abide in me and I in them bear much fruit, because apart from me you can do nothing" (John 15:4–5).

The fruit of the Holy Spirit is absolutely crucial to those who want to discover who they are in Christ and what their calling is. The life of freedom to which we have been called gives time and space for grace and the fruit of the Holy Spirit to grow in our lives. That is precisely why God never seems to be in a hurry to work in our lives. The fruit of the Holy Spirit grows on the tree of life in each of us. When the tree of life is strong in us and there is an abundance of the fruit of the Holy Spirit, our leadership will be Christ-centered.

Part VI

Christ-Centered Gospels

Unfortunately, salvation has become a marketable package in our generation. Salvation is offered to people as something they accept as if it were a bag of groceries. Jesus is to be "accepted as Savior" (whatever that means) and a new mark put on the score board, a tick added to the prayer list. We are all to do church in a certain way, behave in a certain way, speak in a certain way, pray in a certain way, preach in a certain way, and undoubtedly die in a certain way. But I tell you this as a certainty: Jesus will not be boxed in or contained within the confines of our theology—nor in any other box or confinement.

I am persuaded that the enemy of our souls will do everything that he possibly can to deflect us away from being Christ-centered and, in so doing, he will turn Christianity—a love relationship with Jesus—into a set of beliefs, or rules, or a form of orthodoxy. The enemy of our souls will do everything that he possibly can to make us comfortable so that we have no hunger for a deeper relationship with Jesus. He will do everything he possibly can to stop us from reading Scripture as Christ-centered.

The idea that that the four gospel writers were all evangelists is too silly for words. (How I wish that people would not believe what is traditionally repeatedly said without first properly checking it for themselves. How I wish that Bible translators would not insert headings into the text that do not belong there.) Christ-centeredness could never believe that that the gospel writers were evangelists. What Christ-centeredness knows as a certainty is that the four gospel writers were

333

proclaimers. They were proclaiming King Jesus, each in his own way. The gospels are Christ-centered. The gospel writers all present King Jesus. We will shortly look at some examples of how Mark presented King Jesus, but first we will go to John's gospel.

"Now Jesus did many other signs in the presence of his disciples, which are not written in this book. But these are written so that you may come to believe that Jesus is the Messiah, the Son of God, and that through believing you may have life in his name" (John 20:30–31).

I used to read these verses in a particular way, because it seemed that everybody did. And if everyone does so, it must be the right way to read them. I used to read them like this: Now Jesus did many other signs in the presence of his disciples, which are not written in this book. But these are written so that you may *come to believe* that Jesus is the Messiah, the Son of God, and that through *believing* you may have life in his name.

My emphasis was on the words "come to believe" and "believing," because John was deemed to be an evangelist, so it was the "right" way to read it. However, Christ-centeredness takes a different emphasis, because John was writing to a church that was being ripped apart from the inside and whose people were totally confused by the many "Christs" that were vying for their attention and loyalty.

So, the Christ-centered verses read like this: Now Jesus did many other signs in the presence of his disciples, which are not written in this book. But these are written so that you may come to believe that *Jesus* is the Messiah, the Son of God, and that through believing you may have life in *his* name.

Now the emphasis is on the person of Jesus, as it should be. John was pointing to Jesus and proclaiming that he alone was the Christ, the Messiah. Christ-centeredness says that John's gospel was written to reveal King Jesus, as in indeed were the other three gospels. Each gospel writer had his own particular emphasis, because each was showing King Jesus in a particular way. A careful study of each of the Gospels with this in mind would reveal their individual kingly emphasis. The starting foundation looks something like this:

Matthew portrayed Jesus as king in law. Jesus fulfilled the Law, brought in the new covenant, showed the covenant outworking, and demonstrated by words and actions that he had personally fulfilled the Law.

Mark showed Jesus as king in power. Jesus showed "the Way" and the "suffering servant" who suffered rejection by religious leaders and family. Mark's gospel is the "immediate" action gospel.

Luke saw Jesus as king in salvation healing. Jesus was the man of joy, of fellowship, and of human origin who ate meals with people.

John portrayed Jesus as king in control. Jesus was the Word of God and the mystery of God. He was one with God and was humanity and divinity in union as he moved in the way he knew he must go.

A further examination of the Gospels will reveal each gospel writer's key words and insights, all of which point to Jesus, proclaim Jesus, and reveal him as God incarnate. Just as the overall theme of the Scriptures is "Covenant Relationship," so the gospel writers showed that, although the overall theme hadn't changed in the new covenant Scriptures, it had become personal to the man Jesus. He was the center. He is the center.

The Gospels present the revelation that Jesus the Christ really is the very center of everything, that everything revolves around him and is focused on him, and that everything testifies about him and points to him, whether it realizes it or not.

This is what Scripture is all about: Jesus the Christ, God-revealed. Let us now move into Mark's gospel and see some examples of how Mark is Christ-centered.

> The beginning of the good news of Jesus Christ, the Son of God. As it is written in the prophet Isaiah, "See, I am sending my messenger ahead of you, who will prepare your way; the voice of one crying out in the wilderness: 'Prepare the way of the Lord, make his paths straight,'" John the baptizer appeared in the wilderness, proclaiming a baptism of repentance for the forgiveness of sins. And people from the whole Judean countryside and all the people of Jerusalem were going out to him, and were baptized by him in the river Jordan, confessing their sins. Now John was clothed with camel's hair, with a

leather belt around his waist, and he ate locusts and wild honey. He proclaimed, "The one who is more powerful than I is coming after me; I am not worthy to stoop down and untie the thong of his sandals. I have baptized you with water; but he will baptize you with the Holy Spirit." In those days Jesus came from Nazareth of Galilee and was baptized by John in the Jordan. And just as he was coming up out of the water, he saw the heavens torn apart and the Spirit descending like a dove on him. And a voice came from heaven, "You are my Son, the Beloved; with you I am well pleased." And the Spirit immediately drove him out into the wilderness. He was in the wilderness forty days, tempted by Satan; and he was with the wild beasts; and the angels waited on him. (Mark 1:1–13)

It is very likely that Mark got most of his information from Peter, and therefore, in a very real sense, Mark's gospel is really the gospel according to Peter. Mark's gospel was almost certainly written to Christians in Rome, and that would explain why Mark took time to explain Jewish terms and customs to his readers. There would have been no such need if he had been writing to Jews. Furthermore, Mark used several Latin words, some of which are not found anywhere else in the new covenant Scriptures. Mark referred to the old covenant Scriptures far less often than any other gospel writer. Mark also never used the word *law*, which was frequently used by the other gospel writers. Mark also used the Roman way of telling the time. Mark was clearly writing to people who were familiar with terms like baptize and Holy Spirit, because he made no attempt to explain them or their significance. He also assumed that his readers were familiar with Jesus' background and the major events of his life, and he assumed also that they did not need him to explain about John the Baptist.

Mark began his gospel (good news) in the same way that the books of Genesis and John begin: "Beginning." The first verse is the title that describes the whole of the gospel. The whole of Mark's gospel is but the beginning of the gospel that is Jesus the Christ, the Son of God.

Mark's gospel starts and ends with God and is focused on Jesus. For Mark, the gospel wasn't about Jesus; the gospel was Jesus. Mark's gospel set forth the way of Jesus. In Mark 1:2, the word *way* is translated from the Greek *hodos*. Mark used this Greek word quite deliberately and more than once (Mark 8:27; 9:33–34; 10:32, 52). Mark had no time for unnecessary details in his gospel. He was too busy tracing this 'way'. It was the way of Jesus, and only Jesus could lead the way. The whole call and purpose of Mark's gospel was to meet this Jesus for yourself. Mark *was* evangelizing, but not in our modern understanding of the word. The Greek word for evangelize was used commonly for proclamations, such as:

- news of victory from the battlefield
- events related to the emperor, e.g., births, coming of age, and accession
- the endings of wars and the establishment of social order and benefits

Mark proclaimed victory! Mark's proclamations were related to the king—Jesus! Mark proclaimed the ending of internal war and the establishment of a new social order with great benefits! Mark's clarion call was for his readers to meet this Jesus for themselves personally. Throughout Mark's gospel, we continually ask: What will Jesus do next in us? What will Jesus do next in our midst?

The Jewish religious leaders would have said that only Gentile converts and sinners were defiled and therefore needed to be baptized, but Mark has John calling all Israel to be baptized. Down through the centuries, the children of Israel had been waiting for God's prophet, the next one in line who would speak for YHWH and bring forth his word. But Mark recounted that in John the Baptist there had come quite a remarkable change of emphasis. John the Baptist was not pointing heavenward to YHWH; he was pointing earthward to the man Jesus. Since Mark was writing to Gentiles, he did not belabor the old covenant connection. But to those who explored the connection, the old covnant Scriptures would have made fascinating reading.

Mark's gospel had its beginning in the desert wilderness, and he told us nothing of Jesus' birth, background, or pedigree. For Mark, the story of Jesus began with baptism. Indeed, Jesus was totally anonymous. He has to be pointed out by John the Baptist. Neither did Mark get involved in the theology of why Jesus was baptized; he simply told us about it. Water baptism was the physical declaration of relationship with God through Jesus. Water baptism was the outer manifestation of the inner reality. Through water baptism, Jesus publicly declared that he was not living for himself but for his Father in heaven. Such a declaration had to be tested and proved in experience, and when Jesus came up out of the water, all heaven broke loose!

Mark was clear that his account was not about our access to God but about God's access to us. He was coming, ready or not! Mark described the Spirit as one who descended *like* a dove, not as a dove. It was a dove-like descent, but he was not a dove-like Spirit. Mark recorded the Father's approval of Jesus in the personal pronoun: "You are my Son"—not "this is my Son." Mark's focus was on Jesus, and he called his readers to meet Jesus for themselves. But that has important consequences for us, because Jesus is the anointed one of God who is anointed by the Spirit of explosive power (*dunamis*). There's no sugary sweetness in Mark's gospel, no "meek, mild Jesus child." Jesus spoke with authority and acted in power. That was the Jesus that Mark called us to meet for ourselves, and it goes without saying that meeting this Jesus will change our lives forever!

As Jesus was coming up out of the water, heaven was ripped apart, and it would never be closed again. Once again, this is a very forceful word that that suggests that heaven was torn into little pieces beyond the ability of anyone to repair. Heaven was torn open, but only Jesus saw this happen. Mark began his gospel in the desert, but he also began it with the prophecy that was being fulfilled before their very eyes. In the old covenant, the desert (wilderness) was the setting for the showdown between God and Satan. And it still is for you and me! Comfortable places and good days are not where we prove our relationship with Jesus; it is in the desert wilderness during the dry, hard, and lonely times. This is the way of God. This is the only occasion in Mark where the narrator told us that Scripture was here being fulfilled. In the rest of his gospel, Mark had Jesus saying it himself.

Mark took several old covenant quotations and blended them together as one quotation (apparently) from Isaiah. This was a common practice in a culture of oral tradition. The texts that Mark used are from Exodus 23:20, Malachi 3:1, and Isaiah 40:3—the Law and the prophets (including both major and minor prophets). This was a critically important moment in the history of the world, so the Holy Spirit drove Jesus out into the desert wilderness. Mark recorded the explosiveness of the Spirit in the word translated "drove." This is a powerful and dynamic word that means "forcibly shoved." This was no urging; this was forcible shoving. This was not the action of a dove-like Spirit. Indeed, Mark had a lot to teach us about the explosive nature of the kingdom.

The wilderness was where the open heaven would be tested and proved, where the eternal relationship would be tested and proved. That is why there must be a desert wilderness experience for you and me. The children of Israel failed to prove their eternal relationship and wandered in the desert wilderness for forty years. Jesus proved his eternal relationship over forty days in the desert, and he has shown us how to do it too.

The desert wilderness experience is very important, because, what Mark only hints at, Luke says explicitly: "Jesus, full of the Holy Spirit, returned from the Jordan and was led by the Spirit in the wilderness, where for forty days he was tempted by the devil … Then Jesus, filled with the power of the Spirit, returned to Galilee" (Luke 4:1–2, 14).

When Jesus becomes merely "the nice man in heaven," the desert wilderness becomes a place to be avoided. But if you or I will not go into the desert wilderness, then the desert wilderness will come to us. It must! And it will. Because only in the desert wilderness will testing and proving of relationship be completed. After the desert wilderness, Satan would never again be able to personally tempt Jesus to be diverted from the way. It is to be the same for you and me. After our own baptism in water, there will be a time in the desert wilderness.

But wandering aimlessly in the desert wilderness (like the children of Israel did) is not the same as being led by the Holy Spirit into the desert wilderness of testing and proving. As surely as the Holy Spirit led Jesus through the desert wilderness, so the Holy Spirit will lead us through the desert wilderness, if we work with him. If we are yielded and following Jesus, there is no other way. Mark told us that Jesus was not alone. He had angels with him, though he had no human companionship as he made his way through the desert wilderness. But we are in the way together. Don't choose to try and go it alone.

Mark's prologue is an explosive prologue. Where's John's prologue is mystical in nature, Mark's is explosive. It sets an explosive tone for the whole gospel that is to come. The Jewish religious leaders of Jesus' day did not begin to comprehend how this Jesus could be Messiah, the one who would explosively deliver Israel from bondage. Mark's gospel is explosive, but not the explosiveness they expected. Mark's explosive and extraordinary gospel begins with everyone hearing the call to repentance. And as explosive and extraordinary as John the Baptist was, he was speaking of another who would come after him.

John the Baptist effectively said of Jesus: "You ain't seen nothin' yet." John the Baptist was explosive enough in his dress code, his speech, and his actions, but he spoke of the one to come who was as far above him as the heavens are above the earth. John the Baptist said, "I baptize you with water, but he will baptize you with the Holy Spirit." He is far above all your thinking, far above all your imagining, far above all your believing.

This is the one Mark's gospel is about! In church today, this Jesus has been sanitized, disarmed, and made theologically correct. But Mark told us that Jesus is the Christ, the Son of God! And if you don't know this Jesus, then you don't know the real Jesus at all. He is an offense, a scandal, a stumbling-block. Do you really want to know this Jesus?

46

King and the Kingdom

> Now after John was arrested, Jesus came to Galilee, pro-
> claiming the good news of God, and saying, "The time
> is fulfilled, and the kingdom of God has come near;
> repent, and believe in the good news." As Jesus passed
> along the Sea of Galilee, he saw Simon and his brother
> Andrew casting a net into the sea—for they were fish-
> ermen. And Jesus said to them, "Follow me and I will
> make you fish for people." And immediately they left
> their nets and followed him. As he went a little farther,
> he saw James son of Zebedee and his brother John, who
> were in their boat mending the nets. Immediately he
> called them; and they left their father Zebedee in the
> boat with the hired men, and followed him. They went
> to Capernaum; and when the sabbath came, he entered
> the synagogue and taught. They were astounded at his
> teaching, for he taught them as one having authority,
> and not as the scribes. (Mark 1:14–22)

"After John was put in prison" is the NIVs translation, aimed at helping
us understand what has happened. The NRSV here says, "After John
was arrested." But neither of them is what the Greek actually says, which
is: "After John was handed over." Mark's "way" was full of references
to being "handed over," and John the Baptist was the forerunner who
was handed over first. (For more instances of the phrase "handed over,"

check out Mark 1:14; 3:19; 9:31; 10:33; 14:10–11, 21, 41–42, 44; 15:1, 15.) Since the words *prison* (NIV) and *arrested* (NRSV) do not appear in the Greek, Mark introduced a mystery here. Who handed John over? And to whom? The same mystery surrounded Jesus.

What does it mean that "the kingdom of God is near"? The kingdom of God was near because the king was present. The kingdom doesn't appoint a king; the king himself ushers in the kingdom. This King had won his victory in the desert wilderness, and the price of victory was paid at the cross. Jesus won the victory in the desert wilderness and then gave his disciples authority because of that victory. Jesus then saw his disciples enforce that victory. The King's kingdom was extended to all peoples through the cross, and the only way into the kingdom of God is Jesus.

What is happening in our world today, then, is not the battle between good and evil. That battle has already been won in Christ. Rather, it is the breaking in of the future into our present; it is the kingdom of God breaking through to our present reality; and it is the breaking up of our present order of things. To repent and believe the good news is to welcome God's kingdom by handing yourself over to God's King. The way of the kingdom is to hand yourself over to the King. Then you receive the kingdom of God as the kingdom of God receives you, and you become a part of it. For Mark, the kingdom of God is breaking in, breaking through, and breaking up. In verses 14 and 15, Mark began to introduce to us God's coming kingdom, which was breaking in, breaking through, and breaking up. The kingdom of God was near because the King was present. The kingdom of God is the future breaking into and through our present, and it is causing the breakup of that present.

John the Baptist came preaching a "baptism of repentance for the forgiveness of sins," but Jesus came to preach the "good news" of the kingdom of God. For Mark, Jesus' preaching characterized the kingdom of God breaking in, breaking through, and breaking up. Mark's gospel heralded a heavenly disruption of earth and, more significantly, a total disruption of the established order of things. Mark's "way" is full of references to the coming of God's new world. (Check out Mark 4:11, 26, 30; 9:1, 47; 10:14–15, 23–24; 12:34; 14:25; 15:43.) The Jewish people of Jesus' time would have had all sorts of ideas of what this might have meant. Mark made plain that they did not get what they expected, and they did not expect what they got! Therefore, Mark was clearly saying that God was not a mere spectator in human affairs and that his timing is not our timing.

We tend to think that the future should arise out of the present, but Mark is telling us that the future is now breaking into the present. Those who live by the present alone cannot see the future breaking in. Those whose eyes have been opened by the Spirit of God can see the future breaking into our present and the kingdom of God breaking through our present. Those whose eyes have been opened by the Spirit of God can see the breakup of the present order of things. This has cosmic significance!

Radical though all that was, Mark was just as radical as he moved on to the people's reaction to Jesus' teaching. But first, Jesus called his disciples. This was radical in itself, because it was normally the disciples who chose a rabbi. They would normally seek after the rabbi whose presentation of himself impressed them the most. However, Jesus called each of his disciples individually and told them, "Follow me." The prophets of old pointed to YHWH and told the people to follow him, but Jesus pointed to himself and said, "Follow me." This was no ordinary prophet or teacher! The people at large were stunned, because Jesus didn't speak about God; he spoke for God. Indeed, it was even more radical than that: Jesus spoke *as* God.

Jesus preached to the crowds, but he called the individual to follow him. In old covenant times, only YHWH could do that, as it was the right of God alone. No wonder the Jews accused Jesus of blasphemy and asked, "Who does this man think he is?" Mark's account of the calling of the disciples is an explosive and fast-moving account. He did not bother with background or explanation. Jesus spoke and it was so. God himself did that at creation, and only God could do that! Who was this Jesus?

When the King spoke, the kingdom was the result. Becoming a disciple of Jesus was not a human idea or initiative; it was a direct response to God's call in Christ. And the only qualification anyone needs is the willingness to follow. We are to be participators in the kingdom of God, not spectators of it. For Mark, discipleship was all or nothing. It was Mark who recorded Peter's statement, "We have left everything to follow you" (Mark 10:28). No amount of theological training can ever replace the experience of following Jesus personally, because discipleship means learning from Jesus and handing ourselves over to him. But all too often we want God to submit to us and do things our way.

The King taught with great authority—not "I know what I am talking about" but "I know who I am talking about." Knowing God is a lifelong experience, and we need to know the one we are talking about or we will have no authority. Here Mark introduced us to the astonished people's reactions to Jesus' teaching, simply by telling us that it was so, but then he went on to give us tremendous examples of what he was talking about. The King is among us, he was saying. Just listen to the things he said and see the things he did! And so Mark moved on to give us specific examples of the future kingdom of God breaking in, breaking through, and breaking up. In writing to Christians in Rome (Europeans), Mark told us to look at our own lives from this new perspective and begin to see afresh the wondrous purposes of God.

> They went to Capernaum; and when the sabbath came, he entered the synagogue and taught. They were astounded at his teaching, for he taught them as one having authority, and not as the scribes. Just then there was in their synagogue a man with an unclean spirit, and he cried out, "What have you to do with us, Jesus of Nazareth? Have you come to destroy us? I know who you are, the Holy One of God." But Jesus rebuked him, saying, "Be silent, and come out of him!" And the unclean spirit, convulsing him and crying with a loud voice, came out of him. They were all amazed, and they kept on asking one another, "What is this? A new teaching—with authority! He commands even the unclean spirits, and they obey him." At once his fame began to spread throughout the surrounding region of Galilee. (Mark 1:21–28)

Capernaum was a town on the northwest shore of the Sea of Galilee, and it was Jesus' ministry base, his headquarters for the ministry in Galilee. Mark began his account of the Galilean ministry by telling us that Jesus established himself in Capernaum. In Scripture, it is mentioned only in the gospels, yet it was a town of considerable size and importance. How do we know?

- It had a tax collector's office (Mark 2:14).
- A high officer of King Herod Antipas had his office there.
- That high officer built a synagogue there (Matthew 8:5–13; Luke 7:1–10).
- Jesus performed many striking miracles there, such as: the centurion's servant (Matthew 8:5–13), the paralytic lowered through the roof (Mark 2:1–13), and the nobleman's son (John 4:46-54).
- In Capernaum Jesus called Matthew from his tax booth (Matthew 9:9–13).
- Many of Jesus' teachings and discourses were delivered there (Mark 9:33–50).

Because the people of the town did not repent, Jesus foretold the complete ruin of Capernaum (Matthew 11:23–24; Luke 10:15). The town was indeed utterly destroyed, and today we do not even know where the site was. The life we live isn't permanent, and neither is the place or society in which we live. Even the institution of church isn't permanent. Yet we so often live as if all these things and more were permanent. It is our union with God that is permanent, yet we often live as if it had still to happen.

After the desert wilderness temptation, notice where Jesus' first clash with the Enemy took place: in the place of worship! Mark's explosive and action-packed gospel opened with Jesus facing the Enemy—and it was no contest. Mark's opening told us that something of cosmic significance was going on. His emphasis was on the authority of Jesus— his authority over the kingdom of darkness and the authority in which Jesus taught and spoke. When Jesus spoke, things happened! This is the characteristic of YHWH himself. When the man in the synagogue interrupted Jesus, Jesus didn't deal with that man. He dealt with the one who had really interrupted him. Jesus cast the demons out of the place of worship, the holy place, on two levels: out of the synagogue and out of the man.

It is the latter that held great significance for the people of Jesus' day. Here was a man—Jesus—displaying the kind of authority that belonged to YHWH alone. The demons' presence in the man in the synagogue was declaring that nowhere was sacred, but Jesus' action declared that everywhere was sacred. Jesus' action declared that YHWH was in the midst of his people again. YHWH Shammah! The people didn't recognize the face (Jesus), but the authority was familiar. Come, the Sabbath (God's day)! Come, the synagogue (God's people)! Come, the presence (God's man)!

47

Explosion!

As soon as they left the synagogue, they entered the house of Simon and Andrew, with James and John. Now Simon's mother-in-law was in bed with a fever, and they told [Jesus] about her at once. He came and took her by the hand and lifted her up. Then the fever left her, and she began to serve them. That evening, at sundown, they brought to him all who were sick or possessed with demons. And the whole city was gathered around the door. And he cured many who were sick with various diseases, and cast out many demons; and he would not permit the demons to speak, because they knew him. (Mark 1:29–34)

This story begins with "as soon as." The immediacy of Mark is here again. Notice too how the disciples told Jesus about Simon's mother. They told him about her at once—Mark's immediacy again. In order to fully understand why Mark told this story, we need to explore the background a little. In our culture, much of the significance of what happened here is lost, so we need to go back into the old covenant to discover the context. Understanding that context will help us to realize the power of Mark's account here.

In Jesus' day, many people believed that fever was an illness in and of itself, rather than the symptom of disease. This also had theological significance, because many people further believed that fever was an illness that was sent from God as a punishment or chastisement.

"But if you will not obey me, and do not observe all these commandments, if you spurn my statutes, and abhor my ordinances, so that you will not observe all my commandments, and you break my covenant, I in turn will do this to you: I will bring terror on you; consumption and fever that waste the eyes and cause life to pine away" (Leviticus 26:14–16).

"The LORD will afflict you with consumption, fever, inflammation, with fiery heat and drought, and with blight and mildew; they shall pursue you until you perish" (Deuteronomy 28:22).

The finality of these pronouncements meant that, in the people's eyes, no human being could do anything about illnesses such as fever. Only YHWH could put out the fire, because it was believed that it was YHWH who had lit the fire. Mark was therefore making it clear that the cause of the fever was indeed supernatural and not physical, and therefore only YHWH could deal with it. But Mark is clear that God was not the cause of the fever, though he would be the cure of it. Jesus did not say anything to Simon's mother-in-law. Instead he did something he should never have done. Jesus touched her. He took the hand of Simon's mother-in-law, and the fever "left her." The NRSV and NIV translations have been watered down considerably. What the verse actually says is that the fever forsook her; it let go of her; it gave her up. In other words, *it handed her over*. Here Mark has given us another example of "handing over."

Mark was making it clear that the cause of the fever was supernatural, not physical, and that only YHWH could deal with it. Therefore, the fever handed her over because of the authority of YHWH working through this man Jesus. This kind of authority belongs to YHWH alone. Yet here was this man Jesus, exercising exactly that kind of authority. Who was this man? The completeness of Peter's mother-in-law's deliverance was shown by the fact that she immediately served them, but this really should be seen as a response to Jesus rather than as a (female's) duty. Indeed, Mark showed us what she was actually doing here: she was handing herself over to Jesus. Yet again, Mark has given us an example of "handing over." Simon's mother-in-law did not serve them because she was a woman. She served Jesus because she handed herself over to the one who showed the authority of YHWH by delivering her from the fever.

The Sabbath ended in the evening, and on that evening, at sundown, as soon as the Sabbath was over, people brought to Jesus all who were sick or possessed with demons. The whole city was gathered around the door. He cured many who were sick with various diseases, and cast out many demons; and he would not permit the demons to speak, because they knew him. The significance for the communities around Jesus was that Jesus consistently did the things that only YHWH could do. All the diseases handed the people over. All the demons handed the people over. The future kingdom of God was breaking in, breaking through, and breaking up.

This was not about healings or deliverances in and of themselves. It was about a mighty outpouring of YHWH's authority that disrupted the fabric of the universe in that localized area. The evidence was all around. The kingdom of God was near because the King was there.

In our communities and churches today, Jesus will do the things that only YHWH can do. And he will do them through you and me, and in you and me. In our lives, the kingdom is breaking in, breaking through, and breaking up. The kingdom of God is near because the King is near. And that is precisely why Mark's consistent call is for us his readers to hand ourselves over to Jesus.

48

I Am Willing

A leper came to him begging him, and kneeling he said
to him, "If you choose, you can make me clean." Moved
with pity, Jesus stretched out his hand and touched
him, and said to him, "I do choose. Be made clean!"
Immediately the leprosy left him, and he was made clean.
After sternly warning him he sent him away at once, saying to him, "See that you say nothing to anyone; but go,
show yourself to the priest, and offer for your cleansing
what Moses commanded, as a testimony to them." But
he went out and began to proclaim it freely, and to spread
the word, so that Jesus could no longer go into a town
openly, but stayed out in the country; and people came
to him from every quarter. (Mark 1:40–45)

The order in which Mark tells his stories is quite deliberate and reveals
Mark's purpose, though the reason he tells us this story is not immediately
obvious. It is true that the man may not have had actual leprosy, since
the name applied to a number of skin diseases in those days. It is also
true that in the old covenant the healing of leprosy was entirely in the
hands of YHWH alone. The leper was religiously impure, an outcast
who was not to come anywhere near "clean" people. Leprosy was viewed
as a process of turning a person into a living corpse, and only YHWH
could raise the dead. Therefore, Mark was giving us another example of
YHWH's authority demonstrated in Jesus. But there is more.

The man with leprosy broke religious rules by drawing near to Jesus when he should have stayed well away from everybody. Jesus broke religious rules by touching the leper, when he should have sent him away immediately or had him punished. In Jesus' day, almost everyone would have viewed the leper as a sinner who was getting his just deserts from God. Jesus broke religious tradition by healing the man without making any reference to sin. For the Jews of Jesus' day, this would have been unthinkable, for the man was obviously a sinner! But the man drew near and said "if you are willing," not "if you can." Consider the beauty of that! Even this outcast leper had already heard enough about Jesus to go to him. (See Mark 1:28, 33, 37.) Jesus was already well-known, which was why the leper came. And this religiously impure, religiously disobedient, law-breaking outcast said to Jesus, "If you are willing."

Mark's record of Jesus' response is quite remarkable, for there are two readings of verse 41: (1) Jesus was filled with compassion and (2) Jesus was angry. Don't be bound by having to accept only one reading. They can both be true. Compassion for a human being leads to anger at the kingdom of darkness leads to action.

Jesus responded to the call, "if you are willing," with the explosive command, "Be clean!" But it isn't addressed primarily to the man. The way that Jesus spoke here is not the way that Jesus ever spoke to people. Rather, it is exactly the way that Jesus showed the authority of YHWH to the kingdom of darkness. It is exactly the way that Jesus spoke to demons.

Why did Jesus say to the man, "See that you don't tell this to anyone"? It wasn't for Jesus' benefit at all. It was for the leper's own good. Once the healing was proved to be real, then would be the time for testimony, but not until then. Testimony given too soon heaps unnecessary pressure on those who testify:

- before they have had chance to work it through
- before others have seen the clear evidence
- because it all too easily draws attention to people instead of Jesus

When God has worked profoundly in someone's life, that person needs one or two other people to draw near to him to help him work through what has happened. The purpose of miracles is that we might know God better, draw near to him, and hand ourselves over to him. Draw near to Jesus. He is willing! Let him do what only he can do! Hand yourself over to him.

49

The Silent Paralytic

When [Jesus] returned to Capernaum after some days, it was reported that he was at home. So many gathered around that there was no longer room for them, not even in front of the door; and he was speaking the word to them. Then some people came, bringing to him a paralyzed man, carried by four of them. And when they could not bring him to Jesus because of the crowd, they removed the roof above him; and after having dug through it, they let down the mat on which the paralytic lay. When Jesus saw their faith, he said to the paralytic, "Son, your sins are forgiven."

Now some of the scribes were sitting there, questioning in their hearts, "Why does this fellow speak in this way? It is blasphemy! Who can forgive sins but God alone?" At once Jesus perceived in his spirit that they were discussing these questions among themselves; and he said to them, "Why do you raise such questions in your hearts? Which is easier, to say to the paralytic, 'Your sins are forgiven,' or to say, 'Stand up and take your mat and walk'? But so that you may know that the Son of Man has authority on earth to forgive sins"—he said to the paralytic—"I say to you, stand up, take your mat and go to your home." And he stood up, and immediately took the mat and went out before all of them; so that they were all amazed and glorified God, saying, "We have never seen anything like this!" (Mark 2:1–12)

One of the most remarkable things about this account is that the paralytic man, who was central to the story, never said a word. At the beginning of chapter two, Mark told us that Jesus had "come home" to Capernaum, where he and the disciples were based. The crowds were still crushing in around Jesus, and there was still no room to move.

In those days, houses were made of rough, igneous rock (compacted fire lava) without mortar, which could support little more than a sloping, thatched roof consisting of wooden crossbeams overlaid with matted reeds, branches, and dried mud. This roof had to be renewed every autumn before the winter rains set in, and it would not have been difficult to break through the roof or to repair it afterward.

When Jesus saw the faith of those who had dug through the roof, he said to the paralytic, "Son, your sins are forgiven." While Mark had little interest in medical matters (Luke would pick those up later), he once again reported Jesus doing what only YHWH could do: forgiving sin. But Jesus was not treating the symptom. He was treating the cause. Mark was giving us yet more evidence that Jesus is God incarnate.

One of the most significant aspects of a person's healing is that it is very often made possible through the healing of relationships. While this man did not ask, "Why should this happen to me?" he did learn where healing and forgiveness was to be found.

During the Middle Ages when there was no health service, sick people often came to the church for help, but all they got was blame. The common response was: "You have sinned and God is afflicting you. Thank him, and you will suffer so much less torment in the life to come." We would never make that mistake, would we?

When the people had gathered so that there was no room left, not even outside the door, Jesus "preached the word to them." Does that surprise you? In previous crowd scenes, Jesus had healed the sick, cast out demons, and preached in synagogues, but here was Jesus preaching the Word to the crowds around him. Why? Surely there is something here of how Jesus invests in everyone's lives by speaking the Word and having the Spirit thereby test the response that the seed gets. Jesus made a difference then—and also in the days that followed—because he invested his Word in people. That Word is never wasted, and it will not return empty, though it may take a long time to return.

The explosive nature of Mark's gospel is not diluted at all by Mark telling us that Jesus preached the Word, because Mark had already told us that when Jesus spoke, things happened. Mark had already told us that in Jesus lived the authority of YHWH himself. The kingdom of God was breaking in, breaking through, and breaking up, and the seed invested through Jesus' Word would ensure that it continued to break in, break through, and break up in the days, months, and years to come. No wonder, then, that the crowds were amazed, because they had never seen anyone like Jesus. In the days to come, may the communities in which we live, work, and play praise God and say, "We have never seen anything like this!"

50

The Doctor Calls

Jesus went out again beside the sea; the whole crowd gathered around him, and he taught them. As he was walking along, he saw Levi son of Alphaeus sitting at the tax booth, and he said to him, "Follow me." And he got up and followed him. And as he sat at dinner in Levi's house, many tax collectors and sinners were also sitting with Jesus and his disciples—for there were many who followed him. When the scribes of the Pharisees saw that he was eating with sinners and tax collectors, they said to his disciples, "Why does he eat with tax collectors and sinners?" When Jesus heard this, he said to them, "Those who are well have no need of a physician, but those who are sick; I have come to call not the righteous but sinners." (Mark 2:13–17)

Up to this point, a hallmark of this gospel is Mark's use of the word *immediately*, which is translated in various ways by different versions, thus effectively obscuring Mark's hallmark. Although Mark did not actually use this word in relation to the call of Levi, it is inherent in Levi's response, for he "got up and followed him." Jesus' call was responded to immediately.

Tax collectors had tax booths or offices where they collected tolls, tariffs, imposts, and customs duties on behalf of Herod Antipas. They were renowned for their dishonesty and extortion, since they habitually collected more money than they were due, did not always display the regulations that told travelers how much they were to pay, and often made false valuations of goods—as well as accusing people of tax evasion. Levi's booth was positioned at an important intersection of trade routes to get the maximum traffic and therefore the maximum income.

Lepers and sinners were called by Jesus to be his disciples, but religious leaders were not. By getting up and following Jesus, Levi severed his past life completely. Fishermen could always go back to fishing, and indeed some did do so later, but there was no way back for a tax collector who abandoned his post. Levi's action had a remarkable result, for Mark told us that, while Jesus was having dinner at Levi's house, many tax collectors and "sinners" were eating with him. But Jesus was doing far more than preaching at these sinners. He was befriending them! And the Pharisees were appalled.

It is not the healthy who need a doctor, but the sick. Don't misunderstand Jesus, here. He was not saying that tax collectors and sinners were sick but that religious leaders (Pharisees) were healthy. No! Jesus was saying that everyone was sick, but that not everyone would go to the doctor. And even when the doctor called, some of the sick refused his help.

In church, we all too easily and all too often believe that we who have "accepted Jesus" are healthy and that the sinners outside are sick. Nothing could be further from the truth. The "doctor" comes near to heal, not to discuss the plights of others. We all need healing, but we are not all willing to receive it. And if we say that we are healthy and do not need the doctor, then we put ourselves in the same situation as the Pharisees. The question is not: "Do you need healing?" Of course, we all need healing. The question is: "Will you receive healing?" And Mark clearly showed us that we receive healing by receiving the healer, Jesus. The doctor calls. Will you receive him?

> Now John's disciples and the Pharisees were fasting; and people came and said to him, "Why do John's disciples and the disciples of the Pharisees fast, but your disciples do not fast?" Jesus said to them, "The wedding guests cannot fast while the bridegroom is with them, can they? As long as they have the bridegroom with them,

they cannot fast. The days will come when the bridegroom is taken away from them, and then they will fast
on that day. No one sews a piece of unshrunk cloth on
an old cloak; otherwise, the patch pulls away from it,
the new from the old, and a worse tear is made. And no
one puts new wine into old wineskins; otherwise, the
wine will burst the skins, and the wine is lost, and so are
the skins; but one puts new wine into fresh wineskins."
(Mark 2:18–22)

Jesus now faced a question about religious observance. His answer
to the question seemed to be a deliberate avoidance of the issue, but it
is not. Consider the question carefully. They asked why Jesus' disciples
did not fast, but they did not ask why Jesus himself did not fast. Jesus'
response is very interesting, and leads to fascinating conclusions:

- The kingdom of God—which is breaking in, breaking through,
  and breaking up—is not a funeral wake but a wedding party.
- The new cannot be married to the old.
- The new cannot be understood in the context of the old.
- The old has no part in the new.

Jesus is not a reformer; he is a transformer. The new comes through
the old. The kingdom of God breaks up the old, and Mark's gospel is
hallmarked by ripping or tearing:

- heaven torn open at Jesus' baptism (Mark 1:10).
- tearing of cloth (Mark 2:21).
- tearing of wineskins (Mark 2:22).
- Caiaphas' tearing of his garment because of Jesus' claims
  (Mark 14:63)
- temple veil torn in two at Jesus' crucifixion (Mark 15:38)

Mark didn't just say it; he demonstrated it. Authority was torn from
the kingdom of darkness. Initiative was torn from the religious leaders.
Love was torn from the hands of the law.

We must understand that the fasting of Judaism was:

- related to the fear of demons, as it was believed that demons could be warded off by fasting.
- used to gain "brownie points" through the act of self-renunciation.
- used to atone for sins and to avoid further disaster coming upon the sinner.
- used to humiliate oneself before God and to win his favor.
- used as a badge of piety that showed people how spiritual one was.
- connected to the sorrow of bereavement because of the death of a loved one.

All of these belong to the old order of things. But the new had come! Do not misunderstand Jesus. He was not saying that we should never fast at all. Fasting has its time, place, and benefit. Jesus was altogether more radical in his meaning. He was asking, "Why do you want to eat the food of the old kingdom when the new kingdom is here?" The old kingdom was bondage, but when the Son set a person free, that person was free indeed! The old kingdom consisted of a polluted mind, but we are now to think about whatever is true, whatever is noble, whatever is right, whatever is pure, whatever is lovely, and whatever is admirable. The old kingdom was death, but Jesus came to give us a full and overflowing life.

The real purpose of fasting is to wean us off the old and introduce us to the new. When we are being filled with new things, we will fast from the old things. If we really want the new things, we will fast from the old things. Fasting from old things will reduce our appetites for them. We shouldn't merely fast from the old; we should fast to the new. Make this personal! Whether you eat or drink or fast, or whatever you do, do it all for the glory of God.

> One sabbath he was going through the grainfields; and
> as they made their way his disciples began to pluck heads
> of grain. The Pharisees said to him, "Look, why are they

doing what is not lawful on the sabbath?" And he said to them, "Have you never read what David did when he and his companions were hungry and in need of food? He entered the house of God, when Abiathar was high priest, and ate the bread of the Presence, which it is not lawful for any but the priests to eat, and he gave some to his companions." Then he said to them, "The sabbath was made for humankind, and not humankind for the sabbath; so the Son of Man is lord even of the sabbath."

Again he entered the synagogue, and a man was there who had a withered hand. They watched him to see whether he would cure him on the sabbath, so that they might accuse him. And he said to the man who had the withered hand, "Come forward." Then he said to them, "Is it lawful to do good or to do harm on the sabbath, to save life or to kill?" But they were silent. He looked around at them with anger; he was grieved at their hardness of heart and said to the man, "Stretch out your hand." He stretched it out, and his hand was restored. The Pharisees went out and immediately conspired with the Herodians against him, how to destroy him. (Mark 2:23–3:6)

It is somewhat ironic that the Pharisees should accuse God himself of breaking his own religious laws—if, of course, that was what Jesus actually did. Technically speaking, the religious people were finding fault with Jesus' disciples rather than with Jesus himself, but their actions would have been seen to reflect badly upon their rabbi. The law permitted anyone, especially the poor, to pluck ears of grain in a neighbor's field of standing grain, as long as they didn't take a sickle to it (Deuteronomy 23:25). Nevertheless, the Pharisees were classifying Jesus' disciples' action as unlawful. But Jesus did not argue their interpretation of the law. Note the undercurrents that Mark reveals to us.

- The Pharisees believed that Jesus was blaspheming (Mark 2:7).
- The Pharisees accuses Jesus through his disciples (Mark 2:16).

- The Pharisees accused the disciples through Jesus (Mark 2:18).
- The Pharisees again accused the disciples through Jesus (Mark 2:24).
- The Pharisees looked for a reason to accuse Jesus (Mark 3:2).
- The Pharisees plotted to kill Jesus (Mark 3:6).

But the Pharisees completely miss the irony here. God himself had come in the flesh, and he was apparently openly flouting his own religious laws! The Pharisees didn't believe that Jesus was God, but they certainly believed that Jesus was flouting religious laws. Consider the irony here. It was unlawful for Jesus to heal on the Sabbath, but apparently the Pharisees could plot to kill Jesus on the Sabbath! Church history makes it clear that the Pharisees did not have a monopoly on legalism!

What was the Sabbath for? Consider the account of creation in Genesis. Look at God's reaction to the finished creation. He rested. Why did God rest from creating? Was he all tuckered out? Was he shattered? Was he out of breath? No! God rested from work in order to be present with his people. And that—not religious observance—is what the Sabbath is for. The Sabbath was given to people so that God could be present with his people. We are not an afterthought in creation. We are the crowning glory of God's creation. He didn't make people until the rest of creation was fit and ready for them to live in. And when he had made his crowning glory, he wanted to be with them. The Sabbath rest is the manifest presence of God.

> Jesus departed with his disciples to the sea, and a great multitude from Galilee followed him; hearing all that he was doing, they came to him in great numbers from Judea, Jerusalem, Idumea, beyond the Jordan, and the region around Tyre and Sidon. He told his disciples to have a boat ready for him because of the crowd, so that they would not crush him; for he had cured many, so that all who had diseases pressed upon him to touch him. Whenever the unclean spirits saw him, they fell down before him and shouted, "You are the Son of

God!" But he sternly ordered them not to make him known. (Mark 3:7–12)

Jesus' fame seemed to be spreading out of control, and there was nothing he could do about it except to have a way of escape at the ready. The multitude's reaction to Jesus says a lot about him, but it also says a huge amount about how fed-up the people were with the legalistic religion of the Jewish religious leaders. Mark also brought to our attention the reactions of unclean spirits to Jesus, as he summarized the acts of Jesus and brought in themes from earlier parts of the gospel. Jesus could no longer get away from the immense popularity that had gathered around him, and the Son of God was only too well aware of the dangers of fame with crowds whose excitement was fuelled by that popularity. They wanted a hero, and they thought they had one.

The crowds were now coming from a huge geographical area, and this meant that Jesus would find it harder than ever to escape the multitude. As the crowds found him, any semblance of order was lost. The sick and downcast no longer waited for his touch but threw themselves upon him. This exuberant crush of people stood in stark contrast to the grim verdict of the teachers of the Law from Jerusalem. It also explains why those leaders were so worried about Jesus. His surging popularity threatened to undermine their authority over the crowds. The Jewish teachers of the Law were in great danger of losing their control. This was bad enough, but there was Rome to consider.

The unclean spirits continued to know Jesus immediately—that special word used by Mark—and fell before him in surrender, blurting out his identity. Unlike the demon who hailed him as the "Holy One of God," their frequent cry of recognition acknowledged him as "the Son of God" and more closely echoed the heavenly voice at his baptism. The demons uttered an apparently orthodox confession, but they were by no means "well pleased" by the presence of the Son of God. This alone should make us realize that confession on its own is not of great value. Mark did not narrate what effect, if any, their cries had on the crowds or disciples in the stories. He was more interested in the secrecy motif, as Jesus continued to prevent them from making him known.

The multitudes knew of this amazing man who was shaking up the whole region and beyond, but as to who he really was, they did not know yet.

In the first-century context, it would have been considered ominous for demons to shout out a name in recognition. The original readers would not have assumed that the demons were paying him homage but rather that they were attempting to control him by pronouncing his divine name, thereby hoping to impede his deliverance of the persons in their clutches. The translation, "he gave them strict orders not to tell who he was (NIV)," is too mild. Jesus was not merely putting them under a gag order. The verb *epitimao* is frequently translated "rebuke," but even this does not adequately capture its meaning. He also "rebuked" the wind and sea to be still. The muzzling of the demons, like the quelling of the storm, was a sign that Jesus has overcome them. He therefore both expelled and silenced the demons with a word. Mark was highlighting the incredible authority that was in Jesus. It was the kind of authority that:

- made people take notice and follow him
- made demons attempt to control and overcome him
- made the natural order of things around them bend and become fluid

Jesus was not threatened by the demons' attempt to control him, but he did not want his true identity and nature to be made known by them.

51

Jesus Calls the Twelve

[Jesus] went up the mountain and called to him those whom he wanted, and they came to him. And he appointed twelve, whom he also named apostles, to be with him, and to be sent out to proclaim the message, and to have authority to cast out demons. So he appointed the twelve: Simon (to whom he gave the name Peter); James son of Zebedee and John the brother of James (to whom he gave the name Boanerges, that is, Sons of Thunder); and Andrew, and Philip, and Bartholomew, and Matthew, and Thomas, and James son of Alphaeus, and Thaddaeus, and Simon the Cananaean, and Judas Iscariot, who betrayed him. (Mark 3:13–19)

Jesus called his disciples according to the new order of things, and he sent them out according to the new order of things. Jesus' disciples were now the doctors who were calling. They were the new kingdom that was breaking in, breaking through, and breaking up. They were the new Sabbath. Jesus' disciples were the people who were bringing the healing salvation of God, ushering in the new kingdom. They were showing the presence, words, and acts of God. Does that include you and me? The religious leaders of Jesus' day would not have missed the significance of Jesus' actions.

- Jesus chose his disciples, rather than the disciples choosing him.

- Jesus called his disciples by name, as only YHWH could do.
- Twelve disciples reflected the twelve tribes of Israel.
- Critical authority was shifting from a place to a person, from Jerusalem to Jesus.
- Whatever perceived authority the religious leaders had was being swept away.

Before Jesus could send his disciples out, three things had to happen.

- They had to hear his call to come to him, which meant actively listening for the call.
- They had to actually come to Jesus, because hearing on its own was not enough.
- They had to abide with him, which was a relationship, not a geographical, reality.

The foundation, then, is that Jesus still calls today. He still receives people and still abides with them as they abide with him. This is discipleship! And this is the foundation of the church. Still, there are many churches that do not have this foundation. It is Jesus who calls people to follow him, not you and I. This requires a complete change of mind-set. We are to join Jesus in what he is doing, rather than to expect him to join us in what we are doing.

52

Jesus and Beelzebub

Then [Jesus] went home; and the crowd came together again, so that they could not even eat. When his family heard it, they went out to restrain him, for people were saying, "He has gone out of his mind." And the scribes who came down from Jerusalem said, "He has Beelzebul, and by the ruler of the demons he casts out demons." And he called them to him, and spoke to them in parables, "How can Satan cast out Satan? If a kingdom is divided against itself, that kingdom cannot stand. And if a house is divided against itself, that house will not be able to stand. And if Satan has risen up against himself and is divided, he cannot stand, but his end has come. But no one can enter a strong man's house and plunder his property without first tying up the strong man; then indeed the house can be plundered. Truly I tell you, people will be forgiven for their sins and whatever blasphemies they utter; but whoever blasphemes against the Holy Spirit can never have forgiveness, but is guilty of an eternal sin"—for they had said, "He has an unclean spirit." (Mark 3:20–30)

Once again, nobody could move because of the crowds that were thronging around Jesus, but now his own family tried to call an end to the adventure. They went out to restrain him, saying that he was out of his mind. Even as Jesus' own family moved against him, the teachers of the Law were arriving, and they too called a time-out, saying, "He has Beelzebub! By the ruler of the demons he casts out demons."

We would have expected the teachers of the Law to oppose Jesus, but his own family? His family were not there to give advice or friendly counsel. They were there "to restrain him." This is a translation of the Greek word *krateo*, which means "to seize forcibly." It is a forceful and explosive word. (Check out where Mark used the word in Mark 3:21; 6:17; 12:12; 14:1, 44, 46, 49, 51.) Jesus' own family went out to seize him forcibly.

At the time, people would have been shocked at the way Jesus apparently treated his family, because the family was the foundation of social and economic life, the source of one's own identity. To reject one's family was to reject life itself. To be rejected by one's family was to lose one's life. But Jesus, in the authority of YHWH himself, was declaring that there was a new and greater family on earth, a family of which Jesus was the head. Jesus was a transformer, not a reformer, and he was utterly demolishing the old order of things.

The teachers of the Law from Jerusalem had come to bring an end to this crusade of madness, and in the process, they accused God of being the Devil! The teachers of the Law believed that Jesus' ministry had to do with the kingdom of Satan, and they were partially right; but Jesus' ministry had to do with the collapse of the kingdom of darkness, not its advance. Jesus' ministry had to do with the advance of the kingdom of God, not with its defense. Jesus was on the offensive, not the defensive.

Note that it is the kingdom of God that is advancing—not Christianity, church, or denominations, and certainly not our flavor-of-the-month of these things. Jesus was teaching a vital truth that is applicable to all and everything, not just the kingdom of darkness: any house that is divided against itself cannot and will not stand. The individual who is divided against himself or herself cannot and will not stand. A divided heart will tear a person apart.

The undivided heart is the heart that sticks close to Jesus. It abides with him. The undivided church is the church that sticks close to Jesus, encouraging and supporting one another in abiding with Jesus. God's kingdom is undivided. Look around. Is Christianity undivided? Is church undivided? Are denominations undivided?

53

Kingdom Parables

Again he began to teach beside the sea. Such a very large crowd gathered around him that he got into a boat on the sea and sat there, while the whole crowd was beside the sea on the land. He began to teach them many things in parables, and in his teaching he said to them: "Listen! A sower went out to sow. And as he sowed, some seed fell on the path, and the birds came and ate it up. Other seed fell on rocky ground, where it did not have much soil, and it sprang up quickly, since it had no depth of soil. And when the sun rose, it was scorched; and since it had no root, it withered away. Other seed fell among thorns, and the thorns grew up and choked it, and it yielded no grain. Other seed fell into good soil and brought forth grain, growing up and increasing and yielding thirty and sixty and a hundredfold." And he said, "Let anyone with ears to hear listen!"

When he was alone, those who were around him along with the twelve asked him about the parables. And he said to them, "To you has been given the secret of the kingdom of God, but for those outside, everything comes in parables; in order that 'they may indeed look, but not perceive, and may indeed listen, but not understand; so that they may not turn again and be forgiven.'"

And he said to them, "Do you not understand this parable? Then how will you understand all the parables? The sower sows the word. These are the ones on the path where the word is sown: when they hear, Satan immediately comes and takes away the word that is sown in them. And these are the ones sown on rocky ground: when they hear the word, they immediately receive it with joy. But they have no root, and endure only for a while; then, when trouble or persecution arises on account of the word, immediately they fall away. And others are those sown among the thorns: these are the ones who hear the word, but the cares of the world, and the lure of wealth, and the desire for other things come in and choke the word, and it yields nothing. And these are the ones sown on the good soil: they hear the word and accept it and bear fruit, thirty and sixty and a hundredfold." (Mark 4:1–20)

The Greek word for seed is *sperma*. This is an interesting approach by Jesus. He began to teach them many things in parables. Jesus knew the great diversity of people who were on the shore, and so he taught many things. Everybody would get something from the stories he used to teach them. Jesus planted seeds in the people, and then he watched for the seeds to grow. Jesus knew how to recognize when the seeds were growing. Before we go any further, here are two very important points.

1. If this parable makes anything clear at all, it makes clear that comparing yourself to someone else is a futile exercise.
2. It also makes very clear that bearing fruit is not your responsibility. Rather, it is your responsibility to make sure that you are in the right place to bear fruit.

It is easy to think that this parable is centered on people and the sowing of the Word, that we are to sow the Word wherever we go and that the results are up to God. That may be one legitimate interpretation of the parable. But is the parable primarily about that? Was Jesus really telling the disciples that they would sow the Word but have no idea which ground was fertile and which was barren? Could the sower not tell which ground was good and which was bad? Was Jesus telling the disciples that they needed to sow the Word everywhere so that everyone got some, even if Jesus knew that many wouldn't respond? Was Jesus telling the disciples just to sow the Word and leave the results to God? What was Jesus getting at? What was his primary point?

We must first realize that Jesus was teaching the crowds, so he spoke in parables. Jesus seemed surprised that his disciples (not just the twelve) did not understand the parable. Having explained the parable to his disciples, what did Jesus hope that they would learn from it? Let us ask some basic questions in order to understand the depth of what Jesus was teaching here.

1. Who is the sower?
2. What part do we have in this?
3. What does the sower expect us to do?

If the sower is the Holy Spirit of God, then you and I are not the sower. If the Holy Spirit is the sower, then we are to work alongside him, not instead of him. If the Holy Spirit is both the sower and the life-giver, then we are expected to care for those to whom the Holy Spirit gives life. Therefore, are we watching what God the Father, God the Son, and God the Holy Spirit are doing so that we can work with them? It is critical that we do what we can do as we work alongside the God who will do what he can do. It is critical that we do not try to do that which only God can do, and in the doing neglect to do what we can do. The parable of the sower is not so much a call to action as it is a call to watch carefully. We need to do as Jesus did and hear what the Father is saying and do what the Father is doing. We are to watch carefully to see those in whom the seed of God is doing its work.

> He said to them, "Is a lamp brought in to be put under the bushel basket, or under the bed, and not on the lampstand? For there is nothing hidden, except to be

disclosed; nor is anything secret, except to come to light. Let anyone with ears to hear listen!" And he said to them, "Pay attention to what you hear; the measure you give will be the measure you get, and still more will be given you. For to those who have, more will be given; and from those who have nothing, even what they have will be taken away." He also said, "The kingdom of God is as if someone would scatter seed on the ground, and would sleep and rise night and day, and the seed would sprout and grow, he does not know how. The earth produces of itself, first the stalk, then the head, then the full grain in the head. But when the grain is ripe, at once he goes in with his sickle, because the harvest has come."

He also said, "With what can we compare the kingdom of God, or what parable will we use for it? It is like a mustard seed, which, when sown upon the ground, is the smallest of all the seeds on earth; yet when it is sown it grows up and becomes the greatest of all shrubs, and puts forth large branches, so that the birds of the air can make nests in its shade." With many such parables he spoke the word to them, as they were able to hear it; he did not speak to them except in parables, but he explained everything in private to his disciples. (Mark 4:21–34)

Mark was not merely linking these parables to the parable of the sower by placing them here in his gospel. He placed these parables here in order to make their understanding dependent upon the parable of the sower that preceded them and, in doing so, declared that they are to be read, heard, and understood in the context of the parable of the sower.

We are to watch what God is doing. In order to watch what God is doing, discernment is vital. And discernment comes from the Holy Spirit guiding the individual and opening his eyes and ears. Is God's light shining in someone's life? Join the Spirit there. Is God's growth evident in someone's life? Join the Spirit there. Is someone asking very serious questions from the heart? Join the Spirit there.

God is always at work in people's lives. If we don't know that, it is because we are not watching carefully. All too often, we are far too busy living our own lives, and we have neither time nor desire to watch and see what God is doing. If God is at work in people's lives, then there is fruit to be nurtured, growth to be encouraged, and light to be fueled. That which is hidden by God in people's lives is meant to be made known. The seeds that God plants in people's lives are meant to grow into new life, the new life of the kingdom. It is therefore critical that we watch and know what God is doing in people's lives. There is a great danger that we spend time and effort trying to sow into people's lives, when what is needed is the reaping of what God has already sown.

The parable of the sower is all about reaping what the sower has already sown. Why, then, do we seem to think that our primary work is to sow, when that is manifestly the work of God himself? God is at work today in the same way that he has always been. We are called to reap! Why then is so much of our evangelistic focus on sowing? It is the harvest field that needs workers. That is what the parable of the sower is shouting at us, if we will but listen. Therefore, I say it again: if the Holy Spirit is the sower, then we are to work with him, not instead or in spite of him. If the Holy Spirit is both the sower and the life-giver, then we are expected to care for those to whom the Holy Spirit gives life.

Are we watching what God the Holy Spirit, God the Son, and God the Father are doing so that we can work alongside them? It is critical that we do what we can do, as we work alongside the God who will do what he can do. We must not try to do what only God can do, and in the doing neglect to do what we can do. The parable of the sower is not so much a call to action as it is a call to watch carefully. We need to do as Jesus did. We need to hear what the Father is saying and do what the Father is doing. Watch carefully to see those in whom the seed of God is doing its work.

54

Jesus in the Storm

On that day, when evening had come, [Jesus] said to
them, "Let us go across to the other side." And leaving the crowd behind, they took him with them in the
boat, just as he was. Other boats were with him. A great
windstorm arose, and the waves beat into the boat, so
that the boat was already being swamped. But he was
in the stern, asleep on the cushion; and they woke him
up and said to him, "Teacher, do you not care that we
are perishing?" He woke up and rebuked the wind, and
said to the sea, "Peace! Be still!" Then the wind ceased,
and there was a dead calm. He said to them, "Why are
you afraid? Have you still no faith?" And they were
filled with great awe and said to one another, "Who
then is this, that even the wind and the sea obey him?"
(Mark 4:35–41)

Some accounts in Scripture were never meant to be taken only at face
value and accepted unthinkingy. Some Scriptural accounts raise more
questions than they answer. This account of Jesus and his disciples in the
storm is certainly one of them. Therefore, we must not approach it as a
simple story to be swallowed wholesale. We have some heart-thinking
to do around this short account and what it contains. Here are some
questions to meditate on in relation to this account. Quick and easy
answers are not allowed.

- How did Jesus train his disciples to believe in him?
- Since Jesus was not in a classroom with his disciples, what kind of teaching would he employ?
- When the waves were beating against and into the boat and swamping it, how on earth could Jesus possibly be asleep in the midst of that great windstorm?
- How did Mark know that Jesus was asleep?
- How did Peter know that Jesus was asleep?
- Who woke Jesus up?
- How did they wake him up?
- How did Jesus calm the storm?
- Why did Mark not record the rebuke Jesus used?
- What would have happened if the disciples had not "woken" Jesus?

These questions will repay careful and thoughtful meditation. Everybody's life has its storms. Nobody is exempt from them, but it's safer in the water with Jesus than alone in any boat in a storm. Mark taught us that Jesus is the one who stills all the storms of life, but that is not a guarantee of rescue in the way we want and at the time we want. The guarantee is that Jesus is always there with us in the storm. Here in this passage, Jesus did not still the average storm but a furious squall: a great windstorm. The way that Mark recorded this incident, it is possible that he was suggesting that the storm did not have a natural source. As we shall see, this was indeed the case.

In the boat, seasoned and seafaring fishermen were terrified, while the carpenter was apparently asleep on a sandbag (NRSV and NIV say "cushion") that was used for ballast. Since Jesus was apparently asleep and therefore seemingly indifferent to the disciples' plight, they assumed that Jesus simply didn't care. But what had Jesus said? "Let us go across to the other side." He had not prepared for an interrupted journey that was any longer than necessary, because he went "just as he was." The disciples struggled to work out just who Jesus was. The Scriptures would have told them, if only they had known.

> Some went down to the sea in ships, doing business on
> the mighty waters; they saw the deeds of the LORD,

his wondrous works in the deep. For he commanded and raised the stormy wind, which lifted up the waves of the sea. They mounted up to heaven, they went down to the depths; their courage melted away in their calamity; they reeled and staggered like drunkards, and were at their wits' end. Then they cried to the LORD in their trouble, and he brought them out from their distress; he made the storm be still, and the waves of the sea were hushed. Then they were glad because they had quiet, and he brought them to their desired haven. (Psalm 107:23–30)

But in the middle of this crisis, there was only panic. The disciples thought they were going to drown. But what had Jesus said? "Let us go across to the other side." If Jesus said that the boat was going over to the other side, then that was where it was going.

Your greatest security in life, your only security in life, is the presence of Jesus with you on your journey through life. In the midst of where your life is right now, will you call upon Jesus and let him do what he can do? Mark's whole call and purpose is for you to meet Jesus for yourself—again! And again! And again! And again! Not seven times, but seventy times seven. Then Jesus will still the storms that he will still—and he will be with you through the storms that he does not still.

55

The Storm Comes to Jesus

They came to the other side of the sea, to the country of
the Gerasenes. And when he had stepped out of the boat,
immediately a man out of the tombs with an unclean spirit
met him. He lived among the tombs; and no one could
restrain him any more, even with a chain; for he had often
been restrained with shackles and chains, but the chains
he wrenched apart, and the shackles he broke in pieces;
and no one had the strength to subdue him. Night and
day among the tombs and on the mountains he was always howling and bruising himself with stones. When he
saw Jesus from a distance, he ran and bowed down before
him; and he shouted at the top of his voice, "What have
you to do with me, Jesus, Son of the Most High God?
I adjure you by God, do not torment me." For he had
said to him, "Come out of the man, you unclean spirit!"
Then Jesus asked him, "What is your name?" He replied,
"My name is Legion; for we are many." He begged him
earnestly not to send them out of the country. Now there
on the hillside a great herd of swine was feeding; and the
unclean spirits begged him, "Send us into the swine; let
us enter them." So he gave them permission. And the
unclean spirits came out and entered the swine; and the
herd, numbering about two thousand, rushed down the
steep bank into the sea, and were drowned in the sea.

The swineherds ran off and told it in the city and in the country. Then people came to see what it was that had happened. They came to Jesus and saw the demoniac sitting there, clothed and in his right mind, the very man who had had the legion; and they were afraid. Those who had seen what had happened to the demoniac and to the swine reported it. Then they began to beg Jesus to leave their neighborhood. As Jesus was getting into the boat, the man who had been possessed by demons begged him that he might be with him. But Jesus refused, and said to him, "Go home to your friends, and tell them how much the Lord has done for you, and what mercy he has shown you." And he went away and began to proclaim in the Decapolis how much Jesus had done for him; and everyone was amazed. (Mark 5:1–20)

Just as it did on the sea, the storm now came to Jesus. Just as before, this storm also had no natural origin. The region of the Gerasenes was a violent and dangerous place, a place no Jewish rabbi should ever be. Yet this Jewish rabbi took his disciples into the midst of it. Despite popular opinion, this account is not about a power encounter. It is about an authority encounter.

Jesus knew exactly what he was doing and where he was going when he instructed the disciples to cross to the other side of the lake. They were crossing the sea to get to the Gerasenes, an enemy territory if ever there was one. For starters, there were swine there. But there was far more than swine that was unclean. This region was, in fact, an unclean and dangerous place in many senses.

Jesus stepped ashore. The storm that had broken out over the water now found new expression on dry land, as the demon-possessed man immediately rushed at Jesus. The storm on the water had come from a supernatural source, and so did the storm that broke on the land right in front of Jesus. The fierce strength of this demon-possessed man was reiterated in Mark 5:5, which says that no one had the strength to "subdue" him. The Greek word used here (*damazo*) is used for taming a wild animal and it is better translated, "No one was able to tame him." Obviously this demoniac roamed free because all human attempts to constrain him had failed. Only a power more potent than iron bars and chains would ever bridle him. How could a man be so strong that metal could not hold him?

Translating the verb as "tame" also opens up another dimension to the text. It strikes us immediately that something is wrong. One does not normally "tame" human beings; one tames wild animals (or the tongue, as in James 3:8). People treated this man like a wild animal, and he acted like one. He had been banished as an outcast from society and dwelled with those whose sleep would not be disturbed by his shrieks echoing through the night as he lacerated his body with stones. He was condemned to live out his days alone amid the decaying bones of the dead in the tombs, with no one to love him and no one to love. His only food was the decaying food left for the dead.

Jesus had told the evil spirit to come out of the man, which met with immediate evasive tactics. When the demons pronounced Jesus' name, they were basically saying, "We've got the upper hand over you." They also abjured Jesus by the name of God not to torment them, although they themselves had tormented this poor man well past the point of endurance. They invoked the name of God to keep the Son of God off their back—to try to protect themselves.

Jesus seemed to parry these diversionary tactics by asking for the demon's name. The evil spirits evaded the question, however, by giving a number instead of a name: "My name is Legion." This number in a Roman regiment consisted of six thousand foot soldiers and 120 horsemen. No wonder the man was so strong! Now, numbers are not precise in Hebrew thought, but the point is well-made. There were lots of demons inside this man. Jesus, who has just demonstrated his dominion over the sea, did not need to know the names of the evil spirits in order to drive them out. From a Jewish perspective, the scene was a joke: unclean spirits and unclean animals were both wiped out in one fell swoop, and a human being was cleansed.

When the community arrived, they were not frightened by what had happened to the swine but rather by seeing the man now clothed and in his right mind! They did not rejoice at his recovery but were afraid.

What was so scary about seeing a person sitting at the feet of Jesus? The community had desperately tried to tame the man with chains and fetters, all to no avail. Now Jesus had freed him from the chains of demons with only a word. The disciples also expressed fear at Jesus' manifestation of great authority, and they wondered who was this one who with them.

These townspeople did not seem to care that Jesus has such authority. They just wanted him gone from their territory. Instead of giving him the key to the city, they gave him a cold shoulder. The demons had begged Jesus to let them stay in the region, and the townspeople now begged Jesus to leave the region. They considered Jesus more dangerous than the demons. Demons tended to keep to their own turf, but who could control someone with such authority as Jesus clearly possessed? And this rabbi didn't even stick to his own territory!

The community begged Jesus to leave them, and the freed man now begged to be with Jesus. Jesus sent him to his own house so that he could be restored to his family. No one in the entire area could deny that something dramatic had happened to this man. The infamous man who had been possessed by a legion of demons remained to proclaim how he had been delivered by the Lord's mercy. The upshot of this was that the good news of Jesus expanded into the Decapolis.

There is a subtlety here that I have already referred to but have not yet explicitly mentioned: Jesus told the man, "Go home to your family and tell them how much the *Lord* has done for you, and how *he* has had mercy on you." The man was not simply to tell people about the miracle that happened to him but about what that miracle signified—that the Lord himself had been at work. It was personal. Jesus was the one who had healed him, and yet the man was to announce the things that the Lord had done for him. He was therefore to declare by a clear statement that Jesus was Lord, that the demonic forces that controlled the land of the Gerasenes had been removed by the kingdom of God breaking in, breaking through, and breaking up.

All that Jesus did was designed to bring glory to God. To Mark, the name of Jesus was synonymous with "the Lord God." Where Jesus acted, God acted.

It is fascinating how often the words and deeds of Jesus—even seemingly small or insignificant incidents—can be found foretold in the prophetic books of the Old Testament.

> I was ready to be sought out by those who did not ask, to be found by those who did not seek me. I said, "Here I am, here I am," to a nation that did not call on my name. I held out my hands all day long to a rebellious people, who walk in a way that is not good, following their own devices; a people who provoke me to my face continually, sacrificing in gardens and offering incense on bricks; who sit inside tombs, and spend the night in secret places; who eat swine's flesh, with broth of abominable things in their vessels; who say, "Keep to yourself, do not come near me, for I am too holy for you." (Isaiah 65:1–5)

Mark majored on the kind acts of Jesus. Mark showed us that the acts of kindness that Jesus did were acts of power, but they were actually predominantly acts of authority. That made them personal to Jesus.

56

Calling the Doctor

When Jesus had crossed again in the boat to the other side, a great crowd gathered around him; and he was by the sea. Then one of the leaders of the synagogue named Jairus came and, when he saw him, fell at his feet and begged him repeatedly, "My little daughter is at the point of death. Come and lay your hands on her, so that she may be made well, and live." He went with him.

And a large crowd followed him and pressed in on him. Now there was a woman who had been suffering from hemorrhages for twelve years. She had endured much under many physicians, and had spent all that she had; and she was no better, but rather grew worse. She had heard about Jesus, and came up behind him in the crowd and touched his cloak, for she said, "If I but touch his clothes, I will be made well." Immediately her hemorrhage stopped; and she felt in her body that she was healed of her disease. Immediately aware that power had gone forth from him, Jesus turned about in the crowd and said, "Who touched my clothes?" And his disciples said to him, "You see the crowd pressing in on you; how can you say, 'Who touched me?'" He looked all around to see who had done it. But the woman, knowing what had happened to her, came in fear and trembling, fell down before him, and told him the whole truth. He said to her, "Daughter, your faith has made you well; go in peace, and be healed of your disease."

While he was still speaking, some people came from the leader's house to say, "Your daughter is dead. Why trouble the teacher any further?" But overhearing what they said, Jesus said to the leader of the synagogue, "Do not fear, only believe." He allowed no one to follow him except Peter, James, and John, the brother of James. When they came to the house of the leader of the synagogue, he saw a commotion, people weeping and wailing loudly. When he had entered, he said to them, "Why do you make a commotion and weep? The child is not dead but sleeping." And they laughed at him. Then he put them all outside, and took the child's father and mother and those who were with him, and went in where the child was. He took her by the hand and said to her, "Talitha cum," which means, "Little girl, get up!" And immediately the girl got up and began to walk about (she was twelve years of age). At this they were overcome with amazement. He strictly ordered them that no one should know this, and told them to give her something to eat. (Mark 5:21–43)

Mark was doing something both unusual and interesting here. Mark rarely named people in his particular account of Jesus' kingship, but he did so here with this synagogue official. This man was given status by being named, but his walk with Jesus was not straightforward. This synagogue official who waylaid Jesus was named as Jairus, but Jesus' journey to the man's little daughter was interrupted by a woman whom Mark did not name. And yet the account of this woman's encounter with Jesus took up a lot of Mark's narrative here and broke into two sections the account of Jairus and his daughter.

Mark told us that Jairus repeatedly asked Jesus to come and heal his daughter, but Luke did not explicitly record that fact (Luke 8:41). What did Jesus say to Jairus in response to his request to go and heal his daughter? Why did Mark not record Jesus' response(s) to Jairus? Why did Mark think these two incidents were so significant that he recorded both of them together in far greater detail than Doctor Luke did—and in so doing, closely linked them together? How long had the woman suffered from bleeding? How old was Jairus' little daughter? Why did Mark tell us her age only as an aside, like an add-on? Mark told us that the girl was Jairus' little daughter, but Luke recorded that she was his only daughter (Luke 8:42). So many questions.

The suffering of the woman for twelve years stressed her great need and the reason she was so compelled to seek Jesus' help (Mark 9:21; Luke 13:11; Acts 3:2; 9:33; 14:8). The text does not specify the nature of her loss of blood, but it would have been related to uterine bleeding, since that would have made her ritually unclean (Leviticus 15:25–33). Her perpetual bleeding was abnormal, which made it far more serious for her. The woman's impurity was transmissible to others until the problem was cured. Anyone who had contact with her—by lying in her bed, sitting in her chair, or even just by touching her—became unclean and was required to bathe and to launder clothing. Her discharge of blood had caused the woman to be discharged from society, because it made her a major bearer of impurity as a person with a flux. She was therefore similar to the leper who suffered from uncleanness and was excluded from normal social relations. This woman suffered physically, living every day with the signs of decaying mortality as the blood essential for life constantly drained from her body. She suffered socially and psychologically, knowing that she was a contaminant. Her plight was compounded because she had become impoverished after wasting her living on the fruitless cure of physicians.

Jesus has just exorcised a demon from a man that no one could control. Now he healed a woman that no physician could cure and restored a girl's life when all hope was gone. The woman had refused to accept this disease as her lot in life and she boldly took matters into her own hands by touching Jesus' garment (mentioned four times in 5:27–28, 30–31). Earlier Mark told us that many who suffered diseases pushed forward to touch Jesus (3:10). In Mark 6:56, he reported that people begged Jesus to let them touch the hem of his cloak—and that all who touched him were healed. The difference here was that this woman crept up from behind so that she would not be observed, hoping that she could disappear back into the anonymity of the large crowd without anyone knowing of her unlawful contact. When she touched Jesus, her flow of blood immediately stopped.

Because she had experienced healing, she was conscious of Jesus' amazing power and was afraid, much as the disciples had been afraid earlier on the lake when they had witnessed his power over the storm (4:41). This account highlights some things that we would do well to consider carefully in our own day and in our own culture.

- No "Christian" faith is required for God to act in an individual's life. Indeed, this account should make us think carefully about what "Christian" faith actually is.
- No "Christian" faith is required for God to act in our world. The idea that God does nothing in our world except in an answer to prayer is total nonsense. Such an idea is totally unsupportable from the Scriptures and is a relatively modern theology that is based on error. God does not need us.
- There is no formula involved here: no prayer, no laying on of hands, no ceremony, no ritual. The only constant in Mark's account is Jesus himself.
- There is no person of faith involved in this woman's healing— except herself. And this woman of faith was an outcast from society, an unclean, bankrupt, and disobedient woman.

Like the ruler of the synagogue before her, this unnamed woman now prostrated herself before Jesus. Jesus did not let her remain hidden but forced her to step out in faith and be identified. He would not bankrupt her as the physicians had done, but she had to publicly acknowledge her debt to Jesus, that he was the source of her healing. When she did, he blessed her and announced that her faith had not only made her well but that Jesus had restored her as a daughter of Israel by giving back her status in society. Jesus restored her as a daughter of Israel and told her to go in peace (Judges 18:6; 1 Samuel 1:17; 2 Samuel 15:9; Acts 16:36). Faith—not any magical properties in Jesus' clothing—accomplished her healing salvation.

Finally, the King resumed his journey with Jairus. Whatever Jairus had been thinking up to this point, his situation did not improve but actually got worse. So Jairus too had to publicly demonstrate his trust in Jesus as the worst possible news came. The bearers of the bad tidings did not mince words: "Your daughter is dead. Why bother the teacher anymore?" The subliminal message here was that Jesus was only a teacher and that death marked the limit of whatever authority he might have. But just as the woman overcame her fear with her faith, so Jairus was told, "Don't be afraid. Just believe." (The present continuous tense means to keep on believing or sticking to something.) Believe in what? Stick to whom? Who are you that I should stick to you in even my grief? Jairus had shown faith in coming to Jesus in the first place, and now he must continue in faith. And Jesus then took with him only Peter, James, and John. Why?

Jairus obeyed Jesus in leading him to his house, but his faith was again challenged by the grievous chorus of those professional mourners who had already assembled to mourn the little girl's death. They did not have the faith of the woman that Mark had just told us about, and they would certainly have undermined the faith of the father. Jesus' announcement that the girl was not dead but only sleeping met with laughter and derision from the professional mourners. They were not idiots; they knew when someone had died. Of course she was dead. But Mark was showing us that Jesus the King could transform a deadly storm into a great calm, a ferocious brute into a calm and gentle man, death into a calm sleep, and the laughter of scorn into the laughter of joy. The mourners' skepticism put them outside the direct experience of the power of God. There would be no miracles for the scornful throng.

In private—with only the parents and Peter, James, and John—Jesus grasped the little girl's hand to raise her up, and said, *"Talitha koum."* The translation from this bit of Aramaic ("Little girl, get up!") made it clear to the listener that Jesus did not utter some mysterious mumbo jumbo or some magic formula. It was just an ordinary phrase uttered by an extraordinary man. The command to secrecy revealed that Jesus was not pursuing fame. He had consistently avoided publicity and now responded only to those with faith. This causes us to think about the social impact of these two stories and the people involved in them.

The two main characters here interacting with Jesus occupied opposite ends of the economic, social, and religious spectrum. Jairus was a male, a leader of the synagogue. As a man of distinction, he had a name. He also had a family. Jairus had honor and could openly approach Jesus with a direct request, though he showed the greatest deference. Jairus had status. By contrast, the woman was nameless, and her complaint rendered her ritually unclean. She was walking pollution. Her condition therefore separated her from the community and made her unfit to enter the synagogue, let alone the temple. She had no honor and had to slink about and approach Jesus from behind, thinking that she must purloin her healing. She had no status. Moreover, Jairus had a large household and was thus a man of means. The woman had become destitute because of her medical bills. Her complaint made childbearing hopeless and marriage next-to-impossible.

All that these two individuals shared in common was that they had both heard about Jesus, both desperately desired him to do something, and both had run out of other options. Here, then, is an interesting thought: Jesus made the man of honor wait until he had healed the woman of dishonor. Dovetailing the stories of two such dissimilar individuals together revealed that being male, being ritually pure, holding a high religious office, or being a man of means provided no advantage in approaching Jesus. Being female, impure, dishonored, and destitute was no barrier to receiving help.

God always takes the side of those who have been denied rights and privileges—the oppressed and the poor. In God's kingdom, the nobodies became somebodies because of Jesus. Healing salvation and wholeness were not extended to just the lucky few who already had so much of everything else. But neither did Jesus set the lowly over the lofty.

Faith enabled all—honored and dishonored, clean and unclean alike—to come to the merciful Jesus who brought both healing and salvation. In this respect, all were equals before Jesus. One should also note that Jairus was a member of the Jewish establishment that seemed on the whole to be hostile to Jesus. His rank as a leader in a hostile institution did not disqualify him from Jesus' care, because he was willing to lay aside whatever social status he had by humbling himself before Jesus in a desperate plea for help.

Throughout the gospel of Mark, Jesus' frequent contact with what was unclean never rendered him unclean. Quite the reverse: Jesus purged the impurity. He touched a leper and cleansed him. He ventured into a tomb area and drove a legion of demons out of a man and into a herd of pigs. He was touched by one with a hemorrhage, and she was made whole. He touched a dead girl and brought her to life. Jesus did not need to purify himself from the pollution of a person with a flux or from contact with a dead body. Rather, he overcame the pollution.

We may have difficulty in conveying this important idea in our culture, which does not tend to make such distinctions between clean and unclean. Or does it? We actually do treat some diseases as respectable and some as not respectable. For example, we attach no personal blame to someone who suffers a heart attack, but we might regard someone who has contracted a venereal disease quite differently. And what of the person who has AIDS?

Mark was constantly showing that King Jesus had total authority. The good news Mark proclaimed was that in Jesus' presence storms subsided, demons beat a retreat, infirmities were put right, and death lost its hold. As Jesus moved about, he left behind him a trail of transformed scenes and changed situations: fishermen were no longer at their nets, sick people were restored to health, critics were confounded, a storm was stilled, hunger was assuaged, and a dead girl was raised to life. Jesus' presence was an active and instantly transforming presence. He was never a mere observer of a scene or one who waited upon events. He was always the transformer of the scene and the initiator of events. In a very real sense, Jesus the King caused holy havoc!

And he still does that wherever he goes.

Part VII

Conclusion

As we have explored the theme of the Christ-centered life, we have looked together at aspects of Christ-centered living in which I used the experience of my own journey into Christ-centeredness to show that Christ-centeredness is for everyone. If Jesus can do it for me, he can do it for you too—of that I am certain. Believe it and receive him!

We looked at the Law of God—the first five books of the old covenant Scriptures—and saw how the Law itself is Christ-centered and finds its fulfillment in him. We saw that the Law was a consequential law and not a prohibitive law. This enables us to see that God is not an officer of the behavioral police, nor an angry headmaster, but rather a loving father.

We looked at Christ-centered marriage and saw how critical that is for the day and age in which we live. Marriage on earth is the reflection of God himself—no sexuality implied—and we need to be those whose marriages show the world what it means to be Christ-centered.

We then looked at prayer from a Christ-centered perspective and saw how radically different it is from the common concept of prayer as a request for something—which we then receive or not, as the case may be. We saw that prayer is first and foremost the expression of relationship, from life's first cry to our final breath.

We looked at the subject of leadership from a Christ-centered perspective and saw how God has ordained the kind of people we were meant to be in Christ. We discovered our primary responsibility is to be Christ-centered as we are to take responsibility for other people. We saw that godly calling—not human appointment—is important.

We then considered that the Gospels are actually the work of four proclaimers, each of whom declared—from his own perspective—that Jesus is King of all. We spent some time looking at how Mark presented King Jesus.

A Christ-centered life is one in which every Christian should be growing, irrespective of the flavor of Christianity or church he may adhere to. Christ is so central to God's plans for our lives that if we miss Christ, we miss everything. Read the Scriptures with fresh revelation, and let Jesus spring off the pages in a holy encounter, as the Holy Spirit renews your heart and your mind.

This is but the beginning of a Christ-centered foundation. There is so much more to discover in the awesome person of Christ himself. I hope I have laid a foundation on which you build and grow into an intimate and mature relationship with Christ himself and receive the fullness of him who fills all in all. May it be so for his glory alone. Amen.

> I pray that the God of our Lord Jesus Christ, the Father of glory, may give you a spirit of wisdom and revelation as you come to know him, so that, with the eyes of your heart enlightened, you may know what is the hope to which he has called you, what are the riches of his glorious inheritance among the saints, and what is the immeasurable greatness of his power for us who believe, according to the working of his great power. God put this power to work in Christ when he raised him from the dead and seated him at his right hand in the heavenly places, far above all rule and authority and power and dominion, and above every name that is named, not only in this age but also in the age to come. And he has put all things under his feet and has made him the head over all things for the church, which is his body, the fullness of him who fills all in all. (Ephesians 1:17-22)

Lightning Source UK Ltd.
Milton Keynes UK
UKOW051936300613

213022UK00002B/5/P